COMPREHENSION
GOING FORWARD

COMPREHENSION
GOING FORWARD

where we are / what's next ▶

ELLIN OLIVER KEENE / SUSAN ZIMMERMANN / DEBBIE MILLER /

SAMANTHA BENNETT / LESLIE BLAUMAN / CHRYSE HUTCHINS /

STEPHANIE HARVEY / ANNE GOUDVIS / BRAD BUHROW /

GINA CERVETTI / MARJORIE LARNER / CRIS TOVANI /

NANCY COMMINS / ANNE UPCZAK GARCIA / TANNY MCGREGOR /

CODA BY **P. DAVID PEARSON** / **HARVEY "SMOKEY" DANIELS**, EDITOR

HEINEMANN
Portsmouth, NH

Heinemann
361 Hanover Street
Portsmouth, NH 03801–3912
www.heinemann.com

Offices and agents throughout the world

The authors and publisher wish to thank those who have generously given permission to reprint borrowed material:

Inside cover image from *Comprehension and Collaboration: Inquiry Circles in Action* by Harvey Daniels and Stephanie Harvey. Copyright © 2009 by Harvey Daniels and Stephanie Harvey. Published by Heinemann. Reprinted by permission of the publisher.

"Beautiful and Cruel" from *The House on Mango Street* by Sandra Cisneros. Copyright © 1984 by Sandra Cisneros. Published by Vintage Books, a division of Random House, Inc., and in hardcover by Alfred A. Knopf in 1994. Reprinted by permission of Susan Bergholz Literary Services and Bloomsbury Publishing.

Library of Congress Cataloging-in-Publication Data
  Comprehension going forward : where we are and what's next /
Ellin Oliver Keene . . . [et al.].
    p. cm.
  Includes bibliographical references and index.
  ISBN-13: 978-0-325-04163-6
  ISBN-10: 0-325-04163-6
  1. Reading comprehension.   I. Oliver Keene, Ellin.

LB1573.7.C663 2011
372.47—dc22   2010046547

Editor: Harvey Daniels
Production: Lynne Costa
Cover and interior designs: Lisa Anne Fowler
Cover illustration: ©Eyewire/Getty Images DES-051C
Typesetter: House of Equations, Inc.
Manufacturing: Steve Bernier

Printed in the United States of America on acid-free paper
15   14   13   12   11   VP   1   2   3   4   5

$\mathcal{W}$elcome and Introduction

Harvey "Smokey" Daniels

Greetings, dear reader. I am going to introduce you to this very special book in just a moment. But right now, would you kindly read this passage?

// Recommendation Engine //

Ask an Algorithm

Which TV for Me?

I want that Panasonic 103-inch TV. My wife says that's too big. Is she right?
Optimal viewing distance at 1080p = diagonal screen size ÷ 0.84; maximum OVD for 103-inch screen = 122.619 inches.

Recommendation: If seat to screen distance >122.619 inches: Purchase TV; if <122.619 inches: Construct home theater space of necessary size; purchase TV.

Now, let me try to read your mind:

A minute ago, you entered this passage with your normal reading confidence, but soon ran into a bit of difficulty. This bit of text does not cough up meaning so easily. Perhaps you noticed yourself immediately puzzling over the three headings, trying to figure out what genre of text you were about to read. Or maybe you scanned the passage and were daunted by all those goofy fonts and all that symbolic language ahead.

Because you were *monitoring your comprehension*, you could feel that your understanding might be in jeopardy, and so you started making specific mental moves to improve your chances. Probably, you stopped and reread parts of the passage, or slowed down your reading rate. You could feel your thinking become more conscious and intentional.

A lot of *questions* were popping into your head, like "What's a Recommendation Engine?" "What does OVD mean?" "What kind of publication did this come from?" "Why can't they give the measurements in feet instead of inches?" "Which one of those darn symbols means 'more than' and which one means 'less than'?"

You tried to *make connections* between the text and your background knowledge, perhaps about TVs you have owned, certain mathematical operations, or classic spousal debates. Indeed, a huge component of your ability to make sense of this passage was your *schema* for today's high tech gadgets; if you were recently at Best Buy shopping for a new flat-screen, you probably understood this passage better than if you are a housebound technophobe. You were also doing a lot of *inferring*, putting together clues in the text with your own background knowledge in order to gain understanding—"I bet that TV must be *really* expensive."

Along the way, you were *visualizing*, trying to make a mental image of a living room with that huge TV in it. "How big would a 103-inch TV actually be?" Or perhaps you tried to do that math calculation in your mind—or even picked up a pen and worked it out on paper. All through the text, you were constantly trying to *determine importance*, to figure out what were the most crucial facts and what were insignificant details. Probably, you quicky decided that the specific brand of the TV was relatively unimportant and wouldn't help you crack the meaning puzzle.

And for sure you were always trying to *synthesize*, to pull together all the information into a comprehensible whole, a gist or summary of the piece. Only when you fully synthesized all this thinking did you really "get it," and truly comprehend the passage. You realized that this "advice column" from *Wired* magazine (Leckart 2010, 86) is strictly tongue-in-cheek. The husband gets the giant TV either way. The supposed guidance comes from "An Algorithm," a robotic voice answering questions with faux-scientific wisdom. This is a piece of comedy text; maybe not a gut-busting guffaw, but at least a chuckle.

So how successful was I at reading your mind? If I had any success, it is only because I expected you to make the same mental moves that any veteran reader would in this situation. Skilled readers:

> monitor their comprehension
>
> visualize and make sensory images
>
> draw inferences
>
> connect to background knowledge
>
> ask questions of the text
>
> determine what's important
>
> synthesize and summarize

As you will find in this book, there are several ways of labeling and ordering these mental operations, but their existence—their centrality to the reading process—is certain.

In the early 1980s, P. David Pearson and his colleagues conducted the first wave of research studies that led to the identification of these cognitive strategies. Up to that time, reading research had concentrated—perhaps overmuch—on the behaviors of struggling or "dyslexic" readers. But by shifting the focus to the ways *effective* readers operated, Pearson and his colleagues and interpreters (many of whom are contributors to this book) paved the way to specific classroom practices that help students learn to read like skillful readers do (Pearson and Gallagher 1983; Pearson et al. 1992).

Still, even after joining in an experiment like the TV passage, some people still doubt the existence of their own internal cognitive repertoire. "Strategies, schmategies," they scoff. "I just read." It is true that we don't notice ourselves deploying these tools too often. That's because when we adults encounter the vast majority of our everyday text—the newspaper, memos from the principal, etc., we "just understand it." The text clicks along, we get the meaning, no problem. But this process is not magic; it happens because, as seasoned reading "pros," we have long since internalized a repertoire of thinking patterns, and we now mostly use them unconsciously and automatically. *But,* when the text is a little tougher (as this article was for us, and as school materials so often are for kids) we suddenly "hear our brain working" as we shift to more conscious, intentional strategies.

Sometimes people think they only use cognitive strategies with nonfiction, where a more purposeful and stepwise approach seems necessary. With fiction, the story goes, you can just lose yourself, and still gain robust meaning without using any particular strategies. But think of yourself sitting on a summer beach with the latest page-turning novel. Aren't you making mental images of the characters and the setting? Connecting their travails to your own life experiences (She's just like my mother!)? Inferring from clues in the text to make predictions about what might happen next (These two are totally going to sleep together!)? And maybe even questioning the author's decisions (I can't believe the author killed off my favorite character halfway through the book!)?

Perhaps our comprehension strategies work especially quietly when we read a novel. Probably the elemental backbone of narrative allows our understanding of stories to happen deeper in the background. But still, the strategies are inarguably at work in the minds of all skilled readers, in all genres of text, all the time.

This is profound. What we have come to call *proficient reader strategies* are not a fad, not a program, and not the latest bandwagon rolling through Teacher Town. This model will not soon be displaced by the latest Silver Bullet Super Comprehension Software. Far from being transient gimmicks, these strategies describe the way skillful readers think in response to text, and probably always have.

But the essential question for us as educators is this: Knowing that these strategies are real and lie at the heart of reading, what do we do? What actions do we take with our preschoolers, our third graders, our middle and high school kids? How do we work with English language learners, kids with identified learning needs, and students who just (for one reason or another) struggle with learning to read or enjoying reading?

The Purpose and Origins of This Book

This is precisely the range of issues that this book addresses. In these pages, sixteen distinguished authors show what comprehension instruction looks like when it is "done right"; what an amazing range of applications this paradigm can have for all students, across the curriculum; what problems have been encountered and solved (or not); and most importantly, what's left to achieve. As you'll see, each author takes the comprehension strategies as a starting point, and then reaches out toward a different set of applications, extensions, and practices. Many of these authors are "rethinking thinking," modifying the model, and forging ahead. There's plenty of diversity here, different directions in pathfinding and problem solving. But everyone is also connected by the solid and growing research base on comprehension instruction and by our commitment to kids. Our common goal is to provide every child in America with an "All-Access Pass" to literacy.

Many of these contributors have been associated with Denver's remarkable Public Education and Business Coalition (PEBC), founded in 1983. The PEBC is quite a story in itself, emerging over the past twenty-five-plus years as one of the most focused and influential think tanks in the country—not just in recent years, but ever. The list of PEBC-affiliated educators reads like a "who's who" of progressive reading instruction in America. Also among this book's writers are multiple "generations"—at least two waves of comprehension leaders and pioneers. We hear from veterans who hail from the earliest days of the 1980s—and also enjoy the younger voices of next-generation reading leaders. For obvious reasons, I am not about to enumerate who hails from which era.

Among our contributors are four educators who work mainly as researchers, six current elementary and secondary teachers, and eight former teachers who now work as authors and consultants. Most contributors have written at least one book of their own; in the aggregate, these people have published more than fifty titles. (See a sampling on pages 267–72.) They've keynoted every major conference, research symposium, and state reading convention in the country. But perhaps most uniquely, every contributor to this book has taught kids in school or spent hundreds of hours observing great teachers at work. In fact, as far as I can tell, every one of us is working directly with kids *this year*—either full-time, part-time, doing demonstration lessons, or conducting classroom research.

The Editor's Welcome

I came into the comprehension world as a "friend of the family"—a follower, not a founder. My own work on literature circles, content-area literacy, inquiry learning, and small-group collaboration always had a latent awareness of reading-as-thinking (there's a lot of unconscious stuff happening in this field, isn't there?). So when P. David Pearson's work appeared and was translated for me by Ellin Keene, Susan Zimmermann, Stephanie Harvey, Anne Goudvis, Debbie Miller, and Cris Tovani, I was rocked. The comprehension work revolutionized my own practice as a teacher, staff developer, and author. Over the past six or seven years, I've written several books that show my deep debt to the ideas and the people in this volume.

Still, I rather like my semioutsider status. Editing this project has been a happy way for me to testify to the power of this work and to help extend its growth. Because I value the insights that comprehension research has offered me and the learners I serve, I have also been concerned about misapplications and distortions of the work. So a couple of years ago, out of both appreciation and concern, I got the notion of gathering some of my own (mostly unaware) mentors to talk about comprehension's future.

In the fall of 2009, we gathered in Denver for a daylong meeting. The goal was to look over the past, but mainly to think about the future of comprehension instruction—with an eye toward creating a book, if that felt right to everyone. Our meeting was a bit of a reunion as well, since many people who had once worked side by side in Colorado schools had now branched out across the nation, working as consultants with kids and schools in distant locales. As people entered the room, there were enthusiastic greetings, loud laughter, and two identical outfits (which we overcame after much amusement). It was remarkable to see not just the professionalism and the brilliance of these educators, but their warm community with each other. My buddy Brad Buhrow and I had to agree; there was a component of this connection we two might never be part of.

Once the conversation began, people expressed a mixture of satisfaction, pride, surprise, and concern about the extent to which comprehension strategy instruction had become a national movement. People shared success stories of amazing teachers and their high-achieving young readers around the country, of brave principals and districts who had committed to wide implementation of reading-as-thinking instruction. Others talked about problems encountered and sometimes overcome. We wrung our hands over stories of "strategies gone bad"—being taught for their own sake, rather than as tools for deeper thinking. We exchanged notes about recent articles and books that had really impressed us, and worried about the proliferation of shallow comprehension worksheets and lockstep programs (Monday we visualize, Tuesday we infer . . .). We were all trying to jot notes, contribute to the conversation, and listen at the same time. I had to forcibly remind people to eat something as meals appeared.

It was an exhilarating day. At the end, we decided, yes, let's do a book together about what state-of-the-art comprehension looks like—and how it might grow from here.

I've tried to edit this book so that it feels like the meeting in Denver—conversational, energetic, reflective, principled, forward-looking, and leavened with humor. To recreate that sense of lively interaction, the authors have offered comments on each others' chapters, which you'll find in the margins along the way. I've also pulled out the most striking quotes from each author's chapter, both to highlight the biggest of the big ideas and just to savor what fine writers we have among us. Anne Goudvis has kindly collected everyone's three favorite publications—just those very few recent books or articles that really knocked our socks off and advanced our thinking. I hope you enjoy all these features, as well as the rock-solid reasoning that I believe runs through all the chapters.

At a recent meeting of reading educators, Regie Routman pointed out that "we are all born into this world comprehending." What a powerful reminder. As tiny babies, and even before birth, we are making meaning from everything we hear, feel, and see around us. Our whole lives unfold through our growing ability to make sense as we listen, view, and eventually read. There is no topic more important to human development—or to education—than learning how we humans come to understand.

—Harvey "Smokey" Daniels
Santa Fe, NM

References

Pearson, P. David, Laura Roehler, Janice A. Dole, and Gerald G. Duffy. 1992. "Developing Expertise in Reading Comprehension: What Should Be Taught and How Should It Be Taught?" In *What Research Has to Say to the Teacher of Reading*, 2d, edited by Alan Farstrup and S. Jay Samuels. Newark, DE: International Reading Association.

Pearson, P. David, and Margaret C. Gallagher. 1983. "The Instruction of Reading Comprehension." *Contemporary Educational Psychology* 8: 317–44.

Leckart, Steven. "Ask an Algorithm" *Wired* (August 2010): 86.

CHAPTER ONE

Comprehension Instruction Grows Up

Ellin Oliver Keene

Seen and Heard in a School— Could It Be Yours?

"I don't know why we have to make text-to-text, text-to-world, and text-to-self connections again. I did that in elementary and last year," Shanaya, a seventh grader, addresses her teacher impatiently. Her teacher, Jen, tries to explain that she and the other seventh graders are working in more difficult text and in new genres and it's almost like learning a new strategy each year. The strategy is the same, but things are definitely getting tougher and it's important to try the strategy in tougher text. Shanaya seems to consider this and is just about to speak her rebuttal when Jen moves on to think aloud about her connections—but she's worried.

Later that day, Jen and her colleagues huddled around a teachers' lounge table still somewhat sticky from the lunch rush hours ago. They combed through students' work and shared their own set of frustrations. Jen told the group about Shanaya's query and revealed that it was far from the first time she has heard a similar grievance.

"I know that kids need strategy instruction each year in progressively more difficult text and in new genres, but I can't help but think that there's something I'm missing," she told her colleagues. "It's not just that my kids are complaining about learning the same strategies, I think the kids could be going further. Some of their responses are superficial. It's almost like they've figured out the strategy game. 'I made a text-to-text connection . . .'" Her voice trailed off. "Part of me wants to say, 'So what?'"

The other teachers laughed, but expressed similar concerns. Randy, one of Jen's colleagues, spoke up. "I know what you mean and I had just started to believe that my comprehension instruction was working pretty well. I understand the comprehension strategies, I pay attention to how I use them myself, I think aloud using the strategies so my thinking is transparent to kids, I follow up in conferences to ensure that they are applying the strategies, and I try to keep track of their progress using rubrics. I can't quite put my finger on it, but I feel like there's more they could be doing. I don't want this to become rote. When I first started teaching comprehension strategies, they'd never had that kind of instruction before and we were all excited. Now the elementary teachers are working on strategies and I feel like it's up to us to dig deeper."

"That may be true, but I have a friend who teaches elementary and she says that people are saying the same thing there," Sarah added.

Finally, Claire, a seventh grade teacher, said, "Let's record this because I think we're saying the same thing, really, and it could be the direction we've been looking for in terms of our professional learning community topic for this year. We know the kids can understand more deeply, but we need to know how to get them there and we need some way to know when and if they do comprehend more deeply. Is that right?"

She wrote on chart paper:

1. How can we help children understand more deeply?

2. How do we *know* when they comprehend deeply?

"I want to clarify where we're going with this," Justin, an eighth grade teacher, said. "I wouldn't want to stop teaching comprehension strategies. Our scores have gone up, the kids *are* reading more, and they're reading with better comprehension—I think there has even been a spillover to their writing and now the other people on our team are trying to talk to them about how the strategies work in science, social studies, and math," she said.

Others agreed. Comprehension strategy instruction had made a huge difference in students' learning and in their teaching. They reflected on the improvements in students' work over the last several years and commented that there was lots of good news to hold on to, but sensed it was time to take the next step.

A Larger View

That coincides with what I've observed in American classrooms as well. The focus on strategy instruction has been a boost to comprehension in literature and across content areas and has caused us to reexamine our teaching and children's learning in a profound way. I want to pause for a moment to consider some of the changes I've seen in classrooms since we first read about strategy instruction in the 1980s.

Comprehension strategy instruction:

1. *Caused us to become more reflective about our own reading.* Many of us first discovered the power of comprehension strategies by becoming aware of them in our own reading. Teachers typically hadn't been asked to use strategies in our own schooling and when we became conscious of them, we saw immediately how beneficial strategy instruction would be for children. It wasn't long before we were able to extrapolate from our own reading processes to understand how to think aloud for children, making the complex comprehension processes more transparent.

2. *Created a common language between teachers and kids.* At one time it was too easy to conclude that children didn't understand a text or weren't developmentally "ready" to consider abstract ideas when in fact what was missing was a common language for them to use to describe and define their thinking. When teachers and children share the language of comprehension strategies, what we talk about today can be used independently tomorrow and well into the future. Children use the language of strategies to discuss insights and ideas about text and content knowledge in far more depth and across a broader age spectrum than we would have imagined. When children have comprehension strategies in their arsenal, they are far more likely to retain and reapply what they've read. Asking questions, for example, may cause them to continue to ponder as they read further in a text and can be used again in virtually any text they read at any time. Determining importance

helps children focus and retain key ideas from a text, sorting them from the peripheral details. A class can have discussions about how students asked questions or determined importance, no matter what book each child is reading. Strategy language gives children and teachers a common reference point to use in discussions about text and content-area concepts, making it much more likely that they'll use the tool in another context.

3. ***Increased the amount of time spent teaching comprehension.*** In many classrooms teachers now spend far more time teaching comprehension as opposed to "testing" comprehension by merely asking children to retell and answer comprehension questions about text. Comprehension strategies have become a means to focus explicit instruction on strategies proficient readers are known to use (Pearson et al. 1992; Pressley 2002). When teachers think aloud, the mysterious process of understanding becomes visible and audible for children, permitting them to use the same processes when reading independently. Children awaken the "voice in their minds" and let it take them into the depths of books they may not have ventured into without the strategies.

4. ***Generated innovation in classrooms.*** Teachers have imagined myriad ways to approach comprehension strategy instruction— from songs related to the strategies to book club discussions and colorful charts designed to serve as a visible reminder of the strategies. They have worked tirelessly to develop approaches to thinking aloud and gradually releasing responsibility to students to use the strategies independently. In an era when teachers are increasingly asked to use formulaic prescriptions and scripts in their teaching, strategy instruction has reawakened the artistry in our teaching.

5. ***Helped teachers raise expectations for all children.*** Teaching comprehension strategies has helped us see how much is possible for all learners when they're taught to think. Time and again, I'm told of children who typically don't share in a large group or who are identified for special education or were less inclined to think deeply who, when armed with strategies, have the confidence and the language to express their ideas in a way that challenges everyone's thinking about a book. Ours is a nation that gives a great deal

> Comprehension strategy instruction invites creative expression. Teachers and students can embrace the opportunity to deepen thinking through music, the visual arts, movement, and technology. No scripts provided— just a repertoire of approaches to "find a way in" to the minds of learners.
>
> —Tanny

12

of lip service to "higher expectations" but strategy instruction actually goes beyond rhetoric to give form and substance to the notion of teaching children to think at high levels. They rise to the occasion time after time.

6. *Made it acceptable to read slowly with depth and focus.* One of the key benefits of using comprehension strategies is that they actually slow kids down—and that's a good thing! In light of schools' measurement of children's reading based on words per minute and the time children spend with video games whose images change every second, it's worth remembering that the best thinking often takes the longest time. We need to actually teach kids to slow down and consider ideas they encounter in reading—and strategies are the tools we use to do so. If I ask a child to consider his inferences, it's going to take a bit of time. Using strategy instruction, we're learning to ask kids to pause and ponder, to focus on deeper understanding of texts and concepts—and that is a skill that will last long after we've said good-bye at the end of the year.

7. *Focused our instruction on the reader, not just the text.* In teaching comprehension strategies, we focus on how readers can actually get better at reading rather than on how they answer questions and retell. Most comprehension instruction before strategies focused on asking children to recall details from the text. Now we focus instruction on the mental moves proficient readers make to better understand the ideas and concepts in the text. While it's still critically important to focus on the text content, we know now that teaching children to approach and learn content strategically makes it more likely that they'll retain and reapply the concepts about which they read. In the end, aren't we most concerned with having children remember and reuse what they understand—long after we're there to remind them?

8. *Helps children to build a vast bank of content-area knowledge because they use strategies.* Because children are more likely to retain and reapply what they learn when they are metacognitive (aware of their own thinking and able to manipulate it) by teaching strategies, we are also teaching them to "hold on" to content knowledge. If, for example, a child learns about whales and is

> This is a pretty impressive list of accomplishments for a movement barely 25 years old. While there is plenty of room for the refinement of practice and searching for next steps, it feels completely appropriate to savor the significance of the work so far.
>
> —Smokey

asked to connect that new learning with what she already knows about mammals, it's far more likely that she'll remember the new content about whales. If a child is asked to synthesize following a reading about the Civil War, he is forced to make decisions about what was most important from several sources and texts and to interject his opinions and commentary about the content. Personalizing information makes it stick!

Comprehension strategy instruction has yielded a great deal with respect to children learning to use the language of thought. We know that strategy instruction is a tool that leads to deeper understanding, but we haven't yet resolved Jen's initial question. Isn't there more? Couldn't kids go deeper into their understanding of text more consistently? If we name the strategies and discuss them with children, why aren't we naming and discussing deeper comprehension? Do we know what deeper comprehension is?

Couldn't kids go deeper into their understanding of text? Do we know what deeper comprehension is?

A Plan Emerges

Back in the teachers' lounge, Julia underscored her sense that comprehension strategy instruction had been invaluable. "I agree. I just think that they could go deeper, more often," another added. "I guess this is all good news when you think about it. Our kids are doing more than we could have imagined even five years ago. We're just more ambitious for them. We know now that they're able to do more and we want them to!"

Craig, a sixth grade teacher, interjected, "I think we could make these questions the focus of our study group this year. We could do some research, read a professional book or look at journal articles together and get a better sense of what it really means to understand more deeply. And we could experiment with kids, bring their work in to look at . . . As a matter of fact, I think we should *start* by talking to the kids about this—we should see what they think. We can ask them to tell us what it means to understand more deeply. I'd be fascinated to hear what my kids would say if asked what it means to understand more deeply—to go beyond the strategies."

"Let's See What They Say"

The next day, Jen gathered her students around her in the front of the classroom and spoke honestly to them.

"I understand your frustration when you're asked to do something that you believe you've already done. I understand that you've had lots of opportunities when you were younger to learn about the comprehension strategies that help you understand better. Now I think you're ready for the next step." She paused a long moment.

"As your teacher, I want so much for you. I want you to understand some texts so deeply and well that you'll never forget them. I think you're ready to discover things in text that even the author may not have known were there; I think you're ready to talk about what you read in thoughtful and insightful ways with others; I think you can remember far more from your reading than you do right now and I believe you're ready to let books *affect* you in a profound way. I believe you're ready to come into the world of people who read because the characters and conflicts, the events and themes, the information and ideas actually change them. I think you're ready to read with a different outlook—not trying only to make a connection, but exploring how your connections really help you understand more effectively. I want this to be a watershed day—a day when we as a class and you individually change the reader you are into the reader you're able to become." Jen paused a moment. The students stared back. "Uh oh," she thought, but persevered.

"We have to figure out what helps us understand more deeply. We know comprehension strategies are tools to help readers understand—but what does it mean to understand deeply? We have to sort out that question together and I think we can use a portion of a book to help us.

"I'm going to read a short piece from Sandra Cisneros' book *The House on Mango Street.* Some of you are reading that book now; the piece I'm going to read aloud to you is an excerpt from it. You all have your reader's notebooks with you and I want you to begin to think about and take some notes on how you work to understand a text. Then I'm going to ask you to read this piece to yourselves and take more notes on how you work to comprehend. Here's what I mean by that. Think about what happens in your *minds*—what are you thinking about as you read? Do you create images, do you feel as if you're part of the book in some way, do you wonder things about the book? And what happens in your *lives*? What do you *do* to help yourself understand? Do you reread, do you understand more by talking to other readers about the text, do you feel like you want to write or draw to fully understand? What do you do in your life in order to understand? Okay? What do you do in your mind and in your life in order to understand? First I'll read aloud, then you'll read and take notes as you're reading, then we'll share."

Beautiful and Cruel

Sandra Cisneros

I am an ugly daughter. I am the one nobody comes for.

Nenny says she won't wait her whole life for a husband to come and get her, that Minerva's sister left her mother's house by having a baby, but she doesn't want to go that way either. She wants things all her own, to pick and choose. Nenny has pretty eyes and it's easy to talk that way if you are pretty.

My mother says when I get older my dusty hair will settle and my blouse will learn to stay clean, but I have decided not to grow up tame like the others who lay their necks on the threshold waiting for the ball and chain.

In the movies there is always one with red, red lips who is beautiful and cruel. She is the one who drives the men crazy and laughs them all away. Her power is her own. She will not give it away.

I have begun my own quiet war. Simple. Sure. I am one who leaves the table like a man, without putting back the chair or picking up the plate.

Jen read aloud, slowly and expressively and then asked the students to read the text silently. She reminded them of the ideas she wanted them to capture in their reader's notebooks—how did they go about understanding?

"I want you to divide a page in your reader's notebooks into two columns. At the top of one write *In My Mind* and at the top of the other write *My Actions*. In the first column I want to know what you were thinking as you read. Did you experience any emotion; did you gain any new perspective? Did you use strategies as tools to help you comprehend? How did that work? What did you come to understand because of the strategies that you didn't understand before?

"In the second column, *My Actions*, I want you to write about what you actually did, your behaviors during reading. Did you reread, did you take notes? Does discussion help you understand more completely? In that second column I want you to think about the actual moves you make to comprehend."

She was stunned to see them reading and writing furiously. They went back and forth between reading the short piece and writing about their comprehension in their reader's notebooks. Jen asked them to share their thinking with a partner by cautioning them to "remember that you and your partner can talk about the text, but I want you to really focus on what you were thinking and doing while you read."

The pairs talked animatedly for several minutes before Jen brought them back to the large group where they gathered around two easels with chart paper—labeled *In My Mind* and *My Actions*. She asked for volunteers to share not what they shared in their conversation, but what their *partner* said that surprised, excited, or inspired them. After a moment of confusion—in which those students who had raised their hands to share their ideas even before Jen finished the question quickly lowered them and whispered to their partners, "Quick, what did you say, tell me again . . . "—Jen's strategy for getting students to listen in a more thoughtful, fully attentive way was working. Finally, Jasmine raised her hand.

"My partner was Tiffany and she said that she had connections to her sister." Jen knew that this was one of the classic moments when there really must be more depth to their thinking; that the use of the strategy (in this case schematic connections) was the *beginning* of understanding, but not the outcome. She asked, "I understand that Tiffany had a connection to her sister when she read this. Tiffany, can you tell me how that connection helped you understand this piece better?"

Tiffany paused for a long moment. "I just think that my sister thinks she's the pretty one and she acts like it, but it's really just because she's older."

Jen persisted. "Oh, your sister thinks she's the pretty one and acts like that's true. How did thinking about her help you understand this piece better?"

Tiffany must have known then that she was going to have to respond differently. Jen wasn't asking about the connection—she was acknowledging Tiffany's thinking, but pushing beyond it. Schematic connections do support deeper understanding, but what was it that she understood more completely now that she had made the connection?

"Well," Tiffany said, "I guess it was that I felt like being pretty or hot or something is really overrated. I've always believed that people who might not be that good looking have the most to say sometimes. I think it gets better because my dad told me that he was never that handsome and it wasn't until he was in college that he felt that people took what he had to say seriously and really listened to him and stuff . . . "

She was stunned to see them reading and writing so furiously.

"What else, Tiffany?" Jen interjected.

"I don't know, I just . . . " Tiffany paused for a long moment. "I just think that the girl in this piece has some real strength because she's not giving in to what other people might do. She's a character that I'd actually like to know. I'm like; I'm really behind what she's doing. When it says that she's starting her war, she's standing up to what people expect from her and I have always thought and now I think even more that you have to expect a lot from yourself because other people, even your family, may not know what makes you strong and if you're not pretty, sometimes like that girl, you've got to have real power in you, like inside yourself to surprise people who don't expect that much from you. It's like she's learning that it's good to be smart and that's where her power comes from."

"So, Tiffany, it's really interesting to me because all of your thoughts started out as a connection to your sister, but when I asked you how your connections helped you understand the piece more, you had a lot more to say." Other students had hands up and were clearly ready to jump into the conversation but Jen held them off for another moment.

"I want to capture your thinking up on one of these easels, Tiffany. Do you think that what you just described belongs on the *In My Mind* chart paper or the *My Actions* sheet?"

"I would say *In My Mind*," replied Tiffany, "because it was really all just stuff I was thinking about—as a matter of fact, some of it came to me just now as I was talking."

"Exactly. So that tells me that part of your deeper comprehension was *In My Mind* and part of it was *My Actions*."

Jen wrote on the chart paper under *In My Mind*:
You understand deeply when:

- your beliefs are affirmed or strengthened (or changed) by something you read
- you feel like you're "behind" the character—a sense of advocacy

Then she wrote on the chart paper under *My Actions*:
You understand deeply when:

- you talk it out with a partner or in the large group

"Tiffany, you really did both. You talked about how your existing beliefs were affirmed and strengthened and you spoke about how you felt a sense of advocacy—that you really wanted to speak out on the character's behalf in this piece. But you went on to say something that I think is important. You said that part of what you understood, you discovered only as you talked about it. That's true for a lot of us as readers. We're not sure about all we think, feel and believe until we speak to someone about it. You guys helped us understand, in part, how comprehension strategies help us. You made a connection, but what was most interesting is where the connection led you in your understanding. You didn't stop at making a connection, Tiffany, you went on to tell me how the connection helped you understand this text more deeply."

Jen asked several of her students to go beyond the use of a comprehension strategy and to talk about where it led them. When they shared a connection, for example, she pushed them further by asking "How did the connection help you understand more deeply?" and then probing further by merely saying "What else?" She restated what Tiffany and others said, giving them time to think more deeply about how they viewed the piece, and then captured their thinking in a concise way on chart paper.

Jen confessed later that, while she liked the opening to the lesson, she wasn't entirely convinced that it would lead to any significant changes in her students' reading. She couldn't have been more off the mark. Jen's students rallied that day. Her words inspired them. It mattered less that any of them knew exactly how their transformation as readers would come about than the fact that she believed they were capable of much more and she articulated her hope for them. She had a nagging instinct that they could probe meaning further, go deeper, remember and reuse what they read. Jen was determined to herald a new day in her classroom, one in which students were expected to push their thinking further. She hoped that her words that day and in the days to come would be enough to launch them on a journey toward deeper understanding.

In literacy education, we often talk about wanting children to understand more deeply and we wonder why they don't retain and reapply what we've taught, even a few days later. These are important and closely related questions. If students understand more deeply, they are more likely to remember and reuse what they have read and/or learned about. So what does it mean to understand more deeply? I have found that there are certain indicators or markers of deeper understanding—some cognitive and some behavioral—that allow us to talk more specifically with children about what we really mean by deeper comprehension. I refer to the cognitive indicators, or thinking patterns, in the following, as the Outcomes of Understanding and to the behavior indicators as the Dimensions of Understanding (Keene 2008).

Ellin, the charts on pp. 20–23) *alone* have enough food for thought for years of nourishment for me. I am so excited to read this with teachers and help them figure out implications for their classroom practice. You get right to the heart of the purpose of education and help all of us keep our eyes on what matters most. The WHY we read—and the HOW it makes us more human and more humane.

How Do We Really Know if They Comprehend Deeply?

THE OUTCOMES AND DIMENSIONS OF UNDERSTANDING	
OUTCOMES	OUTCOMES
In Our Minds *Thinking patterns that characterize deeper comprehension (narrative text)*	*In Our Minds* *Thinking patterns that characterize deeper comprehension (expository text)*
1. Readers **experience empathy**—we sense that we are somehow in the book. Empathy can include: • **Character empathy** in which we feel we know the characters, experience the same emotions, stand by them in their trials • **Setting empathy** in which we feel a part of the setting • **Conflict empathy** in which we experience the internal and external conflict as if firsthand • **Author empathy** in which we believe we understand why the author wrote as he/she did, how he/she manipulates the reader's understanding with literary tools such as diction, foreshadowing, imagery, voice, and plot structures	1. Learners **describe a fascination** with ideas. This can take several forms: • We begin to **understand leadership**—we explore and begin to understand the lives of those who have made significant contributions to a field and begin to imagine how we might make contributions • We **understand the context and conditions** that lead to important discoveries in the scientific, technological, or social-scientific world • We **understand the problems that lead to discoveries and new solutions**—we have a sense of the elements that make a situation problematic and some sense of the steps to be taken to solve the problem
2. Readers **experience a memorable emotional response**—the sense that what we feel may be part of our emotional life for a long time, we may feel moved to take action to mitigate a conflict in the world	2. Learners **experience a memorable emotional response**—the sense that, because of our emotional response, we may be moved to take action to mitigate a conflict in the world
3. Readers **experience the aesthetic**—we feel a desire to linger with or reread portions of the text we find beautiful, well written, surprising, funny, or moving; we want to experience portions of the book again and we may wish that the book wouldn't end	3. Learners **experience the aesthetic**—we feel a sense of wonder about the complexities and nuances related to a concept we are learning; we may feel compelled to reread portions
4 Readers **ponder**—we feel a desire to **pause and consider** new facets and twists in the text; we want to reread in order to understand more deeply	4. Learners **revisit and rethink**—we choose to reread or explore other texts in order to learn more about a concept; we feel that we want to review and rethink a concept

OUTCOMES	OUTCOMES
In Our Minds *Thinking patterns that characterize deeper comprehension (narrative text)*	*In Our Minds* *Thinking patterns that characterize deeper comprehension (expository text)*
5. Readers find themselves thinking about the book when they're not reading—we **generate new ideas and imagine new possibilities** in characters' lives; our ideas are original, but related to the text	**5.** Learners **generate our own hypotheses and theories** about why and how things happen in the natural and social world
6. Readers **focus, advocate, and evaluate**—we may follow one character or plot element more intensively and may have the sense of being "behind" the character(s) or narrator; we want events to evolve in a particular way; we discern and evaluate the author's success in making the book credible	**6.** Learners **direct our energy to comprehending a few ideas of great import**—we develop a sense of what matters most, what is worth remembering, and have the confidence to focus on important ideas rather than details that are unimportant to the larger text; we **evaluate the information** and make decisions about credibility or bias in what we read
7. Readers **recognize patterns and symbols**—we may experience a moment of insight or begin to use our knowledge of literary tools to recognize themes and motifs as well as symbols and metaphors in stories	**7.** Learners **recognize patterns and text structures** including • **cause/effect**—we use our knowledge of how events relate to one other • **recognize comparisons and contrasts**—we develop a sense of how concepts are similar and different • **chronology**—we sense the general order of development or the progression of a series of ideas • **problem/solution**—when a problem is introduced, we begin to consider solutions and/or to anticipate solutions that may be presented in the text
8. Readers extrapolate from details in the text—we arrive at **global conclusions from focal points** in the text; these conclusions may reach beyond the scope of the text to other people, events, and settings	**8.** Learners **create schema**—we realize how newly learned concepts "fit" into existing background knowledge, that we can make sense in relation to what is already known; that our existing knowledge is accurate or inaccurate (and needs to be revised); we look to a variety of sources to complete schema when we recognize that it is missing

(continued)

THE OUTCOMES AND DIMENSIONS OF UNDERSTANDING (continued)	
OUTCOMES	**OUTCOMES**
In Our Minds *Thinking patterns that characterize deeper comprehension (narrative text)*	*In Our Minds* *Thinking patterns that characterize deeper comprehension (expository text)*
9. Readers **recognize the influence of beliefs/values/opinions**—we may experience a sense of affirmation of existing beliefs/values/opinions and/or sense newly developing beliefs/values/opinions related to the text; we can give evidence to support our beliefs/values/opinions	**9.** Learners **recognize the influence of beliefs/values/opinions**—we may experience a sense of affirmation of existing beliefs/values/opinions and/or sense newly developing beliefs/values/opinions related to the text; we can give evidence to support our beliefs/values/opinions
10. Readers **remember**—we develop a sense of permanence that comes with deeply understanding something; we know that we'll be able to use a concept we understand in a new situation	**10.** Learners **remember**—we develop a sense of permanence that comes with deeply understanding something; we know that we'll be able to use a concept they understand in a new situation

DIMENSIONS OF UNDERSTANDING
OUR ACTIONS
Behaviors associated with understanding (what we might observe in the classroom when children are understanding)
1. Readers are deeply **engaged**—we experience a sense that the world around has disappeared and we are subsumed by the world of the text; we choose to **focus** on particular ideas for longer periods of time, we may need to focus in silence and/or in conversation with others; we **apply fervent attention**; we can observe others concentrating with a focus that is nearly impenetrable
2. Readers want to **leave a written, artistic, or dramatic legacy**—we want to make an observable contribution to the world around us based on what we have learned about characters in fiction or ideas in expository text; we **write (or create art or dramatic depictions)** considering how to apply a writer's style, ideas, and techniques in our own writing; we **consider the audience and purpose** for reading and adapt our comprehension processes accordingly; we **respond and share our thinking accordingly**
3. Readers **show willingness to struggle**—we choose to challenge ourselves in order to understand more deeply; we select and do our best to understand difficult text if that's what it takes to understand a pressing question; we consciously fight any influence of negative self-judgment and seek, with a sense of efficacy, to solve complex problems

OUR ACTIONS (continued)
Behaviors associated with understanding (what we might observe in the classroom when children are understanding)
4. Readers can **describe our progress as readers**—we can describe our own processes, preferences, and progress as a reader; we can describe, for example, how we used a comprehension strategy and how such use improved our understanding; we **define and describe how our thinking has changed** and can ascribe those changes to the use of comprehension strategies or other factors
5. Readers **engage in rigorous discourse**—we speak with others in order to develop deeper understanding and/or defend our ideas; we remain open to **multiple** perspectives and consider others' ideas seriously, often integrating them into our own background knowledge; we **argue/defend**; we may discuss, challenge others' ideas and beliefs, and/or defend our own with evidence from the text and from background knowledge (schema)
6. Readers are **renaissance learners**—we meander among a wide range of topics, interests, genres, and authors and pursue study in areas we find compelling or aesthetically rewarding; we **pursue a compelling question**; we may decide to tackle a topic of intense interest in order to build a knowledge base or satisfy curiosity
7. Readers **discuss and act**—we share emotional reactions and may feel an urge to do something or act in some way to mitigate or resolve related conflicts in the world; we can talk about how a book changed us and caused us to think and act differently in our own lives
8. Readers **experience insight**—we experience and can describe a moment of clarity, of "seeing" for the first time, possibly due to our efforts to recognize patterns and structures in text
9. Readers **remember**—we reapply previously learned concepts and ideas in new learning situations

What Are the Outcomes and Dimensions of Understanding and How Did I Identify Them?

I'm fortunate enough to work with teachers and children all over the country and I often ask them to reflect on how they came to comprehend text. I use the technique that Jen used with her seventh graders: I read a short text aloud, ask them to follow up by reading it silently, and as they do so to make some notes about how they go about comprehending. What is happening in their minds? How do they make sense of the text? What goes on cognitively when we're working to comprehend? What is happening in their lives? What behaviors do they engage in that make the text more understandable? I then ask them to share their insights with a neighbor before we share several with the whole group. Very often, children and adults will say that they made connections, questioned, had mental images, or inferred—all comprehension strategies. I record their ideas and then ask a simple question or two to follow up: What did you understand in this piece because you asked questions (or any of the other strategies)? What do you understand now that you didn't before? These straightforward little questions often lead to some extraordinary insights and active learning behaviors that I characterize as the Outcomes and Dimensions of Understanding.

The Outcomes and Dimensions of Understanding: Hallmarks of Deeper Understanding

The Outcomes of Understanding are, in my view, descriptors of deeper understanding. They were gleaned from hundreds of responses I've recorded from children and adults, usually when the reader was describing strategy use. The reader shared how they were thinking strategically and I merely asked how that strategy helped them understand the piece they were reading. There were usually moments of silence that were uncomfortable (mostly for the teacher) before the reader responded with an insight about the text. When they did, it was often the kind of response that we used to hear only occasionally—surprising, insightful, probing, fresh perspectives that led the entire group into a discussion of new facets of the text that they had not yet discovered. It's deeper understanding.

Very simply, I began to see patterns in those responses and the patterns became the Outcomes. For example, many readers describe moments when they paused to think more about the text, and found that they wanted to reread it in order to contemplate some aspect of the text (see Figure 1, Number 4, p. 20). Many others began with focus on a detail in the text, but led the reader to draw much larger conclusions about the world beyond the text (see Figure 1, Number 8 , p. 21). Take a moment to look at all the Outcomes in Figure 1 now. You'll notice that there are two columns; one for the patterns in thinking I picked up when the adults or children were reading narrative text, another for the patterns that emerged when the readers were reading expository text. Are there any of the Outcomes you don't believe correlate to deeper understanding? Are there others you would add to the list?

I began to realize that, if a child was describing her thinking and it correlated to one of the outcomes, we can reliably predict that she understands quite deeply. She may or may not understand as well elsewhere in the text, but when she describes, for example, how she felt emotionally moved to take some kind of action to mitigate a problem in the world (Figure 1, Number 2, p. 20). I have little doubt that she understands the subtleties of the text. It soon became clear to me that I had discovered some (though perhaps not all) of the hallmarks of higher-level comprehension.

For example, a second grader named Ella shared an inference about the book *One Green Apple* by Eve Bunting. I asked, "What else do you understand in this book because you inferred?" She paused for a moment and then said, "I guess when I had that inference it made me think about the girl with the head scarf when no one else had one. She didn't have any English and she was trying so hard to fit in with what everyone else was doing. When I read that part, my heart started beating really hard, just like if I was her and I didn't know how to use the apple machine and my hands were shaking. I guess I felt like I was her and the things that were happening to her were really happening to me." That comment describes **empathy** for the character (see Figure 1, Number 1, p. 20). Feeling as if you are actually *in* the book, responding as the characters might, experiencing their conflicts as your own is an empathetic response—one of the hallmarks of deeper understanding.

Empathy is just one of the outcomes I've noticed frequently. Children may begin, for example, by describing a question they had while reading; after I ask how their question helped them better understand the text, they go on to say how they found a particular part of the text dense enough with meaning that it was worthy of a second or third reading (see Figure 1, Number 4, p. 20). All readers ponder occasionally—we can increase this occasional happy accident. We can describe to children what it feels like to pause and consider new facets and twists in the text; to want to reread in order to understand more deeply. I found that many of the adults and children with whom I've worked describe a desire to slow down and consider what may be layered underneath the words; they sense that there is something more to understand and feel compelled to actually stop reading and ponder the ideas that are not as obvious upon the first reading. They describe rereading several times to give adequate thought to the ideas embedded there. The original inference *leads* to the Outcome of Understanding.

It was after noticing these patterns that I began to wonder—what would happen if we thought aloud for children about how readers feel empathetic or feel compelled to reread to understand more subtle meanings—

wouldn't they want to be part of that club? Wouldn't they want to be the kind of reader who experiences empathy or the desire to pause and ponder?

What I found, of course, is that children throughout the grade spectrum were fascinated and delighted to be part of that group of readers who experience empathy or a memorable emotional response or are able to reach more global conclusions by extrapolating from a small portion of the text or any one of the Outcomes of Understanding. It takes so little time and effort on our part: ask them to reflect on how using the strategy helped them understand more deeply and wait for the response and name what outcome the child has used! You may well find that there are responses that don't easily fit one of the Outcomes—you and your students will want to add to my list since there isn't any fixed, correct list. These Outcomes are based on my experience; yours may well be different. Whatever you discover, be sure to record it in a visible way in the classroom to serve as a reminder of the pinnacles of understanding for your classroom.

The Dimensions of Understanding also came from a very reliable source—watching and listening to children when they are engaged in understanding. I noticed that there are actually visible and audible manifestations of understanding including, but not limited to, the "Aha!" moments we've all come to love as teachers. These Dimensions-related behaviors, preferences, and propensities are actually visible and/or audible when a child understands deeply. The Dimensions are also hallmarks of deeper understanding.

For example, I watched a fourth grader, Sam—standing at his desk, his chair pushed back, leaning over a book. I got a little closer and noticed that he was reading about space and that he was completely lost in the world of his book. He was fervent, impassioned, almost fanatical (see Figure 2, Number 1, p. 22) about answering questions he had about how scientists design everyday articles for use in a weightless environment. Sam had a pile of books on and around his desk that I'm sure constituted a fire hazard; and as he read, he was designing the interior of a spacecraft. His lines were precise and the various areas labeled: sleeping quarters, kitchen, resting area, and cockpit. Sam rarely looked up and actually became a little annoyed when someone interrupted him. He drew and labeled items throughout his spaceship and referred frequently to books. As I watched and took notes on his behaviors, I thought to myself, "Now that's understanding." Every cell in his body was engaged.

Sam was fervent (see Figure 2, Number 1, p. 22) in his learning, something not uncommon when a child understands. When I talked to Sam about his research, I found that he was clearly grasping the concepts about which he read. He had a question of passionate interest and he was going for it with all his intellectual and even physical energy (at least as much as classroom decorum permitted!). Sam was also exhibiting signs of a renaissance learner (see Figure 2, Number 6, p. 23). A renaissance learner may meander among several topics of interest before concentrating on one. Sam's initial study varied from those of his classmates in that he had garnered permission to explore space (the rest of his class was studying the solar system) from a slightly different angle. He had the chutzpah to ask his teacher if he could take his query in a slightly different direction and she had the wisdom to say yes. Now he had generated his own questions and was pursuing them with passionate interest. No one told him to draw a diagram of his spaceship. He had chosen to do so in order to remember what was important from his research and to have a written record (see Figure 2, Number 2, p. 22). He displayed at least three of the Dimensions of Understanding that day.

Engaging in discourse (see Figure 2, Number 5, p. 23) is another of the Dimensions we see frequently in classrooms. Think back to our earlier example of Jasmine and Tiffany when they shared the comprehension processes they used to understand the little essay "Beautiful and Cruel." Jasmine pointed out that Tiffany had made a connection to her sister when reading the essay and when Jen asked how that connection made a difference in her understanding, Tiffany pursued new ideas by talking about them with the whole class. Discourse is a powerful tool in the process of understanding and children often think that they have to have everything in mind before they raise their hands or turn to another child to share. However, it's in the talking that we come to understand, and children need to be reminded of that frequently.

> Thankfully, we've moved beyond the diorama days of responding to reading! Thanks, Ellin, for sharing Sam's story. He just can't help himself build meaning with his on-the-spot constructed space craft.
>
> —*Chryse*

What Does All This Mean?

The Outcomes and Dimensions of Understanding are patterns of thinking and behavior that appear highly correlated to deeper understanding. But how do we set up a unit of study focused on empathy? I'd like to suggest that there are better, more subtle ways of incorporating the Outcomes and Dimensions into the classroom.

1. *Name the Dimensions and Outcomes for children. Post them around the room.* Naming the Outcomes and Dimensions for

children is crucial if we're going to move to the next stage in comprehension instruction. I'm certainly not suggesting that the Outcomes and Dimensions become a whole new curriculum or, horrors, a scripted set of responses to children's work. I have noticed, however, that when teachers are savvy about the Outcomes and Dimensions, they watch and "catch kids in the act" of using them and then label them for the students. In a first grade classroom, the students had a wide-ranging conversation about empathy and how you know if you are experiencing empathy. During an independent reading period one day as the teacher was conferring with individual students, seven-year-old Lacy burst out, "I got it, I got it, I was empathetic!" (though it came out more like *empafetic* due to some missing teeth). Her teacher smiled and asked the rest of the children to attend to Lacy while she shared the moment in her reading where she felt empathetic. This little punctuation in an otherwise routine day served to remind children that, as important as it is to use strategies as tools to deepen understanding, we still have to ask ourselves—what *is* deeper understanding? To be empathetic is at least part of deeper understanding.

More typically, however, a teacher will discover—in the course of a conference or while children are sharing in a group—that they are displaying one or more of the Outcomes and Dimensions. This is a perfect opportunity to help them give language to something they already do. If, for example, a teacher noticed that a child was extrapolating from a text detail to a larger issue, she might say, "Wait a minute! I just heard something in what you said that I think you need to know. When you just talked about how the girl's head scarf in *One Green Apple* made you think of the ways that head coverings have been thought of in negative ways, you were doing what's called 'focal to global.' You took a focal detail in this text and used it to think way beyond the text. You realized that there is nothing negative about head scarves or other head coverings that people wear unless people talk about them in negative ways. I want to tell the rest of the class and get it on our poster so that others can go from focal to global in their reading."

2. *Think aloud about ways in which you find yourself using the Dimensions and Outcomes in your own reading.* I can hardly overes-

> I've begun doing this—and WOW! While I'm always asking the kids to help me understand how they're understanding—and to reflect on their thinking—this makes it explicit. What I notice most is that kids are using *empathy*—and becoming able to articulate it. Can't wait to see how far they get by the end of the year!
>
> — Leslie

28

timate the importance of showing children how you use the Outcomes and Dimensions of Understanding. When you're reading aloud and thinking aloud about a strategy, go the next step and talk about where that strategy leads you. For example, in a recent demonstration lesson, I was reading *An Angel for Solomon Singer* by Cynthia Rylant and teaching a class of third graders how we create mental images in order to understand more deeply. I shared an image that came to me as the central character, a man one step away from homelessness, wanders the streets of New York City longing for his home in Indiana.

"I had an image on this page," I told them, "and it surprised me a little. All of a sudden, I imagined Solomon as a very young child and I saw him running through wheat fields and climbing trees, breathing fresh air and feeling the wind breezing through the cottonwoods. I could actually even imagine what he wanted to be when he grew up and I don't think his adult life is the way he imagined it. Then I turned to this page where we can see glimpses of his home in Indiana as if they are part of the background he sees as he wanders the streets in New York and it helps me understand his longing more. I can see why he misses the land around his home. I also have to tell you that I find these illustrations so beautiful. I want to study them and study them. I find insight about Solomon when I do. I understand him more. When you find something so beautiful or so compelling that you just have to look at it over and over or read it again and again, you're experiencing an aesthetic sensation (page 20, Number 3). *Aesthetic* means beautiful or appreciating beauty. Let me show you that word on our list of Outcomes of Understanding because I find that I only find something so beautiful that I would label it aesthetically pleasing every once in a while. The word *aesthetic* isn't for an everyday word or two or picture that you kind of like. It's a word to use when you're describing something that is one of the most beautiful things you've ever seen. I'm not sure whether any of you have ever had a moment where you found something aesthetically memorable in a book you were reading or in your life outside school . . . " That's all I needed to say. One little girl said that she found horses aesthetically moving. "Every time we're driving and I see a horse I get goose bumps. I think they are so beautiful. I don't think I'll ever in my whole life think that anything is more beautiful than a horse." Several others raised their hands.

I don't expect that children will remember and use the word *aesthetic* immediately, but given that the word is posted and that the teacher will go back and think aloud about portions of a book or elements from her own life that she finds aesthetically pleasing, they'll start to use the word. Perhaps more importantly, they'll recognize when something in a book is stunning or compelling to dwell in.

In either case, remember to add to anchor charts—one labeled *In My Mind* (for the Outcomes of Understanding) and one labeled *My Actions* (for the Dimensions of Understanding). You will find that children will devise Outcomes and Dimensions that don't appear on the lists I've provided in Figures 1 and 2.

3. *Ask the critical question: How did using that strategy help you understand more?* One of the most important things we can do to help students deepen their understanding is to expect more depth from them each time they share their thinking, and question them in a way that will lead to deeper understanding. When a child raises his hand to share his use of a strategy, for example, ask him to say more. Ask him to say *how* (not if) his image (or any of the other strategies) helped him understand the text more—what does he know now about the text that he didn't know before? If he says, "I don't know," you can always try my favorite line—"I know you don't know, but if you did know, what would you say?" It works nearly every time because it gives the child a chance to think a little longer. If he shares a little more, say "What else?"

The point is that we have to give children extended opportunities to talk about their thinking in order to figure out what they think! Our questions should serve as probes to deeper thinking, and should not lead them to say what we're thinking or want them to say. For instance, if I ask a child, "Did that image make you think that this line was aesthetically beautiful?" I'm leading her to say only "yes." But if I ask a child to think about how she understands the text better because she used the strategy, I'm probing into entirely new territory. Once children know some of the language of

> "*I* know you don't know, but if you did know, what would you say?"

the Outcomes and Dimensions of Understanding, they will be better able to respond—"My image helped me understand that Solomon Singer's life was very lonely and it made me think about other homeless people in the world. I want to do something to try to make homeless peoples' lives easier."

4. *Use the Outcomes and Dimensions as markers of deeper comprehension.* "How do I know if my students understand deeply and well?" "Will they retain and reapply what they have learned?" These are among the most important questions we can ask. We need some indicators to show when a child understands deeply and well. Though it was not my original intent to develop such a set of markers, I realized that, because the Outcomes and Dimensions are the result of observing children who are in the process of understanding well, they are markers of deep comprehension. We just need to remember to observe children carefully, "catch them in the act," and name what they have done. I carry the list of Outcomes and Dimensions with me as I confer with students as a reminder (I can't keep them all in my mind!) to ask more probing questions and help children explore their thinking beyond a superficial retelling or surface-level use of a strategy. Again, the key question: How did the strategy help you understand?

Let's return to Sam, the would-be astronaut for a moment. Sam completed the design for his spaceship interior, complete with accurate information about how loose items are battened down and how astronauts sleep without floating around inside the cabin. His teacher now has a choice—she can ask Sam to share his design with the rest of the class or she and Sam can talk to the rest of the class about the Dimensions Sam exhibited throughout his project. Remember, she noticed that he was concentrating intensely, fervently, and he was acting as a renaissance learner. It turned out that Sam's teacher did both. She asked Sam to conduct a study group of students who wanted to learn what he had learned about the inside of a spaceship. But, more importantly in my view, she told the class what she had seen. She and Sam together defined what it is to learn fervently and described a renaissance learner. This increases the likelihood that they will recognize the same qualities in themselves when they are in the process of understanding. It's strategic—she wasn't just teaching something about space—she's teaching them about what highly effective learners do.

Back to School—Could It Be Yours?

Jen and her colleagues came together two weeks later to discuss their students' responses when asked what they do to understand deeply. Jen's class wasn't the only one that had rallied! Other teachers found that when they labeled and spent time talking about deep understanding, the students actually engaged more predictably in those processes. It was, they decided, important to weave the language of understanding—the Outcomes and Dimensions—into their daily work with students rather than to make it a stand-alone curriculum. They read *To Understand* and talked with students about their own and the students' intellectual mentors. They met every two weeks to discuss how they named and described students' experiences in using the Outcomes and Dimensions and found that the language became an integral part of their daily interactions.

Jen, who at one time felt that her students could do so much more, spoke to them one day in late May. "I'm becoming a bit melancholy about losing you at the end of the year. This year has been a different kind of learning experience than I have ever had and I'm going to miss our conversations. Believe it or not, I've never had the kinds of exchanges with students that I've had with you. I never talked with kids about what they experience when they understand deeply until this year and you've helped me gain insight into your minds and your lives when you understand. You've shown me that you can be empathetic when you read; that you're drawn to certain things aesthetically; that you can choose to take some action to solve a problem based on your reaction to a text; and you've shown me that you develop your own perspectives more effectively when you talk to each other about what you read. I'll never forget when you lost yourselves so completely in your reading that the fire alarm could have gone off and you might have sat right through it! You've learned what it is to be a renaissance learner and to pause and think more deeply about a text rather than just flying through it at high speed. You've taught me what it means to understand deeply, but more importantly you know what it means to understand deeply and you will never again need to find yourself in a situation where you feel overwhelmed or confused. You have a kind of intellectual power that no one can take from you now. I feel great sending you on into the world when you're the confident and agile thinkers I know you to be."

There is more. Students can do more than recite the language of comprehension strategies and, as important as it is to teach strategies, Jen and her colleagues found that students can leverage their use of strategies into far deeper, more permanent understanding. Children want to understand—they're hardwired to understand—and they love to be surprised and challenged by the depth and quality of their own and others' insights. We need to remember to ask the questions that lead to deeper understanding and then stand back! Their insights await us all.

References

Professional Reading

Keene, Ellin Oliver. 2008. *To Understand*. Portsmouth, NH: Heinemann.

Pearson, P. David, Laura Roehler, Janice A. Dole, and Gerald G. Duffy. 1992. "Developing Expertise in Reading Comprehension." In *What Research Has to Say About Reading Instruction*, edited by S. Jay Samuels and Alan Farstrup. Newark, DE: International Reading Association.

Pressley, Michael. 2002. *Reading Instruction That Works*, 2d ed. New York: Guilford Press.

Readings for Students

Bunting, Eve. 2006. *One Green Apple*. New York: Clarion Books.

Cisneros, Sandra. 1994. *The House on Mango Street*. New York: Knopf.

Rylant, Cynthia. 1996. *An Angel for Soloman Singer*. New York: Scholastic.

$\mathcal{B}$ring the Joy Back to Reading

Susan Zimmermann

> When I look back, I am so impressed again with the life-giving power of literature. If I were a young person today, trying to gain a sense of myself in the world, I would do that again by reading, just as I did when I was young.
>
> —MAYA ANGELOU

Several years ago I stayed at a bed and breakfast in Van Wert, Ohio. A spacious, Victorian house with a large front porch, antique furniture, chintz fabrics, and perfectly tended yard, I felt like I was visiting old friends. Early in my stay, after meeting children and grandchildren, the owner—a vivacious blond who did not look like a grandmother—asked me why I was there.

"I'm giving a summer institute on reading comprehension," I told her.

"Can I come?" she laughed. "No, I'm serious," she continued. "I never liked to read much. In school I was always pretty good in math and I'd get As in reading, but I always got Ds in comprehension. I could read, but I couldn't understand."

She could read, but not really. This was not a new lament. For many years, the focus has been on getting kids to decode well. With effort, they crack the decoding puzzle and become fluent readers. They are proud of their accomplishment. Their parents think they are good readers. But like the bed and breakfast owner in Van Wert, many aren't really reading. They're good at the decoding game, but they aren't making sense of what they read. They are skimming the surface of the words. They aren't really thinking. They aren't really reading.

In workshops, I frequently ask participants to jot down their memories of learning to read. After a pause ("my mind's a blank . . . I don't remember anything . . . "), heads bow and pens start moving across pages. When they start sharing, the buzz in the room grows. Everyone has a learning-to-read story—some good, some bad. The "good" stories involve several common themes: (1) someone who read to them—their mom, dad, grandmother, first grade teacher, librarian, older sibling, and so on; (2) ready access to books— lots of books in their homes or frequent trips to the library (or bookmobile); and (3) a book that lit their reading fire—comic books (*Superman* is a big favorite), Nancy Drew, Hardy Boys, Harry Potter, *Charlotte's Web*, and Dr. Seuss. When they look back they remember some book that reached right into their hearts and minds and forever changed them. They are touched, deeply. They realize those squiggles on the page are words packed with meaning that create whole new worlds for them to explore. They hear, see, feel, taste, and smell. They are on a quest for adventure and new information. They pursue new interests. They connect to the characters, make friends, and fight enemies. They learn about planets, dinosaurs, and epic discoveries. Their lives are enhanced. There is nothing they can't learn about. They are hooked. Years later, they remember the sense of power that real reading gave them.

All the memories aren't positive. People in their thirties, forties, fifties, and sixties carry scars from their early days of learning to read—frequently from classrooms. Statements like this are common: "I could read before I started school and all we did was phonics. I started hating to read"; "My teacher told me I was a slow reader and I believed her. To this day, that's how I view myself"; "I had real problems decoding and the other kids made fun of me when we read out loud"; "I never thought school reading was real. It was a game. My real reading happened at home"; "Reading was boring"; "I never could understand why people liked to read. It was just words on a page. It didn't mean anything." People reveal a disinterest in reading, often engendered in school ("I never could read anything that I cared about") and talk about arriving, in college or even years later, at a place where they enjoy reading. Others, to this day, confess to hating to read.

Teachers Really Matter

Something is amiss in American education and teachers are the only people who can fix it—not politicians or administrators or parents, though they can help teachers a great deal. Somewhere along the line we've forgotten that education is not about getting this or that score on a test, but it is about enlarging hearts, minds, and spirits. It's about fulfilling human potential and unleashing human creativity. It's about helping children understand that the world is a place full of wonder, truly *wonder-full*. It's about giving children the tools they will need to participate in a complex global world where we can't imagine today what the next twenty years, let alone century, will bring. It's about remembering the enormous dangers in our nuclear age and that only through education and breaking down barriers will we be able to address those dangers without destroying the world as we know it.

Both of my grandmothers, Beatrice and Florine, lived to be nearly one hundred. Both were born early in the 1900s. Both experienced going from a horse-and-buggy age to a man-on-the-moon age, from typewriters to laptops, from women not having the vote to women serving on the Supreme Court. When they were in school, they had no idea what their century would bring—cars, televisions, microwaves, supersonic transport, computers, fax machines, fast food, the Internet, cell phones, etc. How could they have begun to imagine the breakthroughs and inventions that would occur during their lifetimes? How can we contemplate what our planet will look like in the next one hundred years? Change, it seems, is the only constant and it will continue at warp speed for our children.

Somehow, in our effort to make sure that no child is left behind (or that no child is left untested!) we have forgotten that we need to teach children to be thinkers and problem solvers. We need to nurture their creativity and celebrate their imaginations. We need to find ways to bring intellectual rigor and expansiveness to the classroom so young people will be able to deal with and adapt to the changes they will, no doubt, face—and so that their lives can be as rich and productive as possible. Reading is key because it unlocks the door to the mind. Once that door is opened, the sky is truly the limit.

It is in the classroom that this will occur, not in the halls of Congress or in the meeting rooms of school district offices. Parents, of course, should

Student conversations inside and outside the classroom walls inform us about their interests, curiosities, and questions they have about their world. We just need to listen in.

Kids get very excited to explore questions that are their own. Once they know their questions matter, they keep asking them. Students' curiosities stoke their excitement about learning and understanding.

—Anne & Brad

be major partners in the effort of educating their children. Many are. But studies show that even when the much-desired parental involvement isn't there, good teachers—year after year—can provide the support, skills, and nurturance that a child needs to succeed in school and in life (Center for Public Education 2005). Good teachers matter. Good teachers change lives.

First, Do No Harm

In medicine there is the maxim "First, do no harm." It reminds health care professionals that they must consider the possible harm that any intervention might cause, that they must avoid a "cure that is worse than the ill." We need to adopt that maxim in education. Do nothing that makes a child feel ignorant or inferior; nothing that bores children so they turn off to learning; nothing that underestimates their gifts and potential; nothing that values a test score over a child's imagination. First, do no harm.

How many children are turned off to reading because of what we do to them in school? How many children do we lose because of an attitude toward reading that is dry, clinical, and tied inevitably to tests? How would you feel as an adult reader if everything you read was graded, if you couldn't put a book down when it didn't capture your interest or you thought it was poorly written—or you found something else that interested you ten times more? What child who has access to television, computers, video games, and all the other entertainments of our time is going to choose to read when it is presented as something that is dull, rote, scripted, and boring? Are children going to want to dive into the next book that sparks their interest when reading is presented as something they have to do because they're going to get tested on it—not because it is a way to travel throughout the world, time travel to different centuries, and find out about absolutely anything that piques their curiosity?

Children come into our educational system thirsty for knowledge. They are learning machines. By the time they enter kindergarten most have mastered an oral language without having been taught a thing. They are brilliant linguists. They are sponges. They are intrepid learners, because they are unabashed about trying new things and have no fear of failure. This is key: they're not afraid to be wrong. There is a story about a little six-year-old girl who was in the back of her classroom, drawing like crazy. The teacher comes up and asks her what she's doing. "I'm drawing a picture of God," she says. "But no one knows what God looks like," the teacher responds. "They will in a minute," the little girl says and goes back to drawing furiously.

> Susan is right here. Teachers are the key and in this era we are called upon to make courageous decisions in classrooms—even decisions that defy conventional wisdom and existing policy. Increasingly, good teaching becomes an act of civil disobedience—at least some of the time. Yet isn't that the way that true change has happened in the world?
>
> — *Ellin*

When given the chance, kids are bold and confident. They will go out on a limb and take a chance. They are hardwired to learn and learning happens as they push beyond their comfort zones again and again and again.

When classrooms become places where we demand conformity, where we insist that students find "the right answer" rather than support their position with rigor and originality, we undermine their need to take ownership of their thinking as well as their ability to think outside the box. When the classroom environment is not safe for daring thinking, we undermine creativity—a commodity greatly needed in a society as ever-changing as ours.

Anti-Trivial Pill

Have you ever had this experience? You're walking through a mall past one store after another crammed with merchandise and you ask yourself, "*Who* buys all of this stuff?"

Or you're waiting in the checkout line at the grocery store and you get to that bank of magazines. On one cover after another, there's Brittany or Angelina or Paris or Oprah and you ask yourself, "*Who* reads all of this stuff?"

Or you're sitting in front of the television with the remote, clicking through all of those channels and you're thinking, "*Who* watches all of this stuff?"

We run the risk as a country of becoming very trivial in our focus, of being overwhelmed by the mundane, corrupted by materialism, seduced by celebrity mania. Our children need a counterbalance to this tendency. They need an antitrivial pill. The best antitrivial pill out there is a good book. Through a book, they can connect to people across the ages, travel to places they will never go in their real lives, experience exotic cultures, escape to alien worlds, and learn about absolutely anything. Through a book, they can tap into and deepen their own humanity. It's the best antitrivial pill around and we must give this medicine to our children.

Why the Thinking Strategies Make a Difference

The human enterprise is to think. Why else would we have these amazing brains? When children are thinking, when they are challenged, when they are engaged—they own their learning. They do it because it is theirs and they

are getting something of value from the process. There is a strong commitment to inquiry, to embarking on the quest for new information, and to
learning how to learn. No matter how hard teachers try they can't come close
to teaching students everything they will need to know to function in this
world. It's not possible. That's why reading is fundamental. That's why the
thinking strategies are valuable.

If the bed and breakfast owner in Van Wert had been taught the
thinking strategies as a child, my bet is she would have gotten As in
comprehension as well as "reading." Sometimes teachers say, "Why should
I teach those strategies? I wasn't taught them and I'm a great reader." Well,
they were the lucky ones. In effect, they developed these thinking
strategies—without naming them—at home or in school. They had parents
or teachers who pushed them to think as they read. For each of those lucky
ones, there were unlucky ones who struggled and never broke through, who
got those Ds in comprehension. They were smart, but they simply didn't
know what it meant to comprehend, they didn't know what was involved.
They had never been taught what goes on in the mind when they read. They
had no idea how they could become one of the lucky ones.

It would be like building a house without putting down a foundation
that was reinforced with rebar. Once it's framed in and the walls and roof
go up, it looks fine. But when a strong wind comes along or the ground
settles, the house won't remain standing straight. There is nothing solid
beneath it. It's a real problem and one that can only be solved by addressing
the underlying lack of a sound foundation. It's the same with children and
reading.

The strategies provide a foundation for going deeper; for pushing
beneath the surface; for tackling new, challenging material; for getting more
out of books—and frankly, out of life. If kids have these thinking strategies
in their toolbox and know how to pull them out and use them, consciously
at first and then more and more automatically, they will have at their
command powerful instruments for gaining knowledge for the rest of their
lives. Their reading foundation is firm and unshakeable.

A Means to an End

The thinking strategies are not an end in themselves. They are a means to
an end. The end is avid reading and good thinking. Recently I was working
with a group of high school teachers who had a question: "How do I grade
the students' think-alouds?" I had never heard of grading students'

> When Susan and I
> first wrote *Mosaic of
> Thought,* I don't
> think we were as
> clear as we might
> have been about this
> point. I hope that
> readers come away
> from this book with
> a strong sense that
> strategies are the
> tools readers can
> use to enhance their
> reading experience.
>
> — *Ellin*

I'm reminded here of the time when, sitting at our dinner table, our daughter Elizabeth said that she "hated those strategies." I nearly fainted. But I calmed down when she explained that her teacher was asking students to put "five determining importances" on each page of their reading. No wonder she "hated those strategies"! Obviously, we have to balance the need for student accountability with the need for authentic learning activities.

—Ellin

I have to wonder if avid reading is the goal or is it avid seeking of knowledge, information, and experiences through any means necessary.

—Nancy

think-alouds before and didn't understand the question. As we talked, it became clear. In their zeal to ensure their students used the thinking strategies, they had required them to keep track in writing of each time they made an inference, asked a question, determined what was important, had a mental image, etc. for all of *1984*. The kids were, as you can imagine, going nuts. They were complaining, rightly, that this exercise was so distracting they didn't enjoy reading *1984* at all. Luckily, this concerned group of teachers realized they needed to do something different. Through our discussion, they found a solution—the students would do the exercise for a few pages of the book so the teachers could confirm the students understood the different strategies, then the students could "go for it" and get into their reading zones. They would also write about their reactions to *1984*, but not in the cumbersome and mind-numbing way of noting every single time they used one of the strategies.

We need to impose a "rule of reason" on ourselves. What makes sense? What enhances a student's reading experience? How can we ensure that what we do makes kids like reading more, not less? I think of it this way: one of the most important roles of the teacher is to "encourage" their students. Think of the word *en-courage*—to give courage; "courage implies firmness of mind and will in the face of danger or extreme difficulty" (Webster's 1967). Firmness of mind, stamina in the face of challenge. It takes that when you're learning something new, when you're pushing beyond your comfort zone. The root of *courage* is the French word *coeur*, heart. *Encourage* means to give heart. The role of the teacher is to give our students the heart to take on new challenges, to keep going, and to avoid discouragement (losing heart!). Our goal must be to make ourselves unnecessary so when the students leave our classrooms they have strong hearts and have made giant steps toward independent, flexible, and delighted reading.

The thinking strategies are valuable only if they help students become avid readers who better understand what they read. If the thinking strategies are taught in a way that interferes with reading for understanding or discourages children from getting into their reading zones, then we're doing something wrong. We need to stand back, take stock, make adjustments, and be reasonable.

Slowing Down, Can You Imagine?

"Slow down you move too fast . . . " Those Simon and Garfunkel lyrics stick in my mind. We are a rush culture. Rush to work, rush to the airport, rush to the grocery store, rush to fix dinner, and rush to pick up the kids. *Rush, rush, rush.* Our schools reflect our rushed lives. We try to do too much, and in the process of trying to do it all, something is lost. Time and again teachers ask, "How can we fit it all in? How can we cover everything we have to cover? How can we add one more thing when we're already bursting at the seams? Slow down. I wish!"

We've all crammed for a test, pulled an all-nighter, drunk a few cups of coffee, made it through the exam (and maybe even scored pretty well on it)—and then, a month (or a week or a year) later, it's gone. We wonder if it's possible that we ever knew that material. We retain almost nothing. We never slowed down to process the information. We never made it ours. We stuffed that information into our short-term memories and then promptly forgot it.

The strategies force children to do more than skim the surface. They have to slow down and think. They aren't just remembering the lead character's name or the color of the dog or where the action takes place. They are taking the time to grapple with the underlying ideas—to ponder motivation, to wonder why people behave as they do, to make sense of what they read. They are learning how to *think* when they read (and after they finish reading). They are learning to do what they need to do to understand. They are doing the opposite of rushing. They are being deliberate and thoughtful—full of thought. They can read progressively harder books, because they've developed the tools to tackle challenging material.

> Thank you, Susan, for reminding us of what really matters. Showing kids how to make reading their own is at the core of our work.
>
> —Chryse

We had our house painted last summer. A crew showed up and spent several days just scraping and taping. I wondered if they were ever going to buckle down and get the job done. Then, in one day, they got out their spray guns and painted the whole house. In one day! And it looked great. But only because they had taken the time to do the painstaking prep work. They had to go slow to go fast. With reading it's similar. If we take the time to lay the foundation by teaching decoding skills as well as thinking strategies, children are at a great advantage. They have the foundation they need to become avid readers who know how to make meaning as they read. They're primed to fall in love with books!

> The notion of going slow to go fast is fascinating to me. I know many of our readers will look forward to Tom Newkirk's new book *Slow Reading* where he encourages us to ask children to slow down and think, to dwell in text, to reread and ponder. In too many schools, we're giving students the impression that fast reading is good reading
>
> —Ellin

Practice Really Does Make Perfect

When I was a kid my dad would tell me, "Sue, if you want to get good at something, do it and do it a lot." Advice I loved when I was skiing, but found annoying when I was studying calculus. Martha Graham, the great modern dancer and choreographer, said, "Practice is a means of inviting the perfection desired." Yogi Berra put his personal twist on this with "In theory there is no difference between theory and practice. In practice there is."

Malcolm Gladwell explores the importance of practice in his book *Outliers*, addressing that fascinating question: is there such a thing as sheer, untrained genius? He examines an eclectic array of talents: Bill Joy, a computer geek who in the 1970s rewrote UNIX (still in use today!), a software system developed by AT&T for mainframe computers, and who went on to found Sun Microsystems; Bill Gates, the cofounder of Microsoft; chess grandmasters; musical geniuses like Mozart and the Beatles; and world-class hockey players. In all the cases, he finds that the unifying theme is that they practiced *a lot*. In fact, at least ten thousand hours before they really achieved their genius.

In *Outliers*, Gladwell quotes the neurologist Daniel Levitin, author of *This Is Your Brain on Music: The Science of a Human Obsession*: "The emerging picture from such studies is that ten thousand hours of practice is required to achieve the level of mastery associated with being a world-class expert—in anything. . . . In study after study, of composers, basketball players, fiction writers, ice skaters, concert pianists, chess players, master criminals, and what have you, this number comes up again and again. . . . It seems that it takes the brain this long to assimilate all that it needs to know to achieve true mastery" (2008, 40).

There is a fairly simple reason that we have a reading problem in the U.S.: our kids aren't reading enough. The National Endowment for the Arts study that looked at reading habits in the U.S. (2007) found that the average person between fifteen and twenty-four spends 2.5 hours a day watching television—and seven minutes reading. Other studies report even higher television time. A recent Nielsen Co. study (2009) found that the average American two- to five-year-old spends thirty-two hours a week in front of a television screen; the average six- to eleven-year-old spends twenty-eight hours watching television every week. That's a lot of television. In fact, at that rate, in about seven years the average American child will have become a ten-thousand-hour master of watching television! And that's not looking at the time they spend in front of other screens. A Kaiser Family Foundation study released in January 2010 found that eight- to eighteen-year-olds spend seven hours, thirty-eight minutes using entertainment media (televisions, iPods, MP3 players, cell phones, and video games) every day—more than fifty-three hours a week. I wonder what would happen if we turned off televisions (and other screens) and made books available; if even half of the time that is now devoted to TV watching were spent reading. That would be over thirteen hours a week. Not bad. I'm guessing we'd have many fewer reading problems in our schools. Our kids would be practicing. A lot.

Wayne Gretsky caught something important when he said, "The only way a kid is going to practice is if it's total fun for him . . . and it was for me." He was on to something. He became one of the all-time great hockey players because he loved to play. It was fun. The only way we are going to address our reading problem in the U.S. is by making reading a joyful experience for children. If we teach our children to love reading, they will do it on their own. If we don't, they won't. It's that simple.

The thinking strategies become important here, because students are much more apt to love reading if they are creating vivid mental images as they read, if they are asking questions and making connections, if they realize that the literal words are not enough, and that—through the inferences they make and their synthesis of what they read—the text becomes multidimensional and much more interesting. They want to read because it is a challenging, joyful, life-enriching experience. Then the old adage "the more you read, the better you get, the better you get, the more you read" becomes a reality for them.

So What Do We Do?

We slow down. As Tom Newkirk says in *Holding onto Good Ideas in a Time of Bad Ones*, "In my experience, excellent instruction rarely feels rushed. As a learner, you feel there is time to explore, there is the tolerance of silences, there is the deliberate buildup to an activity, there is the feeling of mental space to work in" (2009, 11). We immerse children in books. We share our reading passions with our students. We let them know how much we value reading and how much it enhances our lives. We make sure there are lots of books available in our classrooms. Media specialists become really important here in helping to round up books that can be carted around or loaned to classrooms. We give time every single day in class for children to read books of their choice. We talk about books, a lot. We model what goes on in the mind of a great reader by doing think-alouds where we stop and show them our own thinking as we read. We get to know our children well enough that we know their interests and feed them books that will capture their imaginations. We encourage our students to write about what they read, to follow their minds and jot it down, and to push deeper with their thinking. We listen carefully and model listening, thereby creating a classroom where ideas are honored and each child is respected. We go public with thinking.

Listening is so powerful. When students know they are listened to—truly listened to and heard—and they feel safe, there is no limit to the risks they'll take and how far their thinking will go. Then to put their thinking up—to make it public—honors them even more. Every child deserves that.

—*Leslie*

We put students' writing up around the room so they see their thinking is valued. We stress the importance of the text and keep going back to it, thereby establishing a rigor in the classroom that says to read carefully and thoughtfully. We put a premium on discussion—that vital opportunity to express thoughts, listen to others, and participate in the iterative process where one thought leads to another and another and another. We set the bar high so that we honor our students' intelligence and abilities.

Why This Is So Important

Last year I worked in Japan. While there I made a trip to the Hiroshima Peace Park. In the middle of the park is the skeletal A-Bomb Dome, the only building near the hypocenter of the bomb that remained standing. A grim reminder, it is a mere prelude to the pictures in the Peace Memorial Museum. On August 5, 1945, photos show Hiroshima as a bustling city with people cramming the streets, stopping at markets, pushing their wooden carts, chatting to one another. The next morning, Hiroshima is an utter and complete wasteland, a vast and hideous wreckage. "Little Boy," the first atomic bomb dropped on humanity, had done its work. It's no news that war is hell and that horrendous deeds are done in its name. However, seeing the destruction from one bomb—and knowing that our nuclear arsenal is now thousands of times more powerful—brings home the stark reality of the magnitude of the stakes. If Hiroshima teaches anything, it is that there must be an effective antidote to war.

Several years ago, I saw the Dalai Lama at the Pepsi Center in downtown Denver. Unlike for rock concerts and hockey games, there was no hoopla, no light show, no music blasting. The Dalai Lama stood on stage in his saffron robe and spoke simply and unassumingly to an audience of sixteen thousand. While he said much of interest, what I took away from that day was one thought. He said he feared education was failing us. He said that the role of education must be "to cultivate warmheartedness and compassion." He said it was essential for the salvation of our world. This is a role of education that goes far beyond testing. It is education that causes hearts and minds to expand, that helps us understand we are all, as human beings, deeply connected and dependent upon one another. It is the antidote to war and destruction, if there is one.

In the United States, we have become testing obsessed. It's not that testing is bad in itself. It can be good. It can help young people synthesize what they've learned and attain a level of understanding that they otherwise

> Susan, you are not exaggerating one bit. I live just 30 miles from Los Alamos National Laboratory, where the Hiroshima and Nagasaki bombs were made—and atomic weapons still being built and "refurbished" every single day. How these weapons eventually get used, not used, or destroyed, has everything to do with what kind of citizens we are growing in our schools right now.
> —Smokey

might not achieve. But too much testing or testing that doesn't enhance thinking is bad. When testing becomes the driving force, everything we do is directed toward the tests. Much that is important is neglected or avoided outright. It's like washing your hands. We know that hand washing is one of the best ways out there to prevent diseases from spreading. Hand washing is a good thing, but not if you wash your hands every five minutes. Then it becomes obsessive-compulsive. It interferes with your life. You're preoccupied with something that causes more harm than good.

Educator Marva Collins put it this way, "Once children learn how to learn, nothing is going to narrow their mind." The better children read, the better they learn. Teachers are in the unique position to cultivate warmheartedness and compassion in our children, to push them to think broadly, to expand their worldviews so that their minds are opened and their hearts enhanced, and to help them experience the captivating joy and delight of reading a book that changes their lives. Reading is key. It might even help save the world.

References

Center for Public Education. 2005. "Teacher Quality and Student Achievement Research Review." Available at www.centerforpubliceducation .org/site/apps/nlnet/content3.aspx?c=lvIXIiN0JwE&b=5114831&ct= 6857791&notoc=1. Accessed October, 2010.

Gladwell, Malcolm. 2008. *Outliers: The Story of Success.* New York: Little Brown & Co.

National Endowment for the Arts. 2007. To Read or Not To Read: A Question of National Consequence, Research Report #47. Washington, D.C. (November).

Newkirk, Tom. 2009. *Holding onto Good Ideas in a Time of Bad Ones: Six Literacy Principles Worth Fighting For.* Portsmouth, NH: Heinemann.

The Nielsen Company. 2009. "TV Viewing Among Kids at an Eight-Year High" (October). Available at http://blog.nielsen.com/nielsenwire/media_ entertainment/tv-viewing-among-kids-at-an-eight-year-high/. Accessed October 2010.

Rideout, Victoria J., Ulla G. Foehr, and Donald F. Roberts. 2010. "Generation M2, Media in the Lives of 8- to 18-Year-Olds." A Kaiser Family Foundation Study, January 2010. Menlo Park, CA: Henry J. Kaiser Family Foundation.

Webster's 7th New Collegiate Dictionary. 1967. Springfield, MA: G. & C. Merriam Company.

CHAPTER THREE

Not So Gradual Release

Teaching Comprehension in the Primary Grades

Debbie Miller

I used to think that comprehension strategy lessons were all about me. I'd spend time finding just the right book, marking the places where it made the most sense to think aloud, and thinking about the language I'd use to best make my point. I'd explain what we were going to be learning that day, why it was important, and how it would help us as readers. And then I'd set about showing kids how. This was my time to teach, and time for children to listen and notice what they saw and heard me doing.

In my comprehension strategy lessons today, I still spend time finding just the right book, marking the places where it makes the most sense to think aloud, and thinking about my language. I explain what we're going to be learning, why it's important, and how it will help us as readers. This is still my time to teach, and it's still time for children to listen and notice what they see and hear me doing.

But now I understand the importance of releasing responsibility to children much earlier than before, inviting them to "have a go" even on day one of launching a new comprehension strategy. Why so early?

Independence is my goal. When we want children to be active, thoughtful, and *independent* readers, our teaching (and their learning situations) must be active and thoughtful, too. Engaging children in the process, and bringing their voices into the mix, deepens and increases their capacity for learning, understanding, and remembering—and scaffolds them for success during independent practice.

I used to wonder, "But are they ready? Are they really ready?"

"Ready for what?" I ask now. "To think?" Of course they're ready! Releasing responsibility to children early and often gives them opportunities right away to practice a strategy, use the language, and think, "Oh! I can do this!" Believing they have what it takes to be successful engages, motivates, and supports them as they work and practice making the link between listening comprehension and using strategies independently in their own reading.

So now there's a little more *we* in my lessons, and a little less *me*. My lessons are much more participatory—they have an interactive, collaborative, let's-figure-this-out-together kind of feel.

Take a listen . . .

"Good morning everyone!" I say to the twenty-three first graders sitting on the rug before me. "Today we're going to be learning something new that readers do to help them understand their reading. I know you already know about how readers make connections and create mental images to help them make sense of, or understand, their reading, right? And on your chart here, I also see that you are just learning about another strategy that readers use—making predictions. Can you share with me a little bit about what predictions are, how you make them, and how they help you as a reader?"

Jeremiah jumps in. "Well here's how it goes for me," he says. "I have all these connections in my head when I read, and then the really big ones, just like go POOF! and they turn into pictures! And the pictures won't stop—they move ahead of the story and then I have my prediction. And it really, really helps me!"

"Wow," I say, writing his words in my notebook. "That's cool. I'm going to have to try that. So when you said it really, really helps you—how exactly does that work?"

"It, um, well it kinda helps me stick with the story. 'Cause I want to find out what happens, like if my prediction comes true or if I have to change my picture."

"What do the rest of you think about that?" I ask. "Turn and talk with someone close to you about Jeremiah's thinking, or share how you go about making predictions."

> I can really relate to what Debbie is saying here. I used to model for five to ten minutes while kids could hardly contain themselves, chomping at the bit to join in. "Hang on a minute, watch me!" I would say to them. Silly me. . . . When kids are so engaged, they need to have a go right away with the teacher dipping in and dipping out. Gradual release is not a linear process, but rather a recursive and dynamic one.
>
> —*Stephanie*

> Debbie captures something key here: she lets go of her own control; she empowers her students and by doing so their level of commitment and engagement soars. That's when real learning takes off.
>
> —*Susan*

Children talk for a minute, and I bring them back with, "Today we're going to learn even more about how readers make predictions, and we're going to use another strategy to help us. Have you ever been reading along—reading the words and looking closely at the pictures—and thought, Oh! I know just what this character is thinking? Maybe you've been in a situation like that before, or maybe you know about someone who has. Has that ever happened to you?

"Yes? Me too! When I do that—when I read the words and look closely at the pictures, it helps me infer—to figure out—what a character is thinking right then and there in the story. When I take the time to do that, it helps me make thoughtful predictions about what the character might say or do next.

"Authors, really excellent authors, don't usually come right out and tell us what their characters are thinking—they trust us, they expect us—to infer, to figure it out for ourselves. They leave us clues along the way, but in the end, it's up to us. Let me show you what I mean in this book, *A Circle of Friends*, by Giora Carmi . . .

". . . take a look at this page right here—do you see the muffin in the little boy's hand, and the look on his face? He looks very pensive—very thoughtful—doesn't he? And maybe just a little bit sad? I'm inferring the little boy is thinking 'Oh! This man is homeless—he lives in the park and he's sound asleep on a park bench. I bet he's going to be hungry when he wakes up.' So you see, I'm inferring what the little boy is thinking—he's worried that the man is going to be hungry. And now, I'm going to make a prediction—I predict the little boy is going to give his muffin to the man.

"Do you see how this works? What did I do first? Then what? That's it exactly. Inferring and predicting work together, don't they? I'm going to write that in my notebook so we won't forget—and later we can add this, and Jeremiah's thinking, to your chart.

"Now, when we turn the page, one of two things will happen. I'll either confirm my prediction—that means what I predicted actually happened—that he shared his muffin with the man, or I'll have to change my thinking—I'll find out that he didn't share his muffin.

"Turn and talk with someone close to you—what do you think? Do you predict the little boy will share his muffin, or do you predict he won't? Use the words, 'I predict . . .' and then explain your thinking—why do you predict he'll share, or why do you predict he won't?

Let's listen in . . .

> "Well," says Briana to Jake, "I predict the little boy is going to give his muffin to the homeless man, 'cause look at his face. See how he's thinking so hard? He's nice and he doesn't want the man to starve. And that man doesn't have a mom to give him money like the little boy does."
>
> J: "But if he's gonna give it to the man, then why did he take a bite out of it?"
>
> B: "Well maybe he just couldn't help himself, you know? Maybe he was hungry, but he knows the man's hungry too. And the man has no hope for food. And the boy is really nice."
>
> J: "I still predict he's going to eat it. Maybe he wants to give it to the man, but he's kind of scared. And Briana—he is a stranger."
>
> B: "I know, but it's called *A Circle of Friends*. Why would they call it that if he's not gonna make a friend?"
>
> "Everyone, let's come back together. Are you ready to find out what happens?"

Turning and Talking in Briana and Jake Style

Asking children to get eye-to-eye and knee-to-knee is one of the most effective ways I know to release responsibility to children and get them talking and thinking about big ideas. It's not that asking children to talk with a partner about something specific is new, but showing them *how* to have a conversation with each other often is.

You might have wondered about Briana and Jake—do first graders really talk like that?

They do when we show them how.

In some classrooms, turning and talking has become, well, perfunctory. Everyone tells us it's a good thing, and so we work to incorporate it into our lessons. But let's think about the *why*. Why is it important to take a few minutes during a lesson for children to share their thinking with each other? Why take the time to show them how?

> Students are capable of brilliance, yet so often the expectations aren't there. When kids see the modeling and trust that you believe they can think at that high level, they rise to those expectations.
>
> —

When we ask children to talk with a partner about big ideas, it:

- sends the message that I trust you—I believe that you have something important to say;

- allows children to become aware of their mental processes and use their words to make them public for themselves and others;

- develops their ability to share, listen, respond, and appreciate a variety of perspectives;

- shifts the spotlight off the teacher and places it directly on the child;

- permits teachers, when we get up and out of our chair and listen in to snippets of children's conversations, to assess where they are in the process, informing our instruction in the moment.

And listen to what Peter Johnston has to say on the subject:

> It [talking with your neighbor about your thinking] helps children to understand that meaning-making is not a matter of getting the right answer, because they quickly learn how different people make different, yet similar, sense. In addition, the more they get to have such personal conversations with their classmates, the more they know them and the less they are able to view them through stereotypes or to put them down. Stereotype and domination are made possible by reducing the complexity of others to the handful of features that mark them as different—as not me. (Johnston 2004, 71)

To show children how, think about what you do when you have a conversation with someone. Model, with a child or another adult, just what it is you want for them. Ask kids what they notice. Help them understand that turning and talking is about interacting with each other, having a conversation, and a give-and-take of ideas. Make it clear it's not just one turn each and we're done! Give them lots of opportunities to practice. Scoot around and listen in. Really listen, and model some more.

The Read-Aloud/Think-Aloud Doesn't End the Lesson!

The inferring/predicting lesson with *A Circle of Friends* continues over two days, and when we finish, I do what Ellin Keene urges us all to do—I ask the children, "What do we understand now about this story that we didn't understand before?" And then I ask, "What did we do that helped us—how did

Give-and-take discussions make spaces for teachers to elaborate on student talk and thinking. By elaborating (clarifying, paraphrasing, and nudging kids to say more) we guide them toward new vocabulary and language structures. We now know, too, that having our students turn and talk in their heritage language provides a bridge to their understanding in English and celebrates their ability to speak another language other than English—something that high-stakes tests don't bother to count as achievement.

—Anne & Brad

we get from there (pointing to the first page) to here (pointing to the last one)?" And, "What are some of the big ideas in this story—what do you think Giora Carmi wants us to learn, understand, and remember?"

When we consistently ask questions like these at the end of strategy focus lessons, we're letting children in on the *why* of strategy instruction. We teach children strategies not so they can rattle them off and know them by name, but because they promote active, metacognitive, independent readers and thinkers—for whom learning, understanding, and remembering are paramount.

Asking children, "How did we get from there to here? What exactly did we do?" invites them to reflect—to think back and think out loud—about the process we used and how it helped them as readers. That way, when it comes time for independent practice, they have some schema for how to go about doing what we're asking them to do—they have a place to begin.

Independent Practice—It's a Big Deal

Here's the thing. We can have the best lessons in the world, but if our comprehension instruction ends here—with the lesson—we're missing the point. Even our youngest readers, even those who haven't yet cracked the code, need to practice applying what we're working so hard to teach them.

Nell Duke writes, "As with decoding, all the explicit instruction in the world will not make students strong readers unless it is accompanied by lots of experience applying their knowledge, skills, and strategies during actual reading" (Duke and Pearson 2002, 207).

For children to "own" strategies, for them to get beyond knowing strategies and onto becoming independent, strategic readers, we want to put them in learning situations so they can actively experiment with using strategies early on. This allows teachers and children to co-construct how, when, and why strategies are used, and for children to individualize and make them their own. When they do, they have a repertoire of strategies they can use flexibly and with purpose.

For example, we say at the end of a whole-group lesson focusing on inferring and making predictions:

> In your reading today, take a good look at the pictures in your book, just like we did in *A Circle of Friends*. Look closely at the character's faces—see if you can do some inferring about what the character is thinking. Then, based on the words and the pictures, and what you know about this particular situation, or stories in general, predict what

> We've totally missed the boat on independent practice in school. Think back to anything you've learned to do really well. Water skiing, cooking, sewing. You may have had some kind of teacher, mentor or model, but their direct lessons were probably just a tiny part of your overall learning time. Think of a weekly half-hour piano lesson, followed by hours of independent practice which, if you didn't do it, you never improved.
>
> —Smokey

might happen next in the story. Good luck! I can't wait to see what you find out!

We've extended an invitation to each child to "see if you can discover," giving them something specific to focus on during independent reading. This call to action is for all children, and gives purpose to their reading, thinking, and the ways they respond.

And while the call to action is for all children, differentiation occurs during the application process. Children will be working in a variety of texts and levels, and yet the charge for each of them is the same—"In your reading today . . . " Everyone is expected to have a go, and everyone can (in a range of ways) participate in the larger conversation about how things went and what they learned about themselves today.

What kinds of books might we put in the hands of our youngest readers, even those who haven't yet cracked the code?

- Wordless books, like Giora Carmi's *A Circle of Friends*, *How to Heal a Broken Wing* by Bob Graham, Barbara Lehman's *Museum Trip*, and Mercer Mayer's *Boy, Dog, and Frog* series are perfect for focus lessons *and* independent practice. We all know that children don't have to decode in order to think, and wordless books allow them to do just that.

- At the end of a read-aloud—whether it be fiction, nonfiction, or poetry—I often say to children, "Is there anyone who would like to do some more thinking about this book?" They've heard me read the text aloud, and now during independent reading time they can go back in—have a better look at the pictures, read the words they can, and maybe (just maybe) gain new understandings!

- Sometimes we overlook children's "easy readers." We know they're perfect for practicing fluency and strategies for decoding, but when it comes to comprehension, we wonder if there is really anything for children to think *about*. It isn't always the case, but sometimes the pictures in these early readers play off the text and serve to get kids thinking beyond the words. When this holds true, asking children to focus on the text and the illustrations is a good way to help children consolidate the surface and deeper structure systems.

Conferring and Individual Instruction

Is it possible to have independent reading without conferring? It's possible, but not wise. When we confer with children, we learn where they are in the application process, and what we can do to move them toward independence. Depending on what children say (or don't say) they're guiding us, helping us pinpoint just where they are and what they're thinking. They're helping us individualize our instruction.

For example, listen to this conference with Jacquie . . .

"Hi Jacquie! What are you reading?"

"*Dad's Headache*."

"*Dad's Headache*? Hmmm . . . I don't know that one—what's it about?"

"A dad who has a headache."

"A dad who has a headache? That's it?"

Jacquie nods.

"OK. How about you read a few pages aloud, and let's see if there's more to it than you think—maybe we can do some inferring like we did with *A Circle of Friends*. Shall we see?"

And Jacquie reads: "PoorDadHehadaheadacheIfeelterriblehesaid."

"Wow!" I say. "You are a really fast reader!"

"I know!" Jacquie says back. "You should time me."

"I'm sorry, Jacquie," I say, "I don't even own a timer—can you believe that?"

"Not even in the kitchen?"

"Nope. Not even in the kitchen. But let's go back to the beginning of the book—I want to show you something. I know you can read the words, but have you ever stopped to look at the pictures? Remember how we did that in *A Circle of Friends*, and how much it helped us do all that thinking—all that inferring and predicting?"

"Yeah, but that book didn't have any words, and my book does."

"You're right, Jacquie. *A Circle of Friends* didn't have any words, and your book does, but I'm wondering if reading the words and looking closely at the pictures will help us. Are you willing to give it a try?"

She shrugs, sighs, and murmurs, "I guess."

"Ah," I say, "I was really hoping you would. Thanks!"

"Let's take a look at this page. I know you can read the words 'We got him some breakfast to make him feel better.' But now, let's look closely at the pictures. See the dad? Look at that face! What do you infer he's thinking?"

Jacquie studies the picture for what seems like forever, and finally says, "It looks like he's going to throw up—see his hand over his mouth? Maybe he's thinking the breakfast they brought is not going to make him feel better?"

I'm so glad that you said that. How does speed equate to comprehension? By the time I get my fourth graders, my mantra is "slow down and think!"

— *Leslie*

I actually applauded here! Too many schools are inadvertently giving children the wrong message about what good readers do. Jacquie was equating good reading with fast reading. I loved Debbie's response and hope that it inspires lots of teachers to use their timers for cooking a great roast rather than checking on children's speed!

— *Ellin*

"Wow, Jacquie. See what you just did? You inferred what the dad was thinking! You read the words, looked really closely at the pictures, and then you stopped and did some thinking, right? So what do you predict the Dad will do?"

"There's no way he's gonna eat that!"

"Listen to you!" I say. "Did you even notice the pictures before?"

"Not really," she says, "and I never knew this book was funny, either."

"This is really working, huh? Let's keep going!"

To ensure Jacquie understands the difference between the words in the text and her thinking, I write her thinking on a sticky note—"That's not going to make me feel better"—and give it to her to place in her book. We do the same for a few pages more, and we get to the page that reads, "We told funny stories to make him feel better . . . "

Knock, knock.

Who's there?

Amos.

Amos who?

A mosquito. Ha, ha, ha!

Jacquie grabs my pencil, peels a sticky note off the pad, and infers what the dad is thinking—"Tat ist fne!" (That isn't funny!)—and predicts that joke is not going to make him feel better, either.

And on the page where she reads, "We walked on our hands to make Dad feel better," she writes, "its nt wrkg" (It's not working).

So no matter how explicit the lesson, without this one-on-one conference Jacquie would, at least on this day, continue marching on through her books—reading them faster, and faster, and faster. And believing that this is what reading is all about.

I end her conference by asking, "So what are you learning about yourself as a reader today, Jacquie?"

And Jacquie, with just a hint of a smile, responds, "Well, I used to read fast, fast, fast. But when I slow down and look at the pictures, I can do all the stuff we did in *A Circle of Friends*. I can feel the story and my book was funny and I didn't know that."

And I respond, with more than a hint of a smile, "I'm not sure everyone knows this, Jacquie. Would you be will willing to share this with everyone? Yes? Thanks so much—we learned a lot together today, didn't we? Do you want to practice what you want to say when you share?"

"Nah," Jacquie says with a grin. "I can do it."

Reflection and Sharing: Think the Reader, Not the Reading

Is it possible to have independent reading without building in time for reflection and sharing? You probably know my answer—it's possible, but not wise! Setting aside time every day for children to reflect, share, and teach brings things full circle—we've taught, children have practiced, and now we're coming back together to talk, inform, and teach each other what we've learned.

I used to think reflection and share sessions were about children sharing their connections, images, and wonderings. One child would share, then another, and another and another. By the time the sixth child shows us a picture of a dog in her book that reminds her of her very own dog who they got at the shelter and who likes to play ball and tag and chewed up one of her daddy's really bright orange Crocs, it's enough to make us all a little weary.

But when we shift the focus of sharing from what children are reading to what they're learning about themselves as readers, the dynamics change. Now children aren't talking (as much!) about dogs and shelters and daddy's really bright orange Crocs. Now they're talking about *themselves* as readers. And that's enough to make us all sit up and listen!

How do we help children, and ourselves, make the shift? Mostly, we confer. We ask open-ended questions. We listen to what they have to say. We notice and name what we see them doing. We teach. And then we ask them what they're learning about themselves as readers. And would they consider sharing these amazing findings?

> Debbie, what you describe here is exactly what the research on formative assessment says. If we slow down and focus on the *learners* by teaching students to self-assess and set goals, and reflect on, keep track of, and share their learning —we can close achievement gaps and ensure that every student gets the education they deserve. I feel like you changed this girl's life with this lesson.
>
> —

Let's go back to Jacquie. If I'd asked her during share time, "Would you like to share something from your reading today?" she'd have probably answered with something like this:

"On this page, I was inferring the dad is going to throw up!"

But when we shift the question from the child's reading to the child as reader—when I ask, "Jacquie, what did you learn about yourself as a reader today?"—this is how she responded instead:

"Well, I used to be the fastest reader. I went zoom, zoom, zoom—I didn't even look at the pictures. But today I did, and, um, it was different, and it made my book feel better. My book is funny and I didn't even know it! Pictures are really good! They make you think."

Now we're getting somewhere!

I want to jump up and down, but I restrain myself and say instead, "Thank you, Jacquie." And then, "Everyone, let's think about what Jacquie shared with us . . . "

And now we're *really* getting somewhere. Now children are taking one child's learning, thinking about it, working to make sense of it for themselves and each other.

Six or seven or eight children didn't share their learning that day. But when we're really digging into the thinking process, one is enough—and tomorrow is another day.

I believe digging into the thinking process ultimately leads to independence. Once we make our thinking visible, and clearly explain the strategy—letting children know why it's important, and how it will help them as readers—we teachers need to move beyond talking *about* strategies and put children in authentic learning situations where they practice applying them. That's what leads to independence.

> This chapter offers one of the loveliest descriptions of the gradual release of responsibility model that I have ever read. The focus on letting go as early and often as possible is an important reminder for me . . . and for every teacher. Thanks, Debbie.
> —*Gina*

References

Duke, Nell, and P. David Pearson. 2002. "Effective Practices for Developing Reading Comprehension." In *What Research Has to Say About Reading Instruction*, 3rd ed, edited by Alan E. Farstrup and S. Jay Samuels. Newark, DE: International Reading Association. 207.

Johnston, Peter. 2004. *Choice Words*. Portland, ME: Stenhouse.

Miller, Debbie. 2002. *Reading with Meaning*. Portland, ME: Stenhouse.

Miller, Debbie. 2008. *Teaching with Intention*. Portland, ME: Stenhouse.

Children's Books Cited

Carmi, Giora. 2003. *A Circle of Friends*. Long Island City, NY: Star Bright Books.

Cowley, Joy. 1996. *Dad's Headache*. Columbus, OH: McGraw Hill/Wright Group Publishing.

Graham, Bob. 2008. *How to Heal a Broken Wing*. Somerville, MA: Candlewick Press.

Lehman, Barbara. 2006. *Museum Trip*. Boston, MA: Houghton Mifflin Publishers.

Meyer, Mercer. 1975. *The Boy, Dog, and Frog* series. New York: Penguin/Dial Books for Young Readers.

CHAPTER FOUR

Fulfilling the Promise of "All Students Can"

Comprehension Strategies as the Verbs of Learning Targets

Samantha Bennett

When students enter Liza Eaton's middle school science classroom at the Odyssey School in Denver, Colorado, they instantly feel empowered because with one quick glance at the front board they are reminded why they are here, what's expected, and how they will get smarter today. As a visitor to Liza's room, I feel empowered too—because I see how attention to a few key structures and routines can have incredible impact on student engagement and student learning.

On the white board in the front of the room are two specific learning targets for this sixty-five-minute class period:

- I can skim my texts to help me decide where to read.

- I can use our long-term target to capture what is important from my texts.

OK, pretty straightforward goal—students will learn how to skim for information, and practice skimming, but there are a few key words here that make me pause and want to know more.

- *I can:* Hmmm, these learning targets are different from the goals/objectives that I see in many classrooms because they are written from the perspective of the student, with clear, student-friendly language. I wonder if kids really use these? Do they care?

- This is a middle school science classroom: Hmmm, the teacher is going to take time to show students how to access information instead of cover terms to know, or facts to memorize. What implications will this have for students? What does this say about Liza's beliefs about the discipline of science?

- If Liza wants students to determine importance, I wonder "What's the bigger purpose of skimming?"

- Hmmm, the phrase "long-term" makes me wonder "How much time do students spend on a single topic?"

The physical spaces of our classrooms are packed with information about what we believe the purpose of education to be and how we "do" school. Two learning targets on Liza's white board, triggered my thinking about student ownership of learning, motivation, and engagement; curriculum design; and Liza's beliefs about the purpose of education. Some of my questions are answered as I continue to look around.

Just above the two daily targets, on an atomic-green piece of paper labeled "Long-Term Target," is written:

- I can analyze a local transportation option for its efficiency and sustainability.

So now I'm thinking, "Oh, that is why students will skim for information today." Students are analyzing transportation in Denver with some key scientific terms: *efficiency* and *sustainability*. I read those terms in the newspaper every day in columns about our use of oil and energy alternatives. These are terms that are central to big ideas that really matter in the real world. I'm more intrigued by the minute; I hope students are too. I can't wait for the lesson to begin.

> Sam, you remind me how important it is to clarify why I do what I do everyday. Do I believe every kid can learn? Yes! Then I need to differentiate and scaffold so each kid can learn. I have all the power in my classroom to make that a reality.
>
> —Cris

A Routine for Buy-In: The Lesson Begins

The students are seated around tables in groups of four. Liza begins the lesson.

LIZA: Thanks for coming in so quietly and opening up your science journals. I see most of you are looking up here at the learning targets for today. So, based on these targets, Michaela, what did you write in your journal as your title of our work today?

MICHAELA: We had "Determining Importance with Text."

LIZA: How did you know that was the title? I don't see any of those words up here at all. How did you know "Determining Importance with Text?"

MICHAELA: We use determining importance to try to decide where to read. And since we are trying to research the different types of energy options and we have so many different articles, it will help us if we focus—like it says in the target, "capture what is important"—in our notes.

LIZA: Good. I love that you used words off the target. That shows me you really thought about it. So how is today going to help us get to this long-term target? BC, what do you think?

BC: Today is going to help us because first off we'll learn more about the efficiency and sustainability of transportation with the texts about our particular fuel and that way we can add to our policy proposals (*see Appendix B*).

LIZA: Ian, can you add to that?

IAN: Yesterday we were just trying to get the information and today we are going to actually go into our assigned energy source, how effective it is, and how sustainable it is.

LIZA: Great, thanks. Any questions about where we are going today? OK, let's get started with the minilesson.

Liza's routine for the opening of class lasted about three minutes, but already students know what they are learning about today, why they are learning about it, and have taken a crack at visualizing how they will spend the next sixty-five minutes based on the learning targets on the board. More than just reading the target out loud, Liza asked students *to think* in order *to comprehend* the target:

- by *synthesizing* (What title would you give today based on the long-term target and the two daily targets?) and

- by *inferring* and *visualizing* (Using your *background knowledge* about the usual flow of class [rituals, routines, structures], the texts that are in front of you, what we did yesterday, and our end goal of writing a transportation policy proposal—how do you envision we'll spend our time today?)

This daily thinking routine matters because it reminds students—in the flurry of multiple classes, multiple teachers, and multiple sets of expectations—where they are now in their learning, and where they are going. This step is crucial because it helps with students' emotional, behavioral, and cognitive engagement from the first minutes of class. All students can both practice and succeed with *inferring, synthesizing*, and *visualizing* in a low-risk environment—there is no "right" answer to the title of the day, as long as you can back it up with evidence from the targets.

Comprehension strategies do not live in a box, to be doled out to students one at time. They are the way we make meaning of the world throughout our days of living and learning together. The better we get at naming them, and asking students explicitly to practice them, the more we will break the idea of "smart" and "not smart." Three minutes a day—do you have that much time?

> This is precisely the kind of structured interactive routine, focused on conceptual development, which can allow students at all levels of language proficiency access the content *if* there are visual supports in place and texts at a variety of reading levels about the topic. It strikes me as particularly helpful that students are working in groups to accomplish the routine.
>
> —Nancy

Smart Is Something You Can Get

We have a compelling job as educators in the United States. We are a nation that believes that *all* of our children should be educated—regardless of background, race, or class—and we actually attempt it on a daily basis. It is very "American-dreamy" to believe that "all means all" when it comes to educating our citizenry from the ages of five to eighteen, but what does it truly look like?

The most exciting work I've seen in education to date is fulfilling the promise of *all students can*—explicitly closing the achievement gap and giving all students access to power in society. It is the use of practices of assessment for learning (Black and Wiliam 1998; Stiggins et al. 2004) within purposeful backward planning for student understanding (Wiggins and McTighe 2005). When teachers know what they want their students to know, do, and understand; determine the concrete evidence before the lessons begin; and share those goals and products with students through systematic routines and rituals; all students *can* become the powerful, thoughtful human beings with whom we want to share our world.

So what do assessment for learning and backward planning have to do with the comprehension strategies? Simply put, the comprehension strategies are the verbs of learning targets for students. They are the *how* of learning for *all* students. They are the *how* to get smarter, the *how* to close the achievement gap, the *how* to learn. They are the skills students need to access and use information—through text, through talk, and through experience. The comprehension strategies are explicit entry points of access for *all* students to get smarter over time; an education that gives them options and helps them make wise choices; an education that gives students power.

What Makes a Great Learning Target?

Learning targets are student-friendly statements of intended learning, and their daily use is part of a systematic process based on the simple premise of "when you know where you are going, it is easier to get there." Learning targets that work best are part of a comprehensive plan for students to acquire knowledge and develop skills within a bigger goal for students to gain understanding of the big ideas of a discipline.

Teachers at the Odyssey School in Denver, Colorado, have been experimenting with learning targets and assessment for learning practices for several years. They created a rubric to analyze each other's assessment plans before the start of each unit. Below is their description of quality learning targets:

- Long-term targets align with the big ideas/enduring understanding
- Written in student-friendly language (that is both rigorous and appropriate)
- Measurable
- Specific and contextualized
- Names the learning, not the task
- Sets of targets are diverse in terms of type (knowledge, skill, reasoning)
- Supporting targets get students to the long-term target
- Supporting targets identify the instructional path students will use to meet long-term targets
- Supporting targets name the small, discreet learning that has to happen to reach the long-term targets

In his scathing and often hilarious article, "What Money Can't Buy: Powerful Overlooked Opportunities for Learning" (2009), Mike Schmoker

Sam, teaching strategies as the "how" to do the thinking is so smart. It has changed how I think about my work with students and adults. Planning like this is a lot of work up front, but it sure cuts down on the day-to-day stress of "what will students do in class today?"

—Cris

(my intellectual crush) argues that we don't need any new research or data, nor do we need any new money to do what is best for student learning. It isn't that we don't know what to do, it is a failure of courage and a failure of will to do what we know works. He posits five practices, that, "In combination . . . would have more impact on learning, on the achievement gap, and on civic, college, and career preparedness than anything we've ever done" (524).

One of the big five (in which the use of italics makes me a little sad) is "Ensure *reasonably* sound lessons in every subject and classroom" (526). Just *reasonably* sound lessons? That's all the hope he has for teachers? Talk about expectations of excellence?! Actually, I kind of like it because I think, "OK, I guess I can plan a *reasonably* sound lesson. I'd better get started." Schmoker continues,

> The work of several eminent educators, over several decades, points to one of the most simple, powerful sets of practices we know. They form the general structure of an effective lesson . . . Effective lessons (most of them anyway) start with teaching only those skills or standards that teachers fully understand and which come directly from the agreed-on curriculum. Then, start the lesson by being scrupulously clear in conveying the purpose of the lesson and how it will be assessed, with a careful description of the criteria necessary to succeed on the assessment. (526)

Aha! Learning targets and matched assessments up front, before the instruction begins. OK. What's next? Schmoker continues,

> The lesson must be taught in manageable steps or "chunks." Between each step, the teacher must "check for understanding" or "formatively" assess (e.g. by circulating, scanning, observing) to ensure that students understand the "chunk" that was just taught. Between chunks, students engage in guided practice replete with teacher modeling (or thinking aloud) with frequent use of student and adult models and exemplars . . . to help students understand the work. (526)

Hmmm, this sounds surprisingly like the workshop model, which I happen to know a little bit about (Bennett 2007)! What's missing from Schmoker's beautiful rendition of the use of learning targets and assessment for learning within the workshop model, however, is how tricky it is to actually write *great* learning targets that name the learning, not the task—and then help students gain a vision of what that looks like within a cohesive, comprehensive unit that meets state standards; and lives within a compelling real-world topic to investigate, with multiple formative assessments for learning along the way that lead to an authentic real-world product/project for students to share their understanding at the end. Whew! Piece of cake, huh?

Actually, what I *love* about Schmoker, is that his focus can help us focus. Just do it, in the words of the brilliant Nike ad campaign executive.

OK, let's do it, together. Liza will show us how.

Let's begin how Liza began—with a plan. Take a look at Liza's Assessment Plan for a semester-long unit on Engines, Energy, and Oil (Appendix A). In it, she outlines fifteen long-term learning targets and the matched assessments: the actual evidence students will create to demonstrate their gain in knowledge, skill, and understanding of the big ideas behind engines, energy, and oil—how they work in the world and why they matter.

Semester-long you say? What? How can she possibly spend an entire semester on one unit? Here's how—this unit combined the uncoverage of Colorado State Science Standards from Chemistry, Physics, and Earth/Space Science, as well as the habits of scientists and huge swathes of the Colorado State Literacy Standards. Over the course of the semester, students met fifteen long-term learning targets, and each day tackled a supporting target (around fifty or so scaffolded steps) that helped them reach the long-term targets.

Following is the plan for one long-term target, connected to students' final demonstration of understanding—a policy proposal for alternative transportation options in Denver. This kind of backward planning, based on the principals of *Understanding by Design* (Wiggins and McTighe 2005), is ubiquitous around the country; but Liza takes her planning even further, because she not only figures out what the "end" looks like, she also figures out what the assessments will be along the way, by brainstorming supporting learning targets—the scaffolded steps that outline the explicit knowledge and skills students will need to demonstrate their under-standing of the long-term target. She also brainstorms the matched assessments up front—the concrete evidence that students have gained the knowledge and acquired the skills that will allow them to write informative, high-quality transportation policy proposals. Her detailed planning, using learning targets with language from a student's perspective, helps her visualize what the days in between the kickoff of the unit and the final product will entail. Notice the sophistication of the

> Hmm . . . what are my long-term targets for the students I'm teaching now?
>
> —Cris

64

LONG-TERM LEARNING TARGETS	ASSESSMENTS
Learning targets that correlate directly with standards and are reported on in a grade and/or progress report	*Summative Assessments that are planned to match long-term targets* • *Formative assessments along the way*
I can advocate for a policy recommendation that will affect the efficiency and sustainability of transportation in Denver. • I can analyze the Cash for Clunkers program to determine how effective the policy is. • I can critique additional policies for their effectiveness. • I can analyze a local transportation option for its efficiency and sustainability. • I can use Science Talks[1] as a way to deepen my understanding about various transportation options. • I can develop a policy that addresses the efficiency and sustainability of transportation energy in Denver. • I can describe my thinking about transportation policy in Denver.	Voice Thread[2] Policy Position Statement (Appendix B) • Extended response • T-chart and final analysis of each policy • T-chart, pro/cons for the variables of energy efficiency, sustainability, cost • Science Talk Ticket Reflections—looking for evidence of deepening ideas. Voice Thread—note catcher/planning sheet • Note catcher/planning sheet
I can identify evidence that will help demonstrate my thinking for my Voice Thread.[2] • I can skim material to help me identify where to read (literacy).	• Annotations on alternative energy texts • Note Catcher/Planning Sheet Quiz: Timed common text—highlighted and annotated

[1] A Science Talk is a classroom routine similar to a Socratic seminar, where students sit in a circle and talk about a big question in science. The purpose is to allow students to ask questions, challenge each other, ask for clarification, and tell stories about science phenomena. The goal is that the students' everyday language becomes a deep intellectual resource that helps them to argue, categorize, organize, and theorize about science. They must back up their thinking about the big question with evidence from texts, notes, experiments, and experience.

[2] Voice Thread is an interactive Web-based communication tool for having conversations around media (images, video, or documents). See www.voicethread.com for models and more information.

"nesting" of interconnected knowledge and skill goals within a larger purpose for student thinking and understanding.

OK, we've all seen plans on paper before. Though this plan is incredibly detailed, it morphed and changed as the students grappled with the knowledge, skills, and understanding over time. Some targets got dropped, and some needed several days (even weeks) to uncover. This plan is not set in stone, but because Liza knows where she is going, she is able to focus her daily attention on what matters most: how *students* are making meaning of the content. How they are coming to know based on their talk, and their writing—in annotations, in exit tickets, in graphic organizers, and (yes) even on old-school quizzes. Student thinking about the content matters most; not student regurgitation of the content.

What does this look like in practice? Let's go back into Liza's middle school classroom to take a closer look. We left off when the students had just finished sharing their thinking about what today's lesson would entail, based on the daily learning targets. Liza continues with her minilesson:

> If all students are going to be able to participate in the talk necessary to accomplish the learning targets, it will be critical that students in the process of acquiring English in school have additional time to work on the language and structure of the expected talk in proficiency level groupings.
>
> —*Nancy*

MINILESSON

LIZA: So you all have articles in your folders. Some of them look like the one I have under the document camera—lots of text, not many pictures, lots of small words. Something that smart researchers do when they have to get through a lot of material is *skim*. Adults don't necessarily read *everything* that is on a piece of paper. Who can share their thinking about this? Leo? What is skimming?

LEO: Umm . . . I can use an example of what happens when you skim. It isn't really taking in *everything*. You read really fast and then you see a word and you stop and say "Oh," and circle it and come back to it. Like if my key word were *hydrogen*, so I see it and then stop and then go back up to the beginning of that sentence and reread to see what it says.

LIZA: Good. So let's separate some of those ideas. I'm hearing a couple of things. I'm hearing about "how to skim" and then "what is skimming." Leo said skimming is reading fast; it's reading little parts.

BC (*shouts out*): Yeah, but with a purpose.

LIZA: Great, BC, with a purpose. So I am not going to ask you to read every single thing in your folder, can you believe it? What is real, is that adults, good researchers, skim to locate where they need to read. Some of this information may not be helpful. I'm going to think aloud to research compressed natural gas for my policy proposal. As I think aloud, I want you to write in your notebooks: What do you see me picking out? What do you see me actually trying to do? What are my strategies as I'm skimming? Hold those in your notebook and I'll ask you to share them when I'm finished thinking aloud.

PAUSE IN SCRIPT

Let's take a minute to step out of the classroom and continue to label Liza's practices: to study the interplay of assessment for learning strategies, elements of backward lesson design, explicit use of the comprehension strategies, and why they all matter for maximum student learning.

Even though Liza has some skilled readers in her science class, she doesn't take for granted that they can all skim text proficiently. Even though some of her students know the basics of how to skim, Liza *trusts* that she can help all of them get better at it today—with complex texts, a sophisticated purpose, and an expectation of a high-quality product for an authentic audience.

Leo feels like he gets "how to skim," but he *trusts* that Liza will show him something that will help him do it smarter or more efficiently today. This mutual trust is based on both the authentic purpose and the authentic process that neither Liza nor Leo can "fake." Leo may have skimmed text before, but not while trying to figure out the efficiency and sustainability of hydrogen as a fuel source in order to write a transportation policy proposal for political leaders in Denver. There is no "game of school" here, there is only getting better at a complex skill for an authentic purpose. I believe Leo trusts Liza and stays engaged for a few reasons:

1. Students are reading complex texts they found on the Internet, intended for adult readers. Leo knows Liza is going to think in front of him in real time, plus she has given him a purpose for listening: to see if he can explicitly name the strategies she is using as she skims to find information. There is no predetermined "right" answer. Leo is functioning as a researcher in real time—observing an expert and looking for concrete steps to hold onto in a multi-faceted reading process.

2. Leo is clear about his targets for today—"I can skim my texts to help me decide where to read" and "I can use our target to capture what is

important from my texts"—and he knows that by the end of class, he will be expected to have evidence to show that he has met those targets.

3. Leo has background knowledge about Liza as a teacher. She has a track record of asking him to do important things, and she usually provides feedback and support to make sure he can.

4. Based on the rituals and routines of science class everyday, Leo knows Liza will stop talking at some point and actually let him dig in and do the work. If he gives her a few minutes of his time, he will have the majority of class to actually skim his articles and collect important information that will help him write his own transportation policy proposal.

You could probably find ten other reasons that Leo trusts Liza and is willing to stick with her through this think-aloud. But what continues to amaze me about this work is how layered and complex every minute of our lessons can be. Again, smart is something you get—even if you are acting smart at the start of the lesson. Every single student can (and will) get smarter every day in Liza's classroom.

What's next? Let's dive back into the lesson, where Liza is about to model her own process of skimming text:

> Students listen with rapt attention when they know the mini-lesson will show them the thinking and reading they are expected to do when it ends. Sam helps us understand how all students can "get smart" when lessons are layered with rich content, explicit comprehension instruction, and expectations to successfully meet learning outcomes.
>
> —*Chryse*

LIZA (*reads aloud from the article about compressed natural gas, then stops and thinks aloud*): As I'm thinking about this and my purpose here, I do need to know, "How is natural gas produced?" This will really help me with my purpose of sustainability. I'm going to pay careful attention to this part and read every word here. (*Liza rereads aloud, then looks up.*) Oh, no, that is not what I wanted, "Where we get it from?" I don't think that helps me. I am going to skip that part. OK, that is all I'm going to model right now. With the person next to you, what did you hear me do as I was thinking aloud?

Liza asks the students to talk in their table groups for a few minutes so all students can articulate their thinking, then she calls the class back together to share some ideas:

LIZA: Morgynne, share with me a little bit. What did you see me do?

MORGYNNE: You were only looking at things that met your purpose. Things that helped you.

LIZA: How could you tell?

MORGYNNE: Because you were like "Ummm . . . this doesn't really help me with efficiency or sustainability . . . I don't need to read this."

LIZA: How do I know what my purpose is?

MORGYNNE: The learning target.

LIZA: Yeah, the learning target up on the board. Our long-term target is, "I can analyze a local transportation option for its efficiency and sustainability." We have a guide for our purpose today. Thank you so much. What else did you see me do?

POULAMI: You put a bracket on places you wanted to pay careful attention to.

LIZA: Yeah, you see I'm identifying, with a bracket here, places that might be helpful later on. Sierra, what else?

SIERRA: You saw if it really connected back to the top.

LIZA: Yeah, that bolded part. We call these text features. I'm going to summarize some things I've heard (*she writes on an anchor chart*):

- I used text features.

- I bracketed.

- I read for a purpose that is connected to my target.

Did I do anything else besides using text features, bracketing things, and reading with a really clear purpose? Leo?

LEO: When you did a bracket, you looked at the text feature first— sometimes you can figure it out pretty quick.

LIZA: So what did I do, what did I decide to read?

LEO: You just read the first sentence or two. You were prioritizing.

LIZA: Leo, I love that you said *prioritizing*, because you are right. I usually go to text features first. The big bold things are there for a reason, but sometimes I need to read a sentence or two in order to decide, "Is this really connected to my target?" before I decide to continue.

BC: I noticed you were using the process of elimination. You thought about each one and tried to figure out which one might work and which one wouldn't. You were like, "OK, is this important?"—kind of narrowing down your search.

MINILESSON

LIZA: Yeah, that is really what skimming is about. I want to narrow it down to determine what is *most* important. I want you to practice for just a minute with this new text. I know a lot of you aren't studying natural gas, but since I am asking you to do this skimming that is really hard with this complex information, I want you to practice. I'm going to ask you to skim and bracket things you want to read more closely. OK, one minute, go! (*One minute passes.*) OK, stop. This is just practice. With the person next to you, what did you decide you are going to read more carefully later?

The students talk in pairs to share their thinking, and then Liza calls the class together to have students share with the whole group:

LIZA: OK, who can share what they figured out?

LEE: Well, there was one section we were questioning, "Is natural gas flammable?" I thought it connects to the target because I need to figure out if it is flammable to see if it is a good energy source for the engine.

LIZA: I love that you are using your background knowledge about the engine and that things have to combust to make energy, at least as far as we know. I like that you are questioning it. You used a new strategy here—making connections to your prior knowledge and asking a question. Great. OK, that is all I'm going to model for now. I'm about to set you free to work— what questions do you have? What are our steps for work time? Yeah—

1. skim,
2. look for what is important about the fuel's efficiency and sustainability, and then
3. capture those reasons on your note catcher (Appendix C).

Any questions? You have thirty-five minutes to dig in . . . go!

END OF SCRIPT

> Content knowledge emerges because students comprehended the text. When they focused on the thinking, the content knowledge emerged. Just like Steph Harvey says, we can't ask student to think about nothing—content is key.
>
> —Cris

Wow. Sixteen minutes into the lesson, and miles deeper in student comprehension of the text and of the complexity of the task ahead of them during the work time. Again, smarter is something you get in Liza's classroom everyday. So what can we label now?

In the first sixteen minutes of class, Liza asked the students to:

- *Infer* about the information certain sections might include based on the bolded words/text features in order to prioritize what to read

- Make *connections* to the learning target—*use background knowledge* about sustainability and efficiency in order to *determine importance* and capture evidence about the efficiency and sustainability of their alternative fuel source

- *Question* and talk back to the text to *synthesize*, and *fix-up/clarify* meaning (with both rereading and making connections to what they already know about gasoline as two major "fix-up" strategies)

- Be *metacognitive* (Is this what I need? Does this make sense? Does this fit with what I already know? Will this help me craft a convincing argument?) in order to collect information and support for their transportation policy position statement

All this was couched in Liza modeling herself as a model of strong work—as an "expert" reader trying to make meaning of a sophisticated science-fact-filled text. In sixteen minutes she asked students to do quick self-assessments, practice and give each other feedback on the skill she was going to release them to do on their own during the work time, and let them share their thinking so far. In sixteen minutes, she asked students to use all of the comprehension strategies outlined by Pearson and colleagues in their proficient reader research (Pearson et al. 1992); to use learning targets to guide their purpose for the day (Stiggins et al. 2004); and to do these things with the real-world purpose and goal of advocating for a policy recommendation regarding the efficiency and sustainability of transportation in Denver (Wiggins and McTighe 2005). Schmoker would be so pleased.

Do comprehension strategies still matter? If your goal is for *all* students to engage—to understand a complex, relevant, important topic, and develop the knowledge and skills of scientists along the way—the answer is yes.

The Verb Matters: Learning Targets and Planning to Do the Work of Thinking

Now that we have a concrete picture of what this work looks like in practice, let's go back to Liza's plan and take a careful look at the verbs of the targets—because this is where she figured out what the students would do to gain knowledge, practice skills, and develop understanding along the way. These verbs are the key to how students will spend their class time in order to get smarter. Let's go back to the targets for the day. The long-term target was:

- I can analyze a local transportation option for its efficiency and sustainability.

The daily targets (scaffolded steps to get to the long-term target) read:

- I can skim my texts to help me decide where to read.
- I can use our long-term target to capture what is important from my texts.

Within each of these active verbs lie other verbs—and resulting actions that are key if students really *can* do the sophisticated thinking we want them to do. Take a look at the verbs of the learning targets from the first part of Liza's plan:

Learning Target Verb and Type K = Knowledge S = Skill R = Reasoning	Implications for Instruction: Scaffolding the Smaller Steps *Teachers must harness minilessons to show students how, work time to let students practice, and debriefs to synthesize and capture thinking from today to help propel learning tomorrow:*
Analyze (S, R)	• Determine importance—know key steps, features, facts • Recognize confusion and ask questions—Does this make sense? What else do I need to know? • Be metacognitive—Does this fit with what I already know? • Make connections—Does this fit with what I already know? Connect new to known • Remember—recall • Synthesize—put some pieces together to make a "new" thing • Conclude—synthesize and make a final call
Skim (S)	• Have a purpose for reading and determine importance • Make connections to background knowledge • Infer from text features and decide where to read • Ask questions that propel you deeper into certain parts of the text, identify and help you clear up confusion
Use (R)	• Determine importance—listen to data/support/articulation of arguments and figure out where they fit into your own schema/background knowledge • Make connections—craft and recraft an argument after you hear others' support/data • Ask questions to clarify ambiguity • Synthesize and articulate arguments • Remember, recall information

This list is not exhaustive, but as you skim the list, you see that it is impossible to do the actions of the learning targets without attending to the comprehension strategies. This in turn has huge implications for the use of time and the design of *reasonably* sound lessons. These are the behaviors students need to practice every day. These are the behaviors that teachers need to model every day. These are the actions that should be explicitly labeled, tracked, and assessed every day—by teachers and by students. The comprehension strategies sit at the heart of this work. It's all in the verbs—the active processes of learning—every minute of every day.

What's Next?

So what's next with comprehension strategies? I don't think it is so much "What's next?" as it is an explicit refocus on their use in learning targets to show students how to make meaning of the world. We must explicitly focus on what we want kids to know, and do, *and* understand—and write specific learning targets for all three purposes of education. I agree with Schmoker—our current crisis doesn't come from not knowing what to do, but from a failure of courage and lack of will to slow down and focus on what matters most. We need to actually *commit* to what we will really go after for a period of time and let students in on our goals. Then we will see the results of our efforts more consistently across grade levels, content areas, and for whole swathes of our school-aged population.

What the research says about assessment for learning and the use of learning targets with students cannot be denied and cannot be ignored. It is too important. Teacher clarity = student ownership and involvement. Teacher clarity = student motivation. Teacher clarity = student empowerment. Teacher clarity = an educated, happy, healthy, fulfilled, giving, and engaged American populace. Teacher clarity = wow.

As Suzanne Plaut writes in her compelling introduction to *The Right to Literacy in Secondary Schools* (2009), "Every teacher plays a role in developing students who can think well and are literate at high levels. [We] must make this work central to [our] mission." (3)

Comprehension strategies are central to this work. Continue to make them a part of your mission.

> Sam, your chapter is a great example of how far the comprehension strategy work has come in these short twenty-five years, and how specific and practical its newest applications can be. Pundits who are clamoring for more classroom rigor should have a look at this!
>
> —Smokey

73

APPENDIX A

Assessment Plan

The development of this Assessment Plan (learning targets and matched assessments) occurred before the first day of the unit. Liza determined importance with the Colorado State Standards, and framed the standards in a real-world compelling topic for students to uncover. She figured out what she wanted students to know, be able to do, and understand—and also what *students would create* to demonstrate their knowledge, skills, and understanding (formative and summative assessments) before her instruction began.

LONG-TERM LEARNING TARGETS	ASSESSMENTS
Learning targets that correlate directly with standards and are reported on in a grade and/or progress report	*Summative assessments that are planned to match long-term targets* • *Formative assessments along the way (bulleted items)*
I can advocate for a policy recommendation that will affect the efficiency and sustainability of transportation in Denver. • I can analyze the Cash for Clunkers program to determine how effective the policy is. • I can critique additional policies for their effectiveness. • I can analyze a local transportation option for its efficiency and sustainability. • I can use science talks as a way to deepen my understanding about various transportation options. • I can develop a policy (Appendix B) that affects the efficiency and sustainability of transportation energy in Denver. • I can describe my thinking about transportation policy in Denver. • I can identify evidence that will help demonstrate my thinking for my voice thread.	Voice Thread[1] Policy Position Statement (Appendix B) • Extended response • T-chart and final analysis of each policy • T-chart, pro/cons for the variables of energy efficiency, sustainability, cost • Science Talk Ticket Reflections—looking for evidence of deepening ideas Voice Thread—note catcher/planning sheet • Note catcher/planning sheet

[1] Voice Thread is an interactive Web-based communication tool for having conversations around media (images, video, or documents). See www.voicethread.com for models and more information.

LONG-TERM LEARNING TARGETS	ASSESSMENTS
Learning targets that correlate directly with standards and are reported on in a grade and/or progress report	*Summative assessments that are planned to match long-term targets* • *Formative assessments along the way (bulleted items)*
I can analyze how the parts of an internal combustion engine work together to improve gas mileage. • I can identify the parts of an internal combustion engine. • I can identify parts of the engine that may affect gas mileage. • I can describe how a problem with one part will affect the engine as a whole.	Concept map—showing how the parts of the internal combustion engine are connected and what their roles are. • Quiz—to identify the parts of an internal combustion engine • Extended response—problem solving—use concept map to hypothesize about gas mileage and what is wrong with the engine when . . .
I can describe why scientists use models to think about and understand the world. (Inquiry)	Extended written response—a paragraph or two • Small routine analyses after each time we work with models (engine, atom, boiling point lab); be sure to activate background knowledge from sixth grade
I can describe how the internal combustion engine transfers energy from gasoline to the wheels. • I can name and define the different kinds of energy. • I can identify the different types of energy in the engine. • I can identify where energy is transferred from one form to another in the engine.	Extended written response—synthesize and explain the flow of energy from one form to another though the engine • Quiz—define types of energy transfer • Concept map—label different types of energy • Exit ticket—where energy is transferred
I can analyze the efficiency of the internal combustion engine.	Voice Thread? • Quiz—efficiency in systems
I can identify potential and kinetic energy in the engine. • I can define kinetic and potential energy.	Labels and descriptions—of kinetic and potential energy added to the concept map • Quiz—on kinetic energy in systems • Quiz—on potential energy in systems

APPENDIX A

LONG-TERM LEARNING TARGETS	ASSESSMENTS
Learning targets that correlate directly with standards and are reported on in a grade and/or progress report	*Summative assessments that are planned to match long-term targets* • *Formative assessments along the way (bulleted items)*
I can analyze the combustion reaction to describe how gasoline provides energy for the engine. • I know what an atom is. • I know what a molecule is. • I know what a chemical (covalent?) bond is.	Picture and caption—of the chemical equation for the combustion reaction • Model—the structure of an atom • Quiz—on basic atomic structure • Model—the structure of a molecule • Quiz—on basic molecular structure • Quiz—what is a chemical bond
I can explain how boiling point is used to make gasoline from oil. • I can describe what causes a phase change. • I know the difference between a compound and a mixture. • I can explain what happens when you distill rubbing alcohol.	Picture and caption—of a compound changing state • Quiz—three phases and effect on atomic structure • Diagram labeling—of the distilling apparatus • Matching—categorize examples as either mixtures or compounds • Lab conclusion
I can analyze the sustainability of our oil reserves. • I can describe the difference between a rock and mineral. • I can represent the geologic formation of oil. • I can mathematically model the formation and consumption of oil.	Voice Thread? • Quiz—geology basics • Picture and caption • Graphing quiz—given a graph students model different variables
I can identify evidence that will help demonstrate my thinking for my Voice Thread.[2] I can skim material to help me identify where to read (literacy).	• Annotations on alternative energy texts • Note catcher/planning sheet Quiz—timed common text, highlighted and annotated

[2] Voice Thread is an interactive Web-based communication tool for having conversations around media (images, video, or documents). See www.voicethread.com for models and more information.

LONG-TERM LEARNING TARGETS	ASSESSMENTS
Learning targets that correlate directly with standards and are reported on in a grade and/or progress report	*Summative assessments that are planned to match long-term targets* • *Formative assessments along the way (bulleted items)*
I can identify resources that will help me answer our research questions (literacy). • I can find resources. • I can evaluate the quality of the resource based on the author. • I can evaluate the quality of the resource based on the content.	T-chart—of all resources found, chose because/didn't choose because . . . • List of search/found articles • Short answer quiz—list of articles for various purposes, why is one more valid than another? • Short response—best text found, why annotated?
I can find information that relates to our research questions (literacy).	Determining importance—T-chart
I can be an active member of a group project by staying on task (collaboration).	Video and reflection • Peer critique • Teacher observation
I can complete my part of a group project on time (collaboration/responsibility).	Individual checklist with peer and teacher signature • Required group calendar with due dates
I can push myself and my group members by asking questions and thinking deeply about our topic (collaboration).	Science talk tickets and reflection (use same format) • Three different practice science talks

EXPEDITION/INVESTIGATION: ENGINES, ENERGY, AND OIL

Standards Addressed (Content and Literacy):

Chemistry

- Understand the basic structure of the atom and be able to distinguish among elements, compounds, mixtures, atoms, and molecules
- Relate the particulate nature of matter to measurable physical properties (pressure, density, phase of matter, temperature) of solids, liquid, and gases
- Describing, measuring (for example, temperature, mass, volume, melting point of a substance), and calculating quantities before and after a chemical or physical change within a system
- Know that mass is conserved in a chemical or physical change
- Differentiating mixtures and substances based on their properties (for example, solubility, boiling points, magnetic properties, densities)

Physics

- Identifying and predicting what will change and what will remain unchanged when matter experiences an external force or energy change
- Describing, measuring (for example, time, distance, mass, force), and calculating quantities that characterize moving objects and their interactions within a system
- Understand that there are different types of energy and those types of energy can be transferred, stored, and changed (kinetic, potential) but overall energy is conserved
- Understand the concepts behind Newton's Laws of Motion (inertia, acceleration, action/reaction, etc.)
- Understand speed and know that acceleration is a change in speed or direction

Earth and Space

- Understand the effects of natural processes that shape Earth's surface (for example, landslides, weathering, erosion, mountain building, volcanic activity)
- Explaining how minerals and rocks form
- Interrelationships exist between minerals, rocks, and soils
- Humans use renewable and nonrenewable resources
- There are consequences for the use of renewable and nonrenewable resources

Literacy

- I can use relevant details to support the narrowed topic; this means my details match my topic and purpose
- I can develop details to support my purpose/thesis or make my message memorable
- This means I can give the reader details that go beyond the obvious
- Determine importance
- Identifying quality resources to use in research
- Skimming to locate where to read

Guiding Questions:

- How do we store and use energy for transportation?
- How can we improve our use of energy for transportation?
- How do scientists and policy makers work together to make innovations in the field of transportation?

Final Product Description

Policy Position Statement

Project Description

As the end of the semester draws near, we are ramping up toward a final project, which has real-world applications. We will be using all of the knowledge and understanding that we have built (and will build) to advocate for a policy that we think Denver (Stapleton neighborhood) should adopt. Together, we will look at the sustainability and efficiency of our current transportation system. After analysis, I will ask you to make a recommendation about what Denver/Stapleton should do to help make our transportation systems more efficient and sustainable.

Target

I can advocate for a policy recommendation that will affect the efficiency and sustainability of transportation in Denver.

Formatting

In order to get our voices out to as many people as possible, we will be formatting our position statements in audible files that we can send to radio stations, policy makers, schools, and community planners to try to bring change. We will be using a program called Voice Thread to record, revise, and perfect our policy recommendations. This program allows us to store our thinking in an easy-to-use format.

Content

Your own final policy statement, recorded on Voice Thread, will need to include:

- A clear description of your position
- A persuasive description of your reasoning

Steps to Get There

We will be using Voice Thread throughout the rest of the semester in order to develop our radio-quality voice. However, you may end up cutting and pasting pieces of our "practice" voice threads into your final policy statement. The "practice" voice threads between now and our final will be:

- Analysis of the efficiency of the internal combustion engine

- Analysis of the sustainability of the internal combustion engine
- Analysis of the efficiency and sustainability of one transportation choice
- Discussion of the pros/cons that could improve the efficiency and sustainability of transportation choices in Denver

Audience

The truth is that the authentic audiences that need to hear your voices demand depth of understanding and analysis in order for your policy statements to be reputable. Together we will find experts and distribute our thinking to:

- Policy makers
- State senators
- Community planners
- Radio stations

Note Catcher

Synthesis of Alternative Transportation Options

Use your Internet resources to help you identify the pros and cons of engines
and use of your alternative transportation option.

	PROS	CONS
Efficiency of engine using your fuel		
Sustainability of your fuel		
Other important pros/cons		

References

Bennett, Samantha. 2007. *That Workshop Book: New Systems and Structures for Classrooms That Read, Write, and Think*. Portsmouth, NH: Heinemann.

Black, Paul, and Dylan Wiliam. 1998. "Inside the Black Box: Raising Standards Through Classroom Assessment." *Phi Delta Kappan* 80 (2): 139–48.

Pearson, P. David, Laura R. Roehler, Janice A. Dole, and Gerald G. Duffy. 1992. "Developing Expertise in Reading Comprehension: What Should Be Taught and Who Should Teach It." In *What Research Has to Say About Reading Instruction*, 2d ed., edited by Jay Samuels and Alan Farstrup. Newark, DE: International Reading Association.

Plaut, Suzanne. 2009. *The Right to Literacy in Secondary Schools*. New York: Teachers College Press.

Schmoker, Mike. 2009. "What Money Can't Buy: Powerful Overlooked Opportunities for Learning." *Phi Delta Kappan* (March): 524–27.

Stiggins, Rick, Judith Arter, Jan Chappuis, and Steve Chappuis. 2004. *Classroom Assessment for Student Learning: Doing It Right—Using It Well*. Portland, OR: Assessment Training Institute.

Wiggins, Grant, and Jay McTighe. 2005. *Understanding by Design*. Alexandria, VA: ASCD.

Building a Better Book Club

Leslie Blauman

When you already have a winning recipe why would you mess with the ingredients? And yet that's exactly what this chapter is about—how do you build a better book club when what you're doing is already successful? It's the quest for comprehension, for continually pushing the kids to understand even more and always setting the bar higher. After twenty-five years of implementing and facilitating book clubs in my classroom, I've found a missing ingredient that enhances the recipe and that's what I want to share—how connecting a whole-class "anchor text" to book clubs pushes the envelope.

A Snapshot of an Anchor Text Lesson

It's October in my fourth grade classroom and the students are gathered in the meeting area; each one with their own copy of *The Tiger Rising* by Kate DiCamillo, a pencil, and a highlighter. I sit in my director's chair with my own copy of the book and a pencil in hand. Behind me is our class anchor chart that holds the class' thinking before we even began the book.

As soon as I ask the students to come to the group with their materials, they hustle up. The energy and enthusiasm is palpable—they love this book. When we left off on the reading the day before, the kids were begging for more—they're ready to dive back into the text today.

I turn to Chapter 11 and instruct the kids to do so in their own books. Then I ask them to turn to the previous page and look at the white space at the end of the chapter. In each child's book they have recorded their thinking here. I read that I wrote, "I think he'll tell Sistine. There are two people that understand." Those were my thoughts as I finished the chapter. "When I read those words it brings me back to my thinking when we left off. That Rob has a secret about the tiger and he finally has two people he trusts. I think this was the first time in the book that I felt he could trust someone. I'm reviewing that with you because I didn't write all that, but just my tracks in the snow on that page brought it all back."

"So what were you thinking as we ended yesterday?" I ask. The day before the students had written, and turned and talked with their classmates, but I want to use their thoughts to focus our reading for the day.

Carolyn's hand shoots up. "I am still thinking about Rob's suitcase. That he has to keep the lid closed on tight. I want to know *why*."

Bennett adds on to her thinking. "I think Rob is really hurting about something and he just won't let it out. I can't figure out why he won't talk to his dad. And all that stuff on his legs—the rash. He could talk to his dad when his dad is putting the cream on."

"I think the rash has to do with his sadness. My mom's a doctor that works with kids and she has talked about how sometimes when you're sad or stressed that you can get rashes. That's weird, huh?" continues Emma.

"Do you think it's sadness or that he gets bullied so much?" Brett wants to know.

"I think his sadness has something to do with the title, too. I highlighted what Willie May said on page 51—'You got to let the sadness rise up.' I'm wondering when Rob can do that. He really wants to talk to someone," observes Ryan.

"So I think it's sadness that gives him the rashes—is that what you're thinking?" continues Brett, as he turns toward Ryan. It's obvious that his thinking has changed due to Ryan's comment. I want to be explicit about that.

"Brett, great comment—why did your thinking change?"

"'Cause of what Ryan said. He used the words from the book."

"Exactly. The reason I'm pointing this out is because that's what book clubs are all about—to bring our questions and thinking to the group and then talk and make new meaning. Thanks for letting me use you guys as an example!"

> Notice how many times Leslie uses the word *thinking* when she talks to her students. It's clear that thinking is front and center in her classroom, so the kids naturally push deeper, because good thinking is what's valued.
>
> —Jason

I bring the discussion to a close. "Phenomenal thinking, you guys. I have to be honest, I am so curious about that suitcase, too. I'm wondering if maybe it's a combination of everything you've touched upon. Shall we keep going and maybe find out today?"

With that segue, I begin reading aloud. Yes—I do the reading out loud, with the kids following along in their own copies. I will read the entire book to the class. We are reading for comprehension and *thinking*, not for fluency. Plus I can read with expression and stop at appropriate points in the text. This is not round-robin reading! I use this whole-class novel as a way for me to model my thinking, while asking the students to stop at particular points in the story and jot their thinking in the margins, and then turn and share. We are co-constructing; scaffolding for future interaction with text. The conversations are rich and the thinking runs deep—*and* all students, no matter their ability, are able to access and understand the text as I am doing the reading.

I tell the kids, "OK, as a teacher, I am furious with the school for allowing this type of behavior. It's obvious that Sistine got in another fight at school and then the boys are bullying her more on the bus. Especially on the bus. There is no way the bus drivers here would know that bullying is going on and not do anything about it. That's what I'm thinking. So I'm going to just jot down in the margin 'it makes me mad' to capture that thinking. My feelings are stronger than that, but that's what I'm leaving as my tracks in the snow."

"Maybe the bus driver is scared of the bullies," Everett piggybacks.

"Or maybe it's just easier to ignore it. Maybe that's the way it is in the South. I don't have much background on a school like that," continues Max.

"I don't care, it's not right. Just not right," Micha responds.

"OK, guys, I'm going to be explicit. Do you notice how just my one comment led to lots more thinking from you? Just like what happened earlier between Brett and Ryan. That's what you'll be doing in your book clubs. Bringing your thinking to the group and then discussing it," I conclude.

And so it goes. Read and think and write our thinking, and then talk about it. Talking and listening and deepening our understanding. A waltz that weaves through our classroom as we work through the novel. But where does it lead? Is it a lesson unto itself or is it laying the foundation for further thinking? To answer that question we need to fast-forward to November.

A Snapshot of a Book Club

Micha, Kylie, Emma, Audrey, Katie, and Carolyn now occupy the class meeting area for their book club, while the rest of the class reads or writes at their desks or around the room. The students not involved in this particular book

> I echo Leslie's sentiment that reading aloud plays an important role in comprehension instruction. It can be freeing to the listener, allowing for increased focus on the thinking. It levels the playing field for readers in a classroom or book club. Sadly, an increasing amount of teachers feel they can't make time for this anymore. Reading aloud to our students is something that we can't afford to delete.
>
> —Tanny

An all girl book club? Some books lend themselves to girls, and some appeal to boys. I'm going to offer books that appeal to both genders, but there are so many wonderful books that if I end up with an all girl group or all boy group once in awhile, that's OK. After we finish one book club, we mix up the groups so kids are not "locked in" with a specific group.

Our first and second graders form a hybrid book club by discussing texts they read at home from their book bags. Many of the students discuss their texts in their new language of English. We begin by posting language frames: I read ___. My favorite part was ___, because ___. What questions and comments do you have? The kids quickly internalize this discourse routine and begin to run the discussion on their own.

— *Anne & Brad*

club have settled in to work before the book club moves to the meeting area. I sit outside the circle of girls, as an observer, scripting their words and "eavesdropping." The girls sit in a circle, each with a copy of *Esperanza Rising* by Pam Munoz Ryan in their lap. The books are peppered with sticky notes marking pages to refer back to their discussion. These sticky notes have writing on them, holding each girl's thinking. The writing mirrors the writing that students did in the margins of *The Tiger Rising*—this is evidence that all our work with the anchor text scaffolded this transfer to independence. The girls lean in toward each other and the conversation is animated. Although reading *Esperanza Rising* is their first foray into book clubs for this year, the girls are comfortable diving right into the conversation because they have met as a group twice before to discuss this book. The conversation flows back to topics they've discussed when they've met earlier. The talk is rich and deep and for anyone observing, it would look as if they had experienced book clubs countless times before.

"I finally like Esperanza. I mean I always liked her as a character, but I thought she was pretty spoiled," says Carolyn.

"Yeah, like what she did to the little girl on the train with the doll was so mean. Her mom sure straightened her out. Even if you're rich, you shouldn't treat someone like that—she wouldn't share her doll. I thought it was cool that Mama made the yarn doll for that little girl. I went and tried it after I read it, and it actually works," comments Audrey.

"But you know I started feeling really sorry for her. Especially the part—remember when she was trying to use a broom to sweep—where everyone laughed at her. It was pretty funny, because you have to be pretty lame not to be able to use a broom, but it also made me feel sad for her. She's lost so much," continues Micha.

Kylie cuts in, "And it's not done—she's lost even more. Mama's sick. I'm really worried about her and I hope Munoz Ryan doesn't kill her off the way they killed the Dad. Do you think that the author would do that?"

Carolyn immediately answers, "Oh, she can't—that would be just too sad. I can't see any happiness if that happens. And you know how it says that the word *esperanza* means *hope*, so there really has to be some hope . . . "

Emma is practically jumping off the floor, "Oh my gosh! That's it! *Hope Rising*. That's the title. Esperanza has hope rising. Think about all the bad stuff and she's rising. I have a sticky note on page 51—everybody go there."

Emma waits while the rest of the group turns to that page and she reads about how Abuelita tells Esperanza about the mountains and valleys of the weaving. Then Emma continues, "*And* it's just like *The Tiger Rising*. Her feelings will rise up. Look at the titles and look at the deeper meaning, guys. Rob's suitcase was like the tiger rising—let all the bad out—and Esperanza is rising, the bad has to be let out."

Carolyn immediately adds on, "You know life is like the peaks and valleys—the highs and lows. I think that's what Abuelita had been trying to say. And look at the book so far—Esperanza has already had a lot of peaks and valleys. I still don't want Mama to die. Too sad."

I had never thought of this. In fact, the kids come up with thoughts that blow me away. At this point I ask if I can join the group and talk for a minute.

"Emma, in fact all of you, what terrific thinking. I'm amazed—I hadn't even thought of that connection. The rising. Fascinating. Here's what I'd love you to do. Emma, could you be the holder of that idea and as you read and finish the rest of the book, see if it continues to fit? I'd love to hear what you discover. And I'd also like you to reflect if you would have been able to make that connection if we hadn't read *The Tiger Rising*."

I shift back out of the circle and the girls go back to their discussion. They stay with the idea of "rising" for quite awhile and then move on to other characters, asking questions, and making predictions. When they feel satisfied with their meeting, they choose how far they want to read for the

Esperanza Rising by Pam Munoz Ryan	
What We Know	**Questions**
Esperanza and her mom go to California	Why doesn't her dad go, too?
Setting—Great Depression	Did they lose their money?
They're rich	What was the tragedy?
Abuelita—"Grandma" in Spanish	Who is she and why doesn't she go too? Why?
Riches to rags	How can they be rich on a ranch?
Starts on a ranch in Mexico	Do they sell the ranch?
1920s/1930s	Does she work as a farmer?
Esperanza has to work	Will they be picking crops?
Mexican camp for workers	What type of farm?
	Is it a vineyard?
Ranch	Like a wine farm?
Starts in 1924	How does Esperanza deal with her new life?
	Why is the title *Esperanza Rising*?

Anchor chart on *Esperanza Rising*, created at the first book club meeting. This shows the group's thinking *before* starting the book.

following week and then head back to their desks. As they walk back, they still are discussing predictions—and hopes. This book has them hooked.

So What? How Do These Two Lessons Fit Together?

Twenty years ago, I started book clubs with my class. The kids and their rich discussions were captured in Stephanie Harvey and Anne Goudvis' *Strategy Instruction in Action* video series (2006). The students were amazing. They loved to read and were voracious readers. Today my students continue that love of reading—and I often think about *why*, especially as I look at the plethora of professional books offering advice on how to get kids reading. What has happened in the world that has destroyed the passion for reading for many of our kids? And why do my students love reading? I always wound up answering my own question with "book clubs." Especially since that's the answer my students resoundingly give me—year after year when I ask.

Was it enough, though? Did my students understand what they were doing and how it helped their learning? My thinking about book clubs has evolved and changed over the years. How has my thinking changed? Such a key question—and a question I ask of my students daily in all subject areas. How has your thinking changed? Why? How has it deepened?

In her chapter, Chryse Hutchins captures lessons and book club discussions in my room. Co-constructing anchor charts of how we listen and talk. Modeling thinking for students. Working through the comprehension strategies in minilessons and then conferring with students to ensure they are using the strategies independently. Students reading and learning and talking in their book club groups. Add these to the focus on anchor texts and there is the recipe for building a better book club. I truly think that adding anchor texts was the last ingredient to creating an award-winning recipe.

If I expect my students to be learners, and to go deeper with their thinking, I must model that. Two professional books pushed my thinking. Ellin Oliver Keene's *To Understand* (2008) brought into play the question of "How do our kids know when they're understanding?" (see Chapter 1). Do our students truly understand how that helps them to go deeper with their thinking? As teachers, do we know when our students understand? Many of us had asked our students to think about their thinking (be metacognitive) *before*, *during*, and *after* reading—but I had never pushed the envelope by asking my students to *explain* how it helped them to understand. I found myself questioning if I had done enough modeling—and being explicit—about what *understanding* meant. Reflecting has always been a key component of my classroom, in all subject areas, yet I've discovered that it needs to be utilized more—along with asking the question "Why?" Why are you thinking that, and how will it help you as a reader (or writer, mathematician, scientist, etc.)? Teachers need to be researchers each and every day—discovering what it is that makes our kids tick.

The second book that affected my thinking and teaching was Harvey Daniels and Steve Zemelman's *Subjects Matter* (2004). They theorize that background knowledge is the "hook" to hang new learning on. Without that "hook," learning often doesn't "stick" for students. My students love this analogy and often refer to their hook getting bigger and stronger so they can hang more on it. And I want to provide the "hook" for their book clubs so that their comprehension is stronger and deeper and more meaningful. While we provide students with background on content learning, don't we also need to provide them with the background—the modeling and practice—on how to hold on to their thinking and then to share and listen with their classmates?

Rethinking Anchor Texts: Adding Whole-Group Novels into the Mix

What is an anchor text? We need to define anchor charts first. If you were to ask my students, they would explain that just as an anchor holds a boat in place, an anchor chart captures class thinking and holds it for the year. Building on that, an anchor text is a shared experience that holds *class* thinking. It anchors future learning and captures and holds much of our thinking.

As I discussed this chapter with Chryse Hutchins, she kept asking how an anchor text, as I was defining it, was different from the picture books, short stories, poetry, and so on that I use in my classroom for minilessons and modeling. Yes—those are "anchor texts," as the students and I co-construct meaning. We hold our thinking on class anchor charts and in their Book Lover's Book (Blauman 2011) and we "turn and talk" about our thinking. Generally, though, these lessons are short and completed during one workshop period. This is a wonderful way of modeling the thinking strategies, but doesn't require holding sustained thinking over a period of time—a necessity when reading a novel. And we often are not explicit with our students about *how* to hold on to thinking throughout a novel—we simply expect our short minilessons to transfer to longer pieces of text. That's not always the case.

Often teachers think of "class novel" as one size fits all. And we all know that our classrooms are not all one size. As students progress through the grades, the gap widens between reading abilities. So how beneficial is placing all students in the same book? What about the child who can't read the text independently? What about the child who reads at an advanced level? Or the child with limited English? In response to these questions, I have to say that the "class novel" is not the answer. Students who can't read it either fake it or fail. Frustration has to run rampant for them. The advanced child? Bored, and where's the challenge? So while class novels are often used for accountability, they usually have an adverse affect on student comprehension—not to mention dulling the desire to read. How, then, do we ensure that all our students are accessing the text and making meaning? My answer to that is to shift the focus from a "class novel" to an "anchor text."

Another typical method of using class novels is for students to answer questions at the end of each chapter. While I understand that with the culture of accountability and wanting to excel at high-stakes tests, I challenge teachers to reflect on how that deepens student understanding *and* makes them love to read the book. When I ask kids about this method, the answer is

Sometimes a student captures it best. Here are Emma's thoughts:

Giving kids packets is like giving a dog a banana instead of giving it to a monkey. It just doesn't make sense and there's no enjoyment for the dog, he'll just toss it away. When you throw out worksheets after books, you know the kids won't like it and it makes the kids not want to read the book anymore. Questions in packets at the ends of books have to be questions that you can answer. I guess they don't get that when you ask questions that have no specific answer it brings deep rich conversations. We read The Tiger Rising. *The author, Kate DiCamillo, followed you the whole way with the suitcase full of worries and Rob finally lets his deep and dark and sad feelings* rise *up and waft away. A month or two later we read as a book club* Esperanza Rising. *The girl in the book had to go to a work camp and her grandma had to stay behind but grandma said that after many mountains and valleys (ups and downs) on her quilt we will be together. It is the same idea of rising.*

always that it ruins the book for them. I realize there is a need for accountability and for grades, but what is the *purpose* of the novel as an anchor text? Is it for a grade or to *model* and *practice* deep thinking and interaction with the text? Which would you rather do as a reader?

A Look at Novels as Anchor Texts

So what exactly is a whole-class novel as an "anchor text"? It's a shared text with the teacher reading it aloud and students following along in their own copies. There are no premade questions at the end of the chapters. Students are responsible for creating and asking their own questions. Students determine what is important in the text and share with their classmates. Isn't that what a true book club is? Students bringing questions, predictions, inferences, and their thinking to their book club group? Why not practice as a class before setting off to do it independently? This is where the aspect of building background knowledge began to change my thinking and impact my teaching.

Typically I do one to two anchor texts each year. I choose rich, well-written novels that lend themselves to deep thinking. And I choose books that will challenge my students. I want books at the upper reading level of my class with lots of literary elements. I want to use these books to teach! Since I do the reading out loud, and the students follow along, all my students can access the text. If the economics of the school allow students to purchase their own books in order to write in them, I have students purchase the books. If not, I have multiple copies available so students can use sticky notes to record their thinking. As I model, I have my own copy of the book and I record my thinking directly in it as an example for my students.

The first time we work with the novel, we co-construct a T-chart to hold our thinking before we begin the book (see p. 92).

The left column is "What We Know"—which is our background knowledge as we start. The right column holds our questions. This chart helps set the purpose and is a model for future charts students will create each time they start a new book club. As we read through our book, we will refer back to this chart to see how our thinking changes and grows. What's most important to emphasize, though, is that this chart reflects the *kids'* thinking. They have ownership of their thinking—and that's what I want for their book clubs.

> Leslie, as someone who has tinkered with literature circles for more than twenty-five years, your idea of reading aloud a whole-class anchor novel is brilliant. So many good things going on here: modeling, community building, developing a language for talking about books. This sure beats handing out those stinkin' role sheets and sending kids off on their own.
>
> —Smokey

The Tiger Rising by Kate DiCamillo	
What We Know	**Questions**
Tiger	What is it about?
Rob finds tiger (p. 1)	Why is the tiger in the book?
Found it in a cage	How does he find the tiger?
Sistine Bailey	Why is the tiger in a cage?
Setting—Florida	Is the tiger nice?
Award winner—National Book Award finalist	Why is a girl riding the tiger? (cover)
	Is it a circus tiger?
DiCamillo—*Winn-Dixie, Desperaux, Edward Tulane*	Who is the man in the background? (cover)
Desperaux—Newbery winner	Who is Sistine Bailey?
Winn-Dixie—Newbery honor	Why is the tiger allowing the girl to ride on its back?
	How can you ride a tiger?
	What does the title mean?
	What is the "tiger rising"?
	What's the motel have to do with it?

The snapshot I wrote at the beginning of this chapter illustrates a typical class discussion as we work through a novel. My main purpose is to model interaction with text, holding thinking and practicing how to have deep discussions. Since we do this in a whole-group setting, the class gets a lot of practice. And since we "turn and talk" frequently, everyone is actively engaged and all voices and thinking are honored and respected. Anchor novels also provide the means to teach such elements as character, setting, plot, conflict, mood, theme, foreshadowing, climax, antagonist, and protagonist *in context* and in an authentic way. I'm going to teach as much as possible through these books! That's why it's so important to be choosey about which novels are worthy of becoming an anchor text.

Upon completion of the novel, my students reflect on what they've learned. I also ask them to reflect on how they've changed as readers and thinkers. I want them to internalize what we've accomplished so that they can transfer it to book clubs. I want to be explicit with the students about how the work we did with the anchor text transfers directly to their upcoming book clubs.

The Deepening Discussions in Book Clubs

So often in classrooms, students talk about their reading in groups, but often these groups are teacher directed. Who has control over these groups? Student book clubs are different. Students have much of the control, and they can handle it because they've practiced extensively and know what to do. They are not structured with specific questions to answer or predetermined roles for the members—students come to discuss *their* thinking. They have ownership over their meetings. Since they've been involved in holding and sharing their thinking, the transition from anchor novels to book clubs is seamless. My role is to facilitate if necessary, but mainly to sit outside the group and eavesdrop, scripting their comments and discussion for my own accountability and to help me teach better. And most importantly, observing if my students are truly understanding. Think of the girls in their book club. From their discussion, it's obvious that they were understanding the text and creating meaning at a deep level.

As we move into book clubs, there is one more important foundational piece—and that is to create our norms. After we finish reading through an anchor text novel, we begin to discuss as a class how we want our book clubs to operate. These become our *norms*. What are our class expectations for behavior and accountability? These norms build on other foundational lessons that have been laid throughout the year (listening, good conversations, etc.). As a whole class, we meet and brainstorm ideas and then the following day revisit these and finalize them. Our chart of norms remains hung in the classroom to guide us.

Here is an example of norms from a fourth grade classroom.

2008

Book Club Norms

- LISTEN (refer to chart!)
- Practice/live by our rules of good conversations
- Eye contact—sit in a circle
- Attention to the book club
- Be there on time
- Bring your book
- Come ready to discuss—Hold your thinking:
  *** Book club section in BLB (Book Lover's Book—the students' reading book)
  *** Sticky notes
  *** Bookmarks
- NO EXCUSES! YOU MUST READ!
  *** Make the commitment to reflect/review prior to the meeting
- Mrs. B. will give five to ten minutes before to prepare
- Have to talk/share thinking/GO DEEP!
- Everyone discusses (flexible)—go deeper—piggyback (no one hogs conversation, though)
- Don't change the subject until it has been totally discussed (thoroughly)
- No "side conversations"
- ASK QUESTIONS
- Respect each other's opinions
- Leave it up to each individual book club about reading ahead, but NO SPOILING THE ENDING!
- Hold emergency meetings if necessary (in case we need to decide if we want to read more before the next meeting)
- Rest of class should be working—quiet and considerate (responsibility)

- Group/class needs to be respectful
- Ten minutes in between groups (for kids to refocus and for Mrs. B to work with any kids that need her)
- Move quietly

Notice the quality and depth of these norms. The only item that I make sure is included is that students *must* come to group prepared and they must have captured their thinking—and not just be "holding it in their heads." Students have a lot of choice over how they hold their thinking; however, in order to join the group, students have to be prepared. The kids hold each other accountable and there is nothing more powerful than when the group informs a member that until they mark their text, they may not participate in the discussion!

Chryse Hutchins' chapter dives into the question of what to do with all the sticky notes once we've used them. I'd like to ponder that thought here. What happens when the book is done? What do the kids do with their thinking? This is another way my instruction has changed over the years. When a book club book is finished, students remove their sticky notes (or however they have recorded their thinking) and decide which ones demonstrate their *best* and *deepest* thinking. They choose vocabulary words, questions, predictions, inferences, and sections that they thought were important to the story. These sticky notes are then put in their Book Lover's Book (Blauman 2011) or a reading notebook. This holds the students accountable and I can quickly go back and check their thinking and interaction with the text.

Is that enough? I'm going to circle back to the beginning and the questions that were the impetus for this chapter: the *why* and *how.* I ask my students how their thinking changed. How did it go? I ask them to reflect on the book club. And each year, using student reflections, I too reflect on book clubs.

In *The Inside Guide to the Reading-Writing Classroom Grades 3–6: Strategies for Extraordinary Teaching,* I wrote that "Student-driven literature conversations *are* the be-all-end-all. So much of the literacy work students and I have done together is unfurled, like a big, color flag, in these conversations. And students love them, citing book talks as the most vital, memorable practice of the year, with the BLB, conferring, and using mentor texts coming in as semi-finalists. Taken together, these classroom practices are the game changers. And it's no accident that *these are the venues where students can talk, share and be listened to.* Think about the power of talk" (216–17).

Brian gives some ideas on how talk helps him to comprehend, and then offers other options for book clubs. He says: "Talking in book clubs helps me understand the book better. That's why whenever I read a book club book, everything's much easier to understand. It would help if other people who are reading books in the same settings and the same time and maybe even about the same people could confer and discuss how the two books have connections. Maybe we could make up things called Lonely Book Clubs and we could read any book we want and see how they make connections to each other. I think that will help me comprehend because if the person reading either the same book or a connecting book, we could add our thoughts together and infer what might come next."

Think about the power we are giving our students when we *teach* them how to notice their thinking and then to discuss it. Talk. Meaningful talk. Merely having students discuss—without scaffolding deep, rich talk—isn't enough.

While taking a couple weeks out of the school year to work through an anchor novel may seem like a lot, the benefits are innumerable. We move through the novel quickly. I want students to see how a book doesn't need to be drawn out. I don't want the process of working through a text and holding thinking to become drudgery. My goal is for the kids to fall in love with the text. I want them devouring books! No overkill. I do an anchor text once (twice as a maximum) for the year and then turn the work over to the kids. That's imperative. And the work in an anchor novel is a *shared* experience, with students doing a great deal of the work. Then they move to using this independently. Isn't that the ultimate goal—to create successful, independent students who *understand*? Here are some of my students' thoughts. I asked them to help me understand. I asked them how an anchor novel facilitated better book clubs. I'm going to step out of the way now and let the kids do the talking.

In the Kids' Words

Kylie:

> I think that if we didn't read these books together I would have not liked the books at all. It really has helped me understand some of the things that I don't because if I don't know something someone else will and it's just so much more meaningful when you're like "Oh, I get that!" and it made me feel more open about talking to the group about the book. I think it gave us more of an idea of what to be asking about, and good questions and how to behave during a book club. I also think it helped with sticking with books.

Max:

> <u>Tiger Rising</u> and <u>Bearstone</u> helped me by . . . (1) When Mrs. B modeled she got me to ask more questions. Now that I realize that the more questions you write down that you get answers to, helps me understand the book better. (2) When I hold my thinking I can do a questions/answer in my book when looking back.

Micha:

> I don't think I would have liked any of the books if I didn't read them in our class. You showed me how to do book clubs. What helped me was before we started the book; we started with our questions and our thinking. It got us on the "thinking train." I had never done that before, but now I'm doing that for my own reading. You pushed us to understand and you gave us the background knowledge. Now we know how to "tag off of each other with our ideas." If we didn't know something for <u>Bearstone,</u> you were our BK!

Anna:

> When we held our thinking it helped me because when we had a question that worked all the way through the book you could look back. This especially helped with <u>The Thief Lord</u> when we did it as a book club. When you talked about our thinking, you showed us how to start a good conversation with our book club. Your modeling was excellent, you really helped us learn to share and get our thinking down, also to look at every possibility of thinking. But one of the main things that helped is that now as a reader even when I'm not reading in a book club I'll still think the same and I will laugh because I feel I am in a book club thinking the same. But it is not just you, it was <u>Tiger Rising</u> and <u>Bearstone</u>—they also helped me about holding my thinking, you and the class, modeling and lastly about my/our thinking.

References

Blauman, Leslie. 2011. *The Inside Guide to the Reading-Writing Classroom: Strategies for Extraordinary Teaching, 3–6.* Portsmouth, NH: Heinemann.

Daniels, Harvey, and Steve Zemelman. 2004. *Subjects Matter: Every Teacher's Guide to Content-Area Reading.* Portsmouth, NH: Heinemann.

Dicamillo, Kate. 2001. *The Tiger Rising.* Somerville, MA: Candlewick Press.

Harvey, Stephanie, and Anne Goudvis. 2006. *Strategy Instruction in Action.* Portland, ME: Stenhouse.

Keene, Ellin Oliver. 2008. *To Understand: New Horizons in Reading Comprehension.* Portsmouth, NH: Heinemann.

Ryan, Pam Munoz. 2000. *Esperanza Rising.* New York: Scholastic.

CHAPTER SIX

Thinking and Talking Our Way Through the Words

Chryse Hutchins

The Power of Confessing

As we fly through the friendly skies, we often find ourselves sharing life stories with complete strangers. Family pictures come out, lost luggage nightmares are exchanged, and before we know it we're into personal airplane confessions. I'm convinced people share things on airplane flights they'd never divulge in other settings. At least it's true when you tell them you're on your way to present a workshop about reading comprehension. That topic unleashes a flood of admissions: "Oh, I could sure use that information! How do I sign up? I'm such a slow reader. I can't remember a thing I read."

One of my favorite comments came from a seatmate who said, "Well, *that* should be a short workshop, you either get what you read or you don't! You just can't teach that stuff. Hey, do you want me to do the speech for you?"

On a flight to Arizona, my most powerful airplane confession was shared by a young golf pro. He told me he just didn't read books.

I wanted to help him out and said he probably read the newspaper or Internet, but was stopped midsentence by the look on his face. He replied, "Oh, I can read, I just can't stay with the print. I don't know what to do with the words."

His response has haunted me for some time now. In classrooms across the country, knowing what to do with the words continues to be the hallmark of comprehension instruction. Students in these classrooms view reading as a two-sided proposition. In addition to figuring out how to recognize and pronounce the words, they are taught to simultaneously listen to their inner voice to figure out what it could all mean. These kids are aware of the internal signals they're receiving from what's visible on the page and use that information to create understanding.

My new acquaintance told me he had no problem with the *word work*. He needed instruction on how to light up those words, to create a personal take on the lines of print. I decided to relate my years of golf lessons to reading. Yes, he'd helped his prospective golf students visualize how to loft the ball, by choosing a higher-numbered club. I shared examples of how he could turn on his "reading camera" to see and feel the words play out in his mind. If his mental image became fuzzy, it was a sign his mind had wandered or he lacked sufficient background knowledge to carry on. This conscious effort to create mental pictures would help him stay with the text longer as the words lived in his mind in a more vibrant way. This made sense to him, as golf is seeing in your head what you want the club to do on the range.

My seatmate certainly understood what it meant to build background knowledge for his students. He constructed his golf lessons so that concepts built one on top of the next, allowing his clients to develop their skills as they tackled the game. He'd ask each participant to remember the standard grip he'd taught them for hitting off the tee, and use that information to slightly modify their grip for putting. I told him he'd more successfully relate to what he read if he activated his own background knowledge and connected this to the words on the page. He'd more purposefully engage with the print when he found a home in the words. In that long flight to Tucson, he began to realize that in addition to reciting the words he needed to see and connect to their meaning.

This young golf pro reminded me of students who have been over-schooled in just one portion of the reading equation. He could say the words, but lost his way in the *meaning making* side of reading. If we want to support readers who know how to negotiate the text, it's important that we

Chryse, you are such a patient teacher. I guess we are never really off duty, are we? Maybe you should have charged him; according to the PGA website, the going rate for a 30-minute private golf lesson is $50. Just saying.

—Smokey

acknowledge that both word work and comprehension instruction play vital roles in our literacy goals. Daily lessons about how reading works in the minds of proficient readers dispels the mystery behind the word work and produces engaged, independent readers.

The Power of Thinking Aloud

When we teachers model our own reading process through a think-aloud, we are showing them what "all those words" actually sound like in the mind of an experienced reader, giving kids the courage and confidence to try themselves. Hearing a teacher isolate confusions, read to confirm a prediction, or confess a lack of background knowledge opens up the thinking path for our readers. Unfortunately, that mentor moment has taken on a life of its own, often filling up the better part of the literacy block. In our enthusiasm to show them the way, we might be overdoing our time on the stage! Going public with our thinking is most effective when it's brief, includes a tangible way to hold thinking, and leaves the students with a clear understanding of why they might use a strategy in the first place. Kids lose the benefit of our think-aloud if their practice time becomes a homework assignment or they trundle off to recess. In-class reading should immediately follow the think-aloud lesson. Taking that think-aloud and doing it for themselves is where the road to independence begins. While our students read, we're on the job—conducting individual or small-group conferences and providing on the spot support for the concept modeled in the daily lesson.

The Power of Holding Our Thinking

I'm reminded of a third grade teacher who once stopped me in the hall. She was carrying a student's chapter book loaded with sticky notes. With a perplexed look on her face she said, "Now what do I do?"

In the beginning, it was all about the sticky notes. Teachers described and marked their thinking with sticky notes and sent kids off to try this independently. The students were immediately successful—marking raised questions, pulling out important information, and adding their thinking to the lines of print. But we soon realized that the goal here was not having a book with rainbow notes cascading off each page. We needed to zero in on *how* the strategy helped a reader better understand what was read. Without numerous experiences to mark, talk about, and examine *why* a thinking

> In my experience, far too many students are denied the thinking work because they don't yet have the decoding down, or they can decode well, but don't yet know how to express in English the concepts represented in print. I wonder whether it is reasonable to allow students to do the thinking work without the text using pictures, movies, or role plays or by listening to someone else do the reading.
>
> —Nancy

strategy enabled them to construct meaning, kids were left in the dark as to how sticky notes helped them at all.

Classroom anchor charts are like giant sticky notes. They offer a place to collectively freeze-frame the comprehension journey: What's leading you to infer? What are you learning about yourself as a reader? How do we go about pulling out important information in our nonfiction texts? What does it sound like in your head when you don't understand? These anchor charts provide a record of the year's ongoing comprehension discoveries and often hold the initials of those who shared in the new findings. Readers of all levels see their ideas made permanent as they share and shape how meaning is built from the words.

Sticky notes, anchor charts, coded text, and response notebooks—all come into their own when they provide the springboard to discussion. As a student once said, "I mark my thinking, so I can remember, even a week later, what I thought in the first place!" Holding on to that inference or compelling fact may then be examined in a number of sharing configurations. Readers can easily recapture their thinking in a conference, in written reflection, with a seatmate, or to enlighten others in a book club. What kids record leads to future lessons and new thinking. Practice in holding on to what matters affords readers an active role in the meaning-making side of reading.

> Wow, I never thought about anchor charts as a large-group sticky note! We get smarter together.
>
> —Cris

The Power of Having Kids Take Responsibility for Their Reading

If we ask our students why they do school reading the response is often, "Because you told us to." We've instructed kids to read to answer our questions or read to uncover what the author had in mind. We've pulled out all the vocabulary they might not know, or sped up a science lesson by bulleting what's important to remember. Our students sit back and marvel at how hard we work to get them to arrive at our conclusions.

Now let's look at what it really means to turn over reading responsibility to our students. I'm thinking of Amanda, a new student arriving midyear in Leslie Blauman's fourth grade class. This nine-year-old quickly noticed that expectations were completely different in this room, where her peers filled the day with a constant stream of reading, writing, talking, and thinking. Where were the workbook pages? How was she to fill out a column with a

> True, teachers and kids can get so caught up in covering the curriculum that we forget that student thinking is way more important than content.
>
> —Cris

heading that read "Lingering Thoughts and Questions"? We could almost hear her say, "You mean *my* questions go here?"

As the students read "About Loving," a short story from *Hey World, Here I Am!* by Jean Little (1986), Leslie crisscrossed the room, holding conferences at each cluster of desks: "Thanks for underlining your confusion here. What will you do to figure out the meaning of this line? Please read it back to me. Do these words make you think of another short story we've read? Why? You've just connected something you've read in the past, which helped you fix your understanding of this piece. Nice work! Keep going with that idea."

With another student: "For you as a reader, how are you going to make this paragraph make sense? We're readers in here. You *are* monitoring your comprehension. You said, 'I don't get this word.' Just like we've practiced in our group work, we underline words we don't know and get help. How would you figure out this word if I wasn't here?"

Leslie paused at Amanda's desk and asked her how it was going. This fourth grader confessed she had some questions about the second paragraph. Leslie encouraged her to record her confusions in the question column, saying "What you just told me lets me into your brain. Write your questions down. Then I can do my best teaching." These encouraging words were just what this new student needed.

Amanda's two-column notes:

"About Loving" by Jean Little, from *Hey World, Here I Am*	
What It's About	**Lingering Thoughts or Questions**
Katherine used to think that her parents didn't notice that she was there. Katherine felt like she was invisible. *Love isn't as simple as she once thought* (big idea). She says, "Talking about it isn't what matters most." My thinking after discussion: Katherine's dad did notice that Katherine didn't like it when her parents weren't loving. All of the things connect.	Why aren't they loving in the beginning? Why in the end? Why did Katherine's dad ask, "Katherine, tell me, what truth?" Did he take notice that Katherine didn't like it when her parents weren't loving? Why didn't they start loving in the beginning? Why didn't Katherine's parents ever notice?

On the right side of the chart Amanda lists the ponderous questions that really mattered to her personal understanding. She would bring them into her four-way sharing session.

The room erupted in discussion as each set of four worked their way through not only Little's short story, but the questions they'd jotted down to bring to the discussion. Leslie flowed from group to group, scripting their conversations and challenging them to talk more about unanswered questions. She kept notes about what students were discovering. Pulling the class back together, Leslie asked each student to write how their thinking had changed after discussion. Five minutes passed and Leslie said, "Now look at your written retell, your questions and lingering thoughts raised by the retell, as well as the sentences you jotted after discussion and draw a line under the part that holds the big idea of this piece."

Amanda returned to her notes, and finally underlined, "Love isn't as simple as she once thought." This self-directed search for meaning was not assigned, but scaffolded by Leslie. The result left Amanda beaming.

The Power of Discussion

If our goal is to create readers who know what to do with the words, having access to other readers is crucial. Reading in isolation rarely affords students the chance to grow their own self-talk. When sharing between all groups, a student might explain how a personal connection painted a vivid mind picture. Other kids follow suit. A group of four students start with a connection and discover it becomes the launch site to inferential thinking. A new fact, added to a research project on whales, leads to deeper questions. Turning to talk about this newfound power paves the way to understanding.

To observe the social structure of discussion groups, let's again return to Leslie Blauman's fourth grade class. We are a group of six educators, assembled early one January morning. As a facilitator for the Public Education and Business Coalition's National Lab, my job was to help the group see and hear all that was possible. Mary, from Vermont, was interested in learning more about reading conferences. Hillary and Dave from Spokane wanted to know how to assess thinking strategies. A literacy coordinator from Dallas just wanted to see how this all worked with real students. Paul, visiting from Cleveland, would be noting how Leslie blended reading and writing. What they scripted that morning was far more than their initial wonderings.

The adults flanked the students as the class gathered on the floor to begin the day. Each teacher held notebooks opened to capture the lesson.

Leslie adjusted a fresh sheet onto her clipboard. "This morning, as I meet with two book clubs, you need to decide what to do. Here are your choices for today":

- Write your rough draft on your interview of our room president.

- Continue working on your research report.

- Read your book club book or your own reading choice.

- Write a letter to me about your reading.

- Finish up your vocabulary for the week.

"Take one minute to decide your first choice and, if you finish, your second choice. I'll be taking a Status of the Class, to hear how you'll be using your time while I script book clubs." Some of the following choices were reported as Leslie quickly called the roll and jotted down their responses: writing inquiry reports about sharks, Chinese water dogs, UFOs, cactus, Greek gods, grizzles, and dragons. Others would be completing weekly vocabulary, while a majority of the students said they planned to prepare for their next book club meeting. One student asked for a library pass to continue his research. Three kids told Leslie they needed a conference with her, so they could independently carry on for the morning.

Leslie addressed her next comments to the two book clubs meeting for the first time that day. "When we wrote our book club norms, you decided each member should be ready to talk. How do we do this? Where could we write down our questions and comments? We've held our thinking lots of different ways. You might keep track of your thinking in a notebook, on a piece of paper, your bookmark, or sticky notes. You find what works for you. You also wanted ten minutes to get ready to meet, and *Sign of the Beaver* will be up first today. Use your ten minutes to decide how you'll get your thinking into the discussion."

The classroom settles as kids work on tasks that really matter to them. Leslie circles the room, conferring with students about their reading and writing. She moves the *Sign of the Beaver* wall chart next to the book club meeting area and calls them up to form a group where all can see and hear one another. Directing their attention to the chart, Leslie said, "Please read the questions you generated last week. I'm going to be on the outside scripting your discussion. Will you let me know if you need me?" With those final words, Leslie seats herself outside the discussion circle and, with clipboard at the ready, gave the kids wait time to begin.

Alex breaks the silence by starting them off. "So, in 1768, Matt is left in the woods by his dad for the summer. He and his father built a log cabin and Matt needs to stay there to guard the place, plus the garden, while his dad goes back to get his mom and sister. Oh, I guess there's a new baby too."

"Yeah," Jessica responds, "and things fall apart when his dad leaves him. Like this guy steals the only gun Matt owns, and he is stung over and over by bees. That was really stupid to put his hand down a bee's nest."

"Well, he's only twelve years old, so give him a break. That's my brother's age and he couldn't do half the things that Matt does. He helped his dad cut the logs, caught and cooked his meals and then was scared by the Indians. I mean, I can't imagine *anyone* his age doing those things," added Allen.

Jeff continues, "The whole Indian thing was pretty freaky. That was something huge I wanted to bring up. What do you think about Matt having to teach that Indian kid how to read? I mean, how *would* you do that? Attean doesn't even really know English and he hates Matt. So now I'm wondering how he'll do that."

"Well, first, he started with the alphabet—you know *A* for *arm*, and so on—but he decided that would take too long, so he started reading him that book," said Allen.

Mary added, "Yeah, it was *Robinson Crusoe*. That part confused me. When the book was added to the story, it just didn't make sense. I had to reread it a couple of times and now I think Matt has a plan. He only read the exciting parts out loud. I think he's trying to trick Attean into liking reading."

Mary continued, "Something that really got my attention was on page 39." She waited as everyone turned to that page. "I tried to visualize how Attean caught the rabbit without a gun, but just couldn't see the thing he made."

"He made a snare out of a root and I think it looked like this," Mark said as he sketched the trap on the board.

Jeff posed the final question as the others shared a similar concern, "What do you think will happen if Matt's family never comes back? How will he survive?"

This group found the answers to their first three charted questions. They assigned themselves forty-five more pages to read by next week's meeting and collectively decided they really liked the book, but were very worried about Matt's fate.

I keep asking myself, who are these students? What are the demographics of this classroom and how much preparation for this kind of interaction did they bring with them from home? I absolutely believe that all kids, no matter what their background, can do this kind of thinking. I just wonder if the work needed to get them here would look different in different settings.

—Nancy

How Did These Kids Get So Far?

The teachers were quiet as we assembled in a small room next to the office to debrief the morning's instruction. To collect our thoughts, I encourage us to review our notes and do some writing. After some reflection time, the woman from Spokane spoke first: "I think we've found our missing assessment piece. The comprehension strategies came through loud and clear as those kids talked about their book club novel. They not only hashed out the plot, but added their opinions, questions, and predictions to the conversation. They had a real discussion about what the story meant and did it without Leslie dragging them through a list of comprehension questions. I scripted Jeff using phrases like, 'Something really huge I want to bring up . . . so now, I'm wondering how . . .'"

She continued, "Leslie, you didn't give your students specific questions to bring up in book club, did you? They brought their own authentic thinking. I also noticed kids spinning off one another's comments and questions. How did you get them to this point?"

This question comes up with every observation in Leslie's classroom. To understand how students have internalized so many of the thinking strategies by January, we must rewind the school calendar, to unearth the structures and practices she begins to build from day one.

Early in the year, as kids sit on the floor, couch, and pillows, Leslie models her thinking from a picture book. Her students have their Book Lover's Book (a reader response option outlined in Leslie's upcoming book, *The Inside Guide to the Reading-Writing Classroom: Strategies for Extraordinary Teaching. 3–6* [2011]) opened to the minilesson section. Not only does Leslie pause to share her thinking, she charts it for all to see: "Let me show you how to jump into the words and then I want you to try it on your own." She gradually invites kids to add their thinking to the story by writing down what it all means to them. Finally, with the support of modeling, listening, and writing, her students turn and explain their thoughts to a neighbor. What's different here is that Leslie physically moves throughout the group's "elbow shares." She crouches low to hear what's being said before bringing the thinking back to the whole group.

In this class, reading is a social act and the best part is sharing it with a friend. To facilitate this, Leslie's students move from elbow shares to partner shares, finding a person with whom they really want to discuss all they've discovered about their reading. A "Good Listening Chart" is generated and the kids practice these skills with this partner: "Today, I'm taking a step back

> *Reading is a social act and the best part is sharing it with a friend.*

because I supported you yesterday. I'm going to read a line out loud from this paragraph. What do you think that means? Because I can't read your mind, we use the white space to leave tracks of thinking in the snow. Was there anything you didn't understand? Yes? You could highlight that line and leave that very question in the snow. Good readers are aware when they don't understand a word or a phrase. They highlight it and get help later. Please leave me a key, so I can understand your coding. As a reader, you need to mark any confusions, then bring them back to your partner share. Don't take the easy way out and say you're done when you still have lingering questions. Marking those questions helps our understanding go deep."

Next, groups of two are merged into groups of four. When Leslie calls for a "compass share," kids quickly find their group along with a cleared space on the floor. Each member carries one of many response options, plus the text at hand. Collectively, they continue to bring meaning to a poem, paragraph, content material, or book.

I listened in as four boys assessed their individually coded paragraph. The word *pewter* glowed with highlighted colors. "Hey, look, we all marked the same word!" Jerry jumped up to find a dictionary and, without taking notice of me, looked up the word to unlock the sentence.

"Does 'gray' fit?"

"Yeah, that makes sense." And they were off, sharing questions they'd jotted in the margins, noting powerful language, puzzling through whole phrases, and pulling out new vocabulary. It was clear that these kids had internalized dozens of minilessons about unmasking meaning.

Meanwhile, with clipboard in hand, Leslie visits each four-way share, nudging, celebrating, assessing, and gleaning new discoveries to bring back to the whole group:

- "As an observer, let me name what you just did. Samantha piggy-backed off of what was just said and the conversation went deeper."

- "Sometimes authors make us think. I'm glad you marked that spot. Tell your group about that."

- "When you think it's kind of confusing as a reader, what do you do? Yes, your group needs to leave me some tracks in the snow, so I know you know that. That confusion is a good place to take your conversation."

- "I'm going to push you to an inference. What does that mean? You guys all marked that line. You, the reader, must work it out. What helped you? Do you see how the strategies are a way into discussion? Let's bring this back to the whole class."

During the next weeks the groups of four are mixed in many ways. Changing up the groups provides access to a variety of perspectives and encourages each member to solidify their own questions and conclusions. Leslie continues to deflect the responsibility of meaning making back to her students: "What will you bring with you to your meeting to show you understand this piece?" Or to debrief after discussion, "Does anyone have a new discovery from your compass share to bring back to the whole class?"

By the time book clubs meet, students have spent hours watching Leslie unzip her thinking. They've read, coded, and shared how a strategy applies to their own reading. Through the interplay of anchor charts, conferences, and written reflections, these kids are ready for the big time.

"How many of you have seen a book club? Your mom might be in one. What does it look like? I have lots of books and I need your help because I don't know what you like to read. You get to choose what you want to read after I do a book talk. And then talk about the book as we read, instead of waiting until we've finished."

Students write their top three book choices on cards, and Leslie forms the groups. Now the fun begins. *The Sign of the Beaver* book club assembles, seated before a blank piece of chart paper. Each member holds a copy of the book. They are encouraged to study the cover, read the back flap, skim several pages, and make discoveries about what they think the book might be about. Drawing a large *T* on the chart paper, Leslie labels one side *What We Know* and the other heading *Questions*. She begins, "Research tells us that if we think about all we know before we start reading, we do a better job of understanding. Let's turn your background knowledge about the blurb on the back into questions you want answered as you read. When you chose this book, what did you want to find out?" Secretary Leslie madly scripts the connections and questions arising from what they have uncovered in the ten-minute preview.

"When you meet for the first time on Monday, how are you going to discuss? Will you go around in a circle? Throw out ideas? Reflect on your questions? Sometimes book clubs get messy. Knowing about the quiet talkers, what should we do to include them? You also must decide a good stopping point. How many pages do you want to read for your first book club meeting? While I meet with the next group, please take ten minutes to do some written reflection about these questions. I'll give you time to share with your group at the end of the day."

The Sign of the Beaver by Elizabeth George Speare	
What We Know	**Questions**
Twelve-year-old boy—Matt	Any siblings?
Setting—Maine—wilderness	When? (Past)
Matt's dad has to bring back rest of family.	How did family get separated? Why?
Indians—Attean—grandfather (Father?) Is chief?	
Matt not prepared for attack of swarming bees	Why would bees attack him? And what happens?
Many months pass with no sign of Dad	Where is he? Is he dead? Why so long?
Attean speaks English	How is Matt surviving?
Attean wants Matt to go with Beaver tribe	Will Matt go? Does Matt learn Indian language?

Successful book clubs depend on time to reflect. After the first round of book club meetings, Leslie asks her students, "What do you like about book club? What didn't work? I did see some frustration while you were meeting today. How can we work that out? How many of you came prepared in your head for book club? How are you holding your thinking? How many wrote ahead? How do you know what to talk about when you meet with your group?"

Readers want to share questions, images, laughs, and tears over words that transform their lives. Sharing sessions play a vital role in Leslie's daily schedule. Students in this classroom and in countless others like it express their thinking and love of reading through discussion. Scripting their book club conversations and taking notes during their small-group discussions or one-on-one conferences provides compelling evidence of students' understanding. Strategic thinking comes through loud and clear as they think out loud about all that reading holds. These students know how to independently think and talk their way through the words.

Chryse, thanks for capturing this. Reflection. Not only for the kids, but for me. I need to hear what the kids say—their thinking informs my instruction and truly helps me to become a more effective teacher.

—Leslie

Reference

Blaumann, Leslie. 2011. *The Inside Guide to the Reading-Writing Classroom: Strategies for Extraordinary Teaching, 3-6.* Portsmouth, NH: Heinemann.

Readings for Students

Little, Jean.1986. *Hey World, Here I Am!* Toronto: Harper and Row.

Speare, Elizabeth George.1983. *The Sign of the Beaver.* New York: Bantam Doubleday Dell.

Comprehension to What End?

Stephanie Harvey

When the quantum physicist and Nobel Laureate Richard Feynman was ten years old, he developed a reputation around the neighborhood as the kid who could fix anything. From as early as he could remember, Feynman loved to take things apart and put them together—toasters, lamps, you name it. Rumors spread that this boy was some sort of genius who seemed to be able to make anything work. A skeptical neighborhood businessman got wind of him, knowing that if there was even a smidgen of truth to these rumors, a kid who could fix anything would be pretty useful around the office. So one morning he asked young Richard to come by and take a look at a broken radio.

Feynman rotated the radio in his hands repeatedly and stared at it for what seemed like an eternity. Exasperated, the businessman finally asked "What are you doing? What is taking you so long? Can you fix it or not?" Feynman paused, looked up at him, and said simply "I'm thinking." After several more moments engrossed in thought, Feynman attached a few wires and repaired it expeditiously. He soon became known not only as the kid who fixed things, but *the kid who fixed things by thinking* (Feynman 1997).

Thinking! What a concept.

A similar story recounts how Albert Einstein's mother would put her five-year-old to bed each night by kissing his forehead, saying good night, and turning out the light. Young Albert, however, did not doze off. An hour or so later when his mother checked on him before turning in herself, she generally found him with his eyes wide, staring at the ceiling. One night she asked him, "Albert what's the matter? Why are you still awake?"

"I am wondering something," he answered.

"What could you possibly be wondering at this hour?" she implored.

"I'm wondering where the light goes."

"What do you mean where the light goes?"

"I am wondering what happens to the light when you flip the switch each night. Where does the light go?" (Harvey 1998).

Thinking and curiosity shine through in these stories and the innovations of these two physicists are a testimony to how inquisitiveness and thoughtfulness can lead to major contributions and big things in life. Unfortunately, when it comes to education, thinking and wonder have been in short supply of late. Real questions and deep thought have evaporated in many schools and been replaced by mind-numbing daily routines—filling in bubbles and blanks, finding the main idea in a paragraph, and listening endlessly to a teacher talk (Pianta et al. 2007) What a shame! Of all places that should be havens for thinking and incubators for wonder, schools ought to top the list.

But too often, it is the schools themselves that drum the thoughtfulness and curiosity right out of kids. Who can't picture a class full of charged-up kindergarteners bursting into school in September brimming with questions: Why is the ocean blue? Why do only tigers and zebras have stripes? Where did the cowboys go? Endless questions that might even drive us nuts, if they were not so enduringly charming. By fifth grade, however, the questions have all but disappeared. Kids get the idea that it is the teacher's job to ask the questions and their job to answer them.

So do schools actually kill off curiosity? Perhaps, but maybe they just wound it, since curiosity and the need to know, though gasping for air, are resilient dispositions. In her essay "The Curiosity Coma," Barbara Logan notes "How do children go from wanting to know everything under the sun to having so few questions? It is very simple. They learn it" (2010,1). Sadly, conventional schooling can suck the life out of wonder and amazement. But

Logan also reminds us that "most kids' curiosity has not been killed: It has simply diverted into a coma. Their questions are trapped inside, awaiting a focused adult to release them" (1). Good news! Unlike death, we can emerge from comas.

And it's time for us to wake up!

— *Leslie*

In late 2009, on his CNN Sunday morning news show *GPS*, Fareed Zakaria asked Google CEO Eric Schmidt what he thought education should look like going forward. Schmidt answered succinctly: "Teaching will be learning how to ask the right questions. I was taught to memorize. Why remember it? Now you just need to learn how to search for it. Instantaneous access really changes your life. What never changes is the need for curiosity. What you really need to do is teach people to be curious."

Curiosity and thoughtfulness are at the center of engaged teaching and learning. No two dispositions will better prepare our kids for what lies ahead. Education is always rife with buzzwords: outcome-based education in the 1980s, scientifically based research in the 2000s, and twenty-first-century skills and career and college readiness in 2010. Regarding the current college and career readiness message, who would argue with creating a curriculum that supports kids to be both career and college ready in the twenty-first century? But what does that look like, exactly? April 2010 marked the twenty-fifth anniversary of the Internet. Hard to believe that during my first twelve years of teaching, online research was not even a concept—let alone an option. Facebook only erupted onto the scene in 2004. Google didn't exist in the early 1990s and now it's a verb. Phones were stationary, for goodness sake. The careers of the future are as much a mystery to us now as Google, Facebook, and iPhones were ten years ago.

In November of 2009, Kylene Beers—the well-known educator, author, and outgoing president of the National Council of Teachers of English (NCTE)—gave her final presidential address. Standing in front of two giant screens, she spoke eloquently as slides of images rolled by, searing the speech in our minds. One of the first images to appear was a medieval map with primitively etched nation states and roiling blue waters rife with dragons and sea monsters. As a portrait of Christopher Columbus followed next, Beers asked us to consider Columbus's plight. He may not have known what lay out there beyond the horizon—*here there be dragons*—but he knew how to read the night sky, how to use a sextant, how to watch the clouds. He knew sailing (Beers 2009).

And although we may not know what our kids will be doing when they leave school in 2012 and beyond, we know kids and we know teaching and learning. So as the high-speed train of time and technology blur, we may not know what careers lay out there undiscovered beyond the horizon, but there is no doubt that our kids will always need to think and to wonder. Yong Zhou, the author of *Catching Up or Leading the Way: Education in the Age of Globalization*, shares that for the United States to remain the world leader in innovation and creativity, it must "cherish individual talents, cultivate creativity, celebrate diversity and inspire curiosity" (Richardson 2009/2010). Passion and wonder are contagious. It is our job as teachers to unleash every ounce of passion and wonder we can muster so our kids catch the curiosity bug rather than lapse into the curiosity coma—or worse, languish as curiosity dies on the vine. Teaching kids to think strategically and ask questions ranks at the top of our list of responsibilities in the twenty-first century.

Teachers get this. In the past twenty years, we have witnessed a "comprehension revolution" (Pearson 2008) in this country. Empowered by the research of P. David Pearson and his many colleagues (Pearson and Gallagher 1983; Pearson et al. 1992; Pearson and Duke 2001) and the work of literacy specialists and classroom practitioners across the country, as well as the authors of this book, great numbers of teachers have implemented explicit comprehension instruction in their literacy practice as well as in their content-area teaching. In the belief that thinking matters, and with a commitment to employing teaching practices based on sound research, they have built in time to teach kids comprehension strategies—to ask questions, make connections, draw inferences, evaluate and synthesize information, and (above all) to monitor their own thinking.

Even in this test-frenzied culture, where too many kids have been driven back to their seats for endless test prep and fill-in-the-blank drill sheets, many teachers have continued to push the comprehension movement forward by teaching their kids to think strategically and wonder expansively across the curriculum. And many report that reading has fundamentally changed in their classrooms as kids learn to think about text—about how it connects to their world, how it spurs questions and wonder, and how it nudges them to infer underlying themes and big ideas. But many also ask, "So what's next? I've taught the comprehension strategies. Now what?"

So thirty years into this comprehension movement and counting is probably as good a time as any to stop and reflect on comprehension instruction. We can begin by asking ourselves, "Comprehension, to what end?"

Comprehension: To What End?

As in previous years, the content/process battle rages in education circles. The content folks stress that *what* we learn matters most, the content of learning. The process group emphasizes that *how* we learn is most critical. But frankly, this is a sham. Neither is useful without the other. Content and process both matter. Arthur Costa says "Cognition and content are inseparable" (2008, 22). We don't teach kids to think so they can ponder their belly button. And there's no good reason to memorize a bunch of disconnected facts without thinking about the information and putting it to work in some way.

Today, even in classrooms where teachers implement explicit comprehension instruction, strategies are too often viewed as an endpoint rather than a starting point. Strategy instruction even becomes perfunctory—kids making connections for the sake of it, teachers designing strategy units replete with fill-in-the-blank inferring packets, districts creating a comprehension scope and sequence that assigns strategies to grade levels (connecting in kindergarten, visualizing in first grade, questioning in second grade), and so on. We don't teach a strategy and then clap our hands together with a "been there, done that" exclamation point. If teaching comprehension means getting out the lesson plans for the synthesizing unit and moving lockstep through it, the "comprehension revolution" has sputtered.

A number of years ago, a middle school teacher raised her hand in a workshop I was leading and explained that she had been teaching synthesizing for about eight weeks. She was wondering when she could quit the synthesizing strategy and move on to something else. This rattled me and I can't actually recall my response. But her sincerity struck me. As an educator, teachers' questions and my attempts to address them drive my thinking and writing. This very question has haunted me for years and has, in many ways, informed much of my recent work. Apparently, I had not been explicit enough about the recursive and dynamic nature of comprehension strategy instruction, about the purpose of teaching kids to be aware of their thinking, about the need to watch kids and listen to them carefully to ascertain whether they are using strategies to gain understanding or just "talking the talk," and about strategies as a means to an end rather than an end in themselves.

We don't teach strategies for strategies' sake. We don't teach kids to make connections so they can be the best connectors in the room. Although we may launch a single strategy to give kids a chance to familiarize

> I have noticed this same debate raging in the English language acquisition communities as if the learning of a second language can be accomplished without finding meaning in the words and syntax.
>
> —*Mayou*

themselves with it and practice, we don't teach strategies in isolation. We work to give kids a repertoire of strategies that they can use flexibly and thoughtfully across various texts, disciplines, and contexts over time. Truly proficient readers use multiple strategies at once, orchestrating their use to construct meaning and expand thinking (Pressley 2002; Guthrie 2003). We teach kids to connect, question, and synthesize—so they can integrate that thinking, acquire knowledge, and act.

A classic story of how strategic thinking leads to understanding and action involves Richard Feynman and retired Air Force General Donald Kutyna, both members of the Space Shuttle Challenger commission. General Kutyna collected and worked on junk cars as a hobby. One day when Feynman was visiting, Kutyna showed him a carburetor and mentioned that some of the seals had disintegrated due to the low temperatures the previous night. These broken seals led the general to make a connection to the shuttle seals; he wondered if perhaps the low temperatures had something to do with the shuttle disaster. The Challenger launch temperature was a mere thirty-six degrees, fifteen degrees cooler than any previous launch. Feynman followed this lead and discovered a weakness in the O-rings—they lacked elasticity in low temperatures and did not seal properly, thus resulting in the catastrophic shuttle explosion. Feynman later shared this at a televised congressional hearing when he simply dropped the O-ring into a glass of ice water and showed how it cracked apart. The shuttle investigation had begun with the question "Why did Challenger explode?" Through their collaboration, Feynman and the general laser-focused on the question, investigated multiple possibilities, connected the carburetor seals and the shuttle O-rings, and ultimately synthesized the information to solve the problem (Feynman 2001).

The threads of strategic thinking weave together in an intricate mental tapestry to address and solve problems. The goal is not completing and getting an A on the inferring packet. Strategy instruction is useful only insofar as it leads our kids to better understand the text, the world, and themselves so they can gain insight and even anticipate hurdles and solve pressing problems.

Harvard professor David Perkins says "Learning is a consequence of thinking . . . Far from thinking coming after knowledge, knowledge comes on the coattails of thinking . . . Knowledge does not just sit there. It functions richly in people's lives so they can learn about and deal with the world" (1992, 8). If General Kutyna had not made the connection between his carburetor and the shuttle and Feynman had not synthesized the information, who knows how long it might have taken to solve the shuttle tragedy? Going way beyond the idea of strategies for the sake of it, we teach kids to make connections and employ thinking strategies so "knowledge does not just sit there"—so they can think about information, learn content, and apply what they know by putting that knowledge to work in the real world every day.

A Comprehension Continuum

Comprehension is not about spitting out facts and filling in blanks. Comprehension is about understanding. When our kids think deeply and expansively about issues, ideas, and concepts, they come to care about them and apply that care and learning to the circumstances in their own situations and experiences (Harvey and Goudvis 2007). We teach comprehension strategies to our students so that they turn information into knowledge and actively use it. Ultimately the goal of comprehension instruction is to foster the active use of knowledge.

To further explore this, let's take a look at a continuum of comprehension (p. 118). This comprehension continuum is comprised of five processes—answering literal questions, retelling, merging thinking with content, acquiring knowledge, and actively using knowledge. The processes along this continuum move from the most elementary to the most sophisticated. But they are not necessarily sequential. Kids do not need to be able to answer literal questions before they can retell, for instance. And we know that children can merge their thinking with information at a very young age, long before being exposed to literal, end-of-text comprehension questions. But they do need to think about information before they can acquire and use knowledge. This continuum represents an array of comprehension processes, a spectrum of understanding. It also includes the teacher language that is associated with each one of these five processes. The more sophisticated the process, the more sophisticated the teacher's questions. Harvey Daniels and I first published this comprehension continuum in our book *Comprehension and Collaboration: Inquiry Circles in Action* (2009). I take this opportunity to expand on the idea here.

Answering Literal Questions

Answering literal questions is the least sophisticated level of comprehension because it does not guarantee understanding or expanded thinking. If a reader can answer a list of literal questions after reading, they might have

We already have enough "selfish" readers that take information in, but do nothing with it. We have to raise readers to take action with the knowledge they gain from text—putting it to work in the world by treating others with more empathy, engaging in powerful discourse, and taking action to improve everything they touch.

—Sam

The continuum on p. 118 really helps classroom teachers like me ask myself: "How many times have I asked students to merely retell or summarize?" and "What can I do to move kids to a deeper understanding of text?"

—Brad

Comprehension Continuum

Answering Literal Questions	Retelling	Merging Thinking with Content	Acquiring Knowledge	Actively Using Knowledge
Answering literal questions shows that learners can skim and scan for answers, pick one out that matches the question, and have short-term recall. Does not demonstrate understanding.	Retelling shows that learners can organize thoughts sequentially and put them into their own words. Shows short-term recall of events in a narrative and bits of information in nonfiction. Does not, in and of itself, demonstrate understanding.	Real understanding takes root when learners merge their thinking with the content by connecting, inferring, questioning, determining importance, synthesizing, and reacting to information. Understanding begins here.	Once learners have merged their thinking with the content, they can begin to acquire knowledge and insight. They can learn, understand, and remember. Shows deeper understanding.	With new insights and understandings, learners can actively use knowledge and apply what they have learned to the experiences, situations, and circumstances in their daily lives to expand understanding and even take action.

Teacher Language	Teacher Language	Teacher Language	Teacher Language	Teacher Language
How many...? What is...? Where did...? Who was...? When did ...?	What happened in the story? What was it about? What happened first? Next? Last? What did the character do after that? Retell what you read or heard. Try using your own words to explain what happened.	What do you think? What did the text make you think about? What does this remind you of? Has anything like this ever happened to you? What do you wonder? What do you visualize? What can you infer from this? How does it make you feel? Do you have any reactions? Say more about that....	What did you learn that you think is important to remember? What if anything new did you learn? Why does it matter? What do you think the author most wants you to get out of this? What do you think are some of the big ideas here? What do you think is the main issue here? Why? What makes you think that? How did you come up with that?	Why do you want to remember this? What do you want to do about this? Why do you care? How do you think you can help? Is there a way you can get involved? Do you think you can make a difference? What is your plan?

From *Comprehension Going Forward*. Portsmouth, NH: Heinemann. © 2009 by Stephanie Harvey and Harvey Daniels from *Comprehension and Collaboration*. Heinemann, Portsmouth, NH.

understood the material *or not*. If they can't answer those questions, they still might have understood it *or not*. But most frequently, a student can easily answer literal questions but doesn't understand the information. If we ask the question "What is symbiosis?" after repeating the definition on numerous occasions during a two-week unit on marine biology, most kids can quite readily pick out the correct multiple choice answer: "(C) A long-term interaction between species that results in a persistent relationship from which both organisms benefit." But if we ask them to write a paragraph explaining how symbiosis impacts ocean ecology, blank stares often greet us. A question of that sort requires thinking and understanding.

So what *does* answering literal questions reveal? It might show that the learner has some short-term recall. Or recently, particularly in the test reading department, it shows that the reader can skim and scan the answers and pick out the one that best matches the test question. Ultimately, the most useful reason to ask a literal question may be to find out if the student even read it: "Hey Jake, where did that story take place?" "Uhhh, Alaska?"—and it was set in Hawaii; now that's diagnostic information. Simply put, recall does not equal understanding.

The questions that teachers ask to get at literal comprehension are as low level as the process itself—the What? Where? Who? When? questions that permeate conventional comprehension tasks and reduce the text to its lowest common denominator: Where did Atticus go to law school? What color was Scout's bedroom? Who washed Dill's shirts? (Lee 1960). Every time we give kids a list of those literal end-of-text comprehension questions, we are implicitly telling them that their thinking doesn't matter. Kids learn that their questions must not be that important and that the questions that matter come from the teacher, the publisher, or the test. These literal questions narrow kids' thinking channels rather than expand them. They limit imagination and curiosity rather than driving it. So sadly, many kids quit asking their own.

Retelling

Retelling is a more sophisticated process than merely answering literal questions. Retelling calls for the reader to put the ideas into their own words and shape them into their own thoughts: "Retellings require children to think more conceptually, to look at the bigger picture rather than answering specific questions about the text" (Gibson, Gold, and Sgouros 2003). And there is abundant evidence to suggest that retelling can improve comprehension.

But in primary grades, we have elevated retelling to the crowning achievement in reading comprehension! Just because students can retell a story doesn't mean they understand it. Let me illustrate with a retelling of *Goldilocks and the Three Bears.* A basic retelling might go like this: "A girl wanders into a cabin in the woods and discovers that no one is home. She eats the soup, sits in a chair, breaks it, and goes to sleep in a bed upstairs. Soon three bears come home and chase her off." A more elaborate retelling follows here: "A spirited child in a pink-checked pinafore skips merrily through the woods, her long golden locks bouncing on her shoulders. She catches a glimpse of an inviting log cabin in the distance. As she approaches, she notices a crack in the front door and peers in. Her nostrils meet the curling steam of porridge simmering on the stove. She tiptoes in and dips the ladle into the porridge, taking a sip that warms her through and though as she sits down on a small wooden chair . . . " You get the drift of this more elaborate retelling and it is likely that a child who creates this second retell may grasp the story more completely than the child who provided the more basic retell. However, neither of these retellings definitively demonstrates understanding. A more complete understanding of the story might be revealed through an inference or a synthesis such as "It is not a very good idea to go sneaking into people's houses when they are not at home." A quick gist that illuminates the lesson or underlying theme might provide better evidence of pure understanding than either of these Goldilocks retellings.

We can get some good information from retelling, however. According to Owocki, retelling helps children think their way through a text, thereby enhancing their understanding (1999). Retelling the events of a story or the sections of a chapter shows that the learner can organize thoughts sequentially. And recalling some facts in a nonfiction piece shows that the reader has some short-term memory of fragments of information. Additionally, a great way to find out if a child has read or heard a story is to ask them to retell what they remember. But probably the best information we can get from retelling is identifying kids who can't do it. Most kids should be able to retell pieces of a story they have heard or provide some basic information from a reading. Kids who *repeatedly* have difficulty retelling a story or picking out some information to share either orally, in writing, or through drawing may need a closer look.

Teacher's questions such as "What happened in the story?" "What was it mostly about?" and "What happened first, next, and last?" are the kinds of questions we associate with retelling. Although more sophisticated than literal comprehension questions, since they require the learner to shape the answer into their own thought, these retelling prompts do not necessarily get at the deeper, more expansive meaning we hope our kids glean as they read, listen and view. But these retelling questions can alert us to whether the student has a general idea of the content of the piece. In the end, retelling is a foundational skill that is undoubtedly higher-level than answering literal questions. But retelling in and of itself does not demonstrate understanding.

Merging Thinking with Content

True comprehension *begins* here. Real understanding takes root when learners merge their thinking with the content and react to the information. According to Costa, "Learning to think begins with recognizing how we are thinking, by listening to ourselves and our own reactions and realizing how our thoughts encapsulate us" (2008, 23). "Comprehension is the inner conversation we have with text, the voice in our head that speaks to us as we read, listen, and view. It is the voice that says *Huh, I don't get this part* when we are confused, the voice that says *Wow, I never knew that before* when we meet new information, the voice that says *If anything ever happens to this character, I will never get up in the morning.* That's comprehension—how our thinking evolves, expands, and changes" (Harvey and Daniels 2009, 29).

We explicitly teach kids to stop, think, and react (STR) to information encouraging them to merge their thinking with text, images, videos, artifacts, and any other resources. We teach the terminology associated with thinking. We might ask, "Did you remember to merge your thinking with the information? Do you have any reactions? What are you wondering?" Jotting or drawing reactions, thoughts, ideas, and questions leads to engaged thinking and active reading. When kids add their own thinking to the text, images, and features, they construct meaning by paying attention to their inner conversation rather than merely running their eyes across the page, passively reading words but not thinking about the ideas behind them.

When beginning a content unit, we often have kids jot their reactions to images. When launching a World War II social studies unit, for example, we might distribute different images related to the time period—D-Day, Japanese internment, Navajo code talkers, Tuskegee airman, Nazi SS troops. We encourage kids to jot down anything they wonder, connect to, or infer from the images. When showing videos, we encourage kids to stop, jot their

> Steph, this is a core truth. We proficient readers really do have a voice in our heads (the comprehension one, not the crazy one) that's in dialogue with any text we read. But because veteran readers do this cognitive work mostly unconsciously, we may even deny it is happening. That's why it is so important, as Cris and Ellin discuss on page 181, that teachers occasionally read some really hard text, to remind ourselves of the strategies being deployed in our own heads.
> —Smokey

thinking, and turn and talk to a partner so they can process the information. They can use the same annotation technique with text—jotting thoughts and questions in the margins as well as on sticky notes. Active learners interact with text and resources. The comprehension strategies we have written about reflect the most common ways that learners interact and merge their thinking—connecting, questioning, visualizing, determining importance, inferring, and synthesizing.

When nudging learners to merge their thinking with the content, we concentrate on asking questions that prompt thinking and draw kids out. Questions such as "What does this remind you of?" "What are you wondering?" and "What can you infer from this?" nudge learners to consider their own thoughts and questions as they respond. These questions are derived mostly from the language and underlying concepts that kids have experienced through their comprehension strategy learning. Questions such as these expand thinking rather than limit it.

Acquiring Knowledge

Once readers begin to consciously merge their thinking with the content, they are able to acquire knowledge and gain insight. Active learners turn information into knowledge by merging their thinking with the content. Indeed, a primary reason to read, listen, view, and think is to gain knowledge. Not so in my youth, however. A decent school player, I merely wrote down what the teacher said and crammed on Thursday night to get ready for the test. In fact, in my case, knowledge did sit there *just* long enough for Friday's quiz, but then promptly vanished just in time for Friday night lights! My grades were fine; I learned little. Memorizing discrete isolated facts does not help us acquire lasting knowledge; that requires thinking about the information and working with it. As we acquire knowledge and think about what we are learning, new insights and understandings emerge and we can generate new knowledge.

Content matters. As a matter of fact, it is the content that is seductive. I have never met a child that I cannot interest in something in this wild, wonderful world. Kids show up every day eager to learn and ready to explore—black holes, the Civil War, African animals, ancient Greece. Kids have a deep need to know. We must be those "focused adults" to whom Barbara Logan refers in "The Curiosity Coma," teachers who set up an environment that nurtures their natural curiosity. You can't think about

> Steph hits the nail on the head! We don't read in the abstract. We read to deepen and broaden our understanding of this complex, marvelous world we live in. Great material, fiction and nonfiction, is what will grab kids' imaginations and pique their passions.
>
> —*Anne*

nothing. Classrooms that stimulate wonder are filled to bursting with texts, images, and artifacts on every imaginable topic so kids always have much to ponder.

When we walk into a classroom that promotes active learning and knowledge acquisition, we know it. No kids sitting quietly in rows, raising their hands while waiting for the teacher to call on them, or laying splayed across the desk twirling their hair and staring out a window. Instead they are spread throughout the room—one small group hovers over an aquarium, taking notes on the tadpoles in a spirited exchange about what they notice; a pair of kids at the computer discover why malaria wrecks such devastation in third-world countries and consider what can be done; several students on the floor, paintbrushes in hand, add the final touches to a map of ancient Egypt as sticky notes with question marks spill out of their mummy books; three kids at the smart board devise multiple ways to solve an equation rather than merely one way; a lone student curled up in the reading corner devours *The Secret Garden*.

The teacher is not up front with a whip and chair all day. She gathers the kids to model her thinking, share her own curiosity, and teach. But she doesn't hold them too long. As if fishing for trout, it is "catch and release" as I have heard Cris Tovani say. She catches them briefly to model a strategy or share some information, and then releases them to do the work as she moves about the room—checking in with small groups and touching base with individuals and pairs as they read, write, draw, view, talk, listen, investigate, think, and work their way through the day. Classrooms that promote active learning fairly burst with enthusiastic, curious kids who simply can't resist investigating the questions, issues, ideas, and topics at hand. In classrooms like this, kids work hard and never lack for thinking because there is so much to think about.

So what does the teacher's language sound like in an active learning room like this? The questions ratchet up, incorporating both content and process and prompting both thinking and learning: What did you learn that you think is important to remember? What do you think the writer most wants you to get out of this? What do you think are some of the big ideas here? Why does this matter? These questions require a consideration of both content and process. To answer, kids have to deal with the content they have learned as well as their thinking about the content—deciding what is important to remember, considering the writer's ideas, and merging their thinking with the information to infer the big ideas. All of these actions combine their strategy knowledge with their content knowledge to address questions and ideas. Rather than content and process as polar opposites, they are interdependent and inextricably linked.

Actively Using Knowledge

With new knowledge comes insights that can potentially change the way humans function in the world. As David Perkins puts it, "There is little gain in simply having knowledge and even understanding it for a quiz if that same knowledge does not get put to work on a more worldly occasion: puzzling over a public issue, shopping in a supermarket, deciding for whom to vote . . . and so on" (1992, 6) . When we think about information and acquire knowledge, we can integrate it and actively apply it to experiences, situations, and circumstances in our daily lives. We can make informed choices about how to act, behave, persuade, and take action.

The active use of knowledge means that kids are inspired to make a difference in the world.

P. David Pearson reminds us that "rich talk about text" is central to learning and understanding. When kids interact with each other—discussing ideas, issues, and topics of significance—learning and understanding soar. "Discussion with peers serves as both a forum through which students can sharpen their cognitive skills and deepen their involvement and a motivation for engagement in reading" (Pearson, Cervetti, and Tilson 2008, 76). When learners merge their thinking with the themes in literature, the big ideas in history, or the concepts in science and engage in spirited discussions with each other, they are more likely to acquire knowledge and act.

Sometimes the active use of knowledge means kids learn something new, incorporate that information, and apply it in their daily lives. Listening to and having a lively discussion about Tomie DePaola's *The Art Lesson* (1997) is a wonderful way for first graders to learn about how passion and practice can lead to excelling at something, possibly applying this new insight in their own lives when the time arises. Reflecting on Jacqueline Woodson's *The Other Side* (2001)—a story of how two girls in the deep South, one white and one black, forge a friendship in spite of segregation laws—can lead sixth graders to a deeper understanding of that time period as well as a heightened sensitivity about how to treat one another now. Reading and discussing Michael Pollan's *Food Rules* (2009) might spearhead high school kids to make better, more informed choices about the food they eat every day.

Other times, the active use of knowledge means that kids are inspired to make a difference in the world, form a plan, and take action. A group of middle-class eighth graders in south Florida read an article and discovered that kids in poor communities have less access to books than kids in middle-class neighborhoods. The article suggested that the achievement gap between middle-class kids and kids in poverty was in large part due to this very fact. It had never occurred to these eighth graders that any kids in America lacked books. They pretty much took for granted their own extensive school libraries, as well as their personal collections. This new information hit them like a ton of bricks. They immersed themselves in the topic, reading, viewing, talking, and listening to everything they could get their hands on. Some were saddened, some were outraged; all were disillusioned by the inequities. They took several tacks in response, including raising money to buy books for a nearby Title 1 school, selecting many of the books personally after reading and reviewing them, and writing letters to the state school board demanding an explanation of why their school library collection was far superior to that of the less affluent school. Acquiring new knowledge led them to care, which spurred them to take action.

When teachers foster an environment that encourages kids to take action, the questions evolve as well. Questions such as "Why do you care?" "What do you want to do about this?" and "What is your plan?" echo throughout the room. These questions are the avenues that navigate a way into action.

Concluding Thoughts

As we consider these five processes on the comprehension continuum, one can't help but notice that even today there are schools and districts whose entire comprehension curriculum consists of merely answering literal questions and retelling. Worse, when I started teaching in 1972, answering literal questions was it; retelling was nary a blip on the radar screen. Understanding will suffocate in rooms like these and curiosity will lapse into coma. Comprehension gets a foothold when learners merge their thinking with the information, *but that is not the end of comprehension. That is just the beginning.*

Strategies alone do not improve learning. Understanding is a recursive and dynamic process, not a linear one. For learning to flourish, we must foster a culture of thinking where our kids are continually interacting with the text, the teacher, and each other. We model our thinking, share our own curiosity, and flood the room with compelling text, media, and resources so that our kids can immerse themselves in rich content, read about it, connect to it, wonder about it, talk about it, infer from it, investigate it, and build a knowledge base that may spur them to act on it. When we model and practice thinking as a means to actively using knowledge, kids who have read and discussed *The Other Side* might think more carefully about racism today, high schoolers who have read Michael Pollan just might eat healthier, and eighth graders who have looked poverty in the eye may stand up against issues of inequity that they were blind to before their newfound knowledge.

In the early summer of 2010, Larry King interviewed Microsoft founder Bill Gates and his father on his show one night. He asked the senior Mr. Gates if there was anything that still surprised him about his son. Bill Gates' father answered that he was still astonished by his son's curiosity—"My son is the most curious person I have ever met," he said proudly. For the "comprehension revolution" to continue its forward march, we need to be astonished by our kids' curiosity and amazed by the superb quality of their thinking. We need to focus on their thinking, revel in their wonder, teach strategies for understanding, foster deep conversation, and support them to turn information into knowledge. If we do this, they will undoubtedly be ready for whatever comes their way in the twenty-first century.

References

Beers, Kylene. 2009. "Sailing Over the Edge: Navigating the Uncharted Waters of a World Gone Flat." Presidential address at National Council of Teachers of English Annual Convention Philadelphia, November 22.

Costa, Arthur. 2008. "The Thoughtfilled Curriculum." *Ed Leadership* February: 20–24.

DePaola, Tomie. 1997. *The Art Lesson.* New York: Putnam.

Feynman, Richard. 1997. *Surely You're Joking, Mr. Feynman.* New York: W. W. Norton.

Feynman, Richard. 2001. *What Do You Care What Other People Think? Further Adventures of a Curious Character.* New York: W. W. Norton.

Gibson, Akimi, Judith Gold, and Charissa Sgouros. 2003. "The Power of Story Retelling." *The Tutor* Spring.

Guthrie, John. 2003. "Concept Oriented Reading Instruction." In *Rethinking Reading Comprehension*, edited by Anne P. Sweet and Catherine E. Snow, 115–127. New York: Guilford.

Harvey, Stephanie. 1998. *Nonfiction Matters.* York, ME: Stenhouse.

Harvey, Stephanie, and Anne Goudvis. 2007. *Strategies That Work.* Portland, ME: Stenhouse.

Harvey, Stephanie, and Harvey Daniels. 2009. *Comprehension and Collaboration: Inquiry Circles in Action.* Portsmouth, NH: Heinemann.

Lee, Harper. 1960. *To Kill a Mockingbird.* Philadelphia, PA: J. B. Lippincott.

Logan, Barbara. 2010. "The Curiosity Coma: Online in The EI Point of View The Efficacy Institute Inc. Available at: http://efficacy.org/Resources/The EIPointofview

Owocki, Gretchen. 1999. *Literacy Through Play.* Portsmouth, NH: Heinemann.

Pearson, P. David. 2008. "Teaching Comprehension 24/7." Keynote speech at the Colorado Council of the International Reading Association Conference. Denver, CO, February 7.

Pearson, P. David, Gina N. Cervetti, and Jennifer L. Tilson. 2008. "Reading for Understanding." In *Powerful Learning*, edited by Darling Hammond. San Francisco: Josey Bass.

Pearson, P. David, and Margaret C. Gallagher. 1983. "The Instruction of Reading Comprehension." *Contemporary Educational Psychology* 8: 317–44.

Pearson, P. David, Laura R. Roehler, Janice A. Dole, and Gerald G. Duffy. 1992. "Developing Expertise in Reading Comprehension: What Should Be Taught and Who Should Teach It." In *What Research Has to Say About Reading Instruction*, 2d ed., edited by Jay Samuels and Alan Farstrup. Newark, DE: International Reading Association.

Pearson, P. David, and Nell Duke. 2001. "Comprehension Instruction in Primary Grades." In *Comprehension Instruction Research Based Practices*, edited by Cathy Collins Blaock and Michael Pressley. New York: Guilford.

Perkins, David. 1992. *Smart Schools: Better Thinking and Learning for Every Child.* New York: Free Press.

Pianta, Robert, Jay Belsky, Renate Houts, and Fred Morrison. 2007. "Opportunities to Learn in America's Classrooms." *Science* 315 (March 30): 1795–96.

Pollan, Michael. 2009. *Food Rules.* New York: Penguin.

Pressley, Michael. 2002. *Reading Instruction That Works*, 2d ed. New York: Guilford.

Richardson, Joan. 2009/2010. "Playing Catch Up with Developing Nations Makes No Sense for US: An Interview with Yong Zhou." *Kappan* 91 (4): 15–20.

Woodson, Jacqueline. 2001. *The Other Side.* New York: Putnam.

CHAPTER EIGHT

History Lessons

Anne Goudvis and Brad Buhrow

> Every effort must be made in childhood to teach the young to use
> their own minds. For one thing is sure, if they don't make up their
> own minds, someone will do it for them.
>
> —ELEANOR ROOSEVELT

It's time for the fifth grade study of "westward expansion" and kids know
the drill. After the students read and the teacher briefly reviews the "Going
West" section of the textbook, they turn to the end of the chapter and
begin writing answers to questions like these:

- Why was it so important to build a transcontinental railroad?

- Name two landforms that the Oregon Trail crossed.

When finished, kids answer a "higher-level thinking" question, such as:

- Would you rather be a miner in the West in the 1870s or a home-
  steader in the Great Plains? Explain.

On Friday there's a test covering the chapter vocabulary and some of the
same questions.

Sound familiar? Most of us remember this ritual from our elementary days—but in some cases, little has changed. According to one survey: "Students in the United States, at all grade levels, found social studies to be one of the least interesting, most irrelevant subjects in the school curriculum" (Loewen 2007, 330).

Why do kids feel this way? Perhaps it's because students experience history and social studies as a passive slog through the textbook—with its authoritative voice, generalizations, and endless stream of facts. When the textbook becomes the default social studies curriculum, a litany of facts serves as the main source and sole measure of kids' learning. It's tempting to simply "tell" kids what's in the textbook because the information is so dense and there is so much of it to cover. The result is passive learning—recalling the information for Friday's test and then promptly forgetting it. Instead, students should be reading to learn history, grappling with and constructing the information and ideas for themselves.

In his hard-hitting critique of high school American history textbooks, *Lies My Teacher Told Me: Everything Your American History Textbook Got Wrong*, Loewen suggests taking a more critical stance toward these tomes:

> The stories that history books tell are predictable; every problem has already been solved, or is about to be solved. Textbooks exclude conflict or real suspense. . . . Textbooks keep students in the dark about the nature of history. History is furious debate informed by evidence and reason. Textbooks encourage students to believe that history is facts to be learned. (2007, 5, 8)

But we can't simply blame the textbooks, because there's a mixed message out there. At the same time that demands for a rigorous, content-rich curriculum reverberate from one coast to the other, many elementary schools have put social studies on the back burner. With the No Child Left Behind focus on math and reading, most states don't assess history in the elementary grades. The result? Social studies and history have been squeezed into an ever smaller corner of the school day or abandoned altogether (Harvey and Goudvis 2007).

It doesn't have to be this way. We stand with the history buffs and many teachers who refuse to narrow the curriculum, despite the stranglehold that high-stakes tests in "basic" subjects like math and reading have on it. When you think about it, in a democracy, what's more basic than teaching history and social studies? If students are to become knowledgeable, thoughtful citizens they need to engage in conversations, discussions, and debates

This is such an important distinction. Passively memorizing information from a text could not be further from how historians actually read.

—Gina

I am reminded of those surveys that show Americans' lack of knowledge of basic information about the world and our history—often presented as humorous, but as a teacher it makes me sad.

—Maryann

about events past and present, understand people with different perspectives and opinions, and read widely to become informed about ideas and issues that affect their nation and their world.

As we work with kids in many different classrooms, we've noticed that thoughtful, consistent instruction in reading and thinking strategies encourages them to become more engaged, active readers who (most importantly) more fully understand what they are reading. The next step, then, is to focus on comprehension instruction in the service of a discipline—in this case history. As Pearson et al. point out:

> Scholars have argued that without systematic attention to reading and writing in subjects like science and history, students will leave schools with an impoverished sense of what it means to use the tools of literacy for learning or even to reason within various disciplines. (Pearson, Moje, and Greenleaf 2010, 459–63)

Historical Literacy

Our approach is to embed reading and thinking strategies in our history and social studies teaching so that, as Pearson et al. suggest, students learn to read and reason through different historical sources and materials. While it makes sense to use reading strategies to help kids tackle the textbook, that's not enough. Comprehension instruction in history emphasizes asking and answering questions, drawing inferences and conclusions based on evidence, and synthesizing information across different sources to build students' understanding. Teaching historical literacy means we merge thoughtful, foundational literacy practices with challenging, engaging resources to immerse kids in historical ways of thinking.

If kids are engaged in historical literacy practices, what might this look like?

Students would do the following:

- Read and reason through many different kinds of sources about the past, connecting to the experiences, dilemmas, discoveries, and reflections of people from other times and places.

- Ask their own authentic questions, just like historians do.

- Learn to read critically— to understand different purposes and perspectives, asking, Who wrote this? Why did they write it? What's their perspective?

Anne and Brad's plea for more time for reading, thinking, and learning about history is a clarion call. How will our students ever participate fully and thoughtfully in a democracy if they have so little time to learn about it?

— Stephanie

- Try out ways of thinking about history—inferring, analyzing and interpreting facts and evidence to discover themes and important ideas.

Rather than skimming the surface of the textbook, they read rich and engaging trade books, short articles, primary sources, and historical fiction picture books. Delving into specific topics requires students to sort and sift all the information they take in, determining what's important to remember and synthesizing different perspectives. If kids encounter conflicting information, they keep reading and dig deeper to reconcile and explain their findings. They are immersed in what history is all about, namely

> enduring human dramas and dilemmas, fascinating mysteries, and an amazing cast of historical characters involved in events that exemplify the best and worst of human experiences. (Bain 2007, 210)

Voilà . . . our approach to historical literacy . . . a way to learn about and experience other people, places, and times so that kids no longer view the subject as "uninteresting" and "irrelevant" but rather as relevant, engaging, and even fascinating.

Putting Historical Literacy to Work

In Matthew Reif's fifth grade class in Prince George's County, Maryland, we carved out time by combining the literacy block and the time allocated to social studies each week; after all, this was literacy, just historical literacy for a change. Building on several articles in the basal anthology about "westward expansion" that had piqued the kids' interest, we determined that this topic offered plenty of opportunities for teaching kids how to read and reason through historical sources.

Kids in Matthew's classroom were well versed in using comprehension strategies as tools for learning in the literacy block. They sorted and sifted information to get at important ideas. Students monitored their understanding, left tracks of their thinking, and asked lots of questions. They were enthusiastic readers and thinkers, who eagerly crammed their twenty-nine growing bodies onto the small rug in the front of the classroom to engage in wide-ranging and sometimes heated discussions.

For starters, we abandoned the textbook, headed for the library, and fired up the computer to find resources. The first step to building historical literacy was to fill the classroom with challenging, engaging materials. We collected photographs, letters, trade books, historical fiction picture books, newspaper articles, paintings and other artwork, and magazines to create a multisource, multigenre, multiperspective curriculum (Allington and Johnston 2002). Short articles and picture books filled classroom tables: everything from oral histories of Native American children to the stories of Exodusters who left the south to settle on the plains of Kansas to tales of Annie Oakley and her Wild West shows. We grabbed every kid-friendly source we could lay our hands on, including a historical fiction "account" of Lewis and Clark's journey from the perspective of Seaman, Clark's dog (Eubank 2010). What kid could resist reading about the Lewis and Clark expedition from the point of view of a Newfoundland? Our goal was straightforward—if kids were going to acquire knowledge about this topic, they had to read, write, draw, talk, question, view, debate, and discuss engaging historical texts and materials. We wanted kids to get excited about the topic, of course. But most of all, we wanted them to build their knowledge store and grasp ways of thinking about and exploring the past—and to question, interpret, reason through, and "think flexibly about multiple sources of information" (Juel et al. 2010).

To illustrate how we revamped comprehension instruction from a disciplinary perspective, we've come up with eight practices that introduce kids to "doing history" with the goal of furthering historical literacy. These practices are based on Prince George's county standards and key concepts, the national core curriculum standards, and advice from historians knowledgeable about teaching history in the elementary grades (Levstik and Barton 2001; Zarnowski 2006).

We outline briefly the purpose of each of these instructional practices, describing each practice and showing how we teach kids new ways to read and think about history so they more fully understand the ideas and issues central to our topic. We had some key concepts and ideas we wanted kids to understand. Our goal was to explore and "unpack" the common notion of westward expansion as "manifest destiny," making sure we included people, events, and points of view that are often glossed over or left out of textbook chapters. We began with a series of lessons that focused on teaching kids to monitor their understanding as they read different kinds of sources and documents. Throughout the study we collected and paid close attention to the kids' questions, inferences, and interpretations as they read and discussed texts of all kinds. Then we developed subsequent lessons based on our analysis of and reflection on kids' learning—responding to their content knowledge as well as introducing them to strategies as tools for reading and learning in the discipline. While we describe how we taught the lessons with the topic of westward expansion, these practices can be adapted for many topics and texts.

1. *Make Students' Background Knowledge About the Topic Visible and Public*

> *Purpose:*   Explore and discuss kids' background knowledge, including the preconceptions and questions they bring with them.

> *Practice:*   Discuss, record, and "map" kids' thinking on a large chart— constructing a map of their background knowledge and initial questions.

Charting kids' background knowledge allowed us to make what kids already knew and their thinking "visible" (Ritchhart 2002) so we could examine it and make it public from the get-go. The discussion provided a window into kids' thinking so we could build on the accurate information they already had as well as uncover misconceptions to address.

Kids (spurred by other students' comments and prior knowledge) shared what they thought they knew about the topic and came up with thought-provoking questions (see Figure 1). For example, when one child noted that some people were forced to go west, another wondered aloud

Figure 1 Students' background knowledge and questions

133

"Who was forced to go west? Why were people forced to go west?" These questions added a new twist to the more typical question of why pioneers moved west. Rather than just a warm-up, the kids were engaged because they knew their thinking mattered and that their questions were the most important ones.

2. *Give Kids Opportunities to Read Extensively and Interact with Texts*

> *Purpose:* Kids read to learn, coding the text with their thinking—their reactions, questions, connections, and new learning.

> *Practice:* As kids learned new information, this prompted more questions. We created lists of kids' questions, which they investigated on their own and in small groups.

David Pearson says, "Today's new knowledge is tomorrow's background knowledge." To learn new information and build their store of knowledge, students had to do some serious reading, so we encouraged kids to choose materials that grabbed their interest. They read and responded to a variety of texts, coding their thinking in the margins or on sticky notes: reacting to new information, asking questions, drawing inferences, and connecting to previous learning. As they came together to share what they were learning from their reading, Matthew led a discussion and added kids' thoughts and comments to the map we had created, paying special attention to their questions.

> **MATTHEW:** Now that we've done some reading about why people went west and what happened along the way, go ahead and turn and talk about any additional questions you have. Then we'll come back together and discuss and jot down some of what you have been learning, as well as your questions. (*After a few minutes, Matthew brought the kids back together.*)

> **JEROME:** If the Native Americans were here first, whose land was it?

> **ANNE:** That's a really interesting question, Jerome. Let's talk about it . . . what do we know about whose land it was?

> **GEORGE:** I think that the Spanish owned the land before the U.S. government owned it.

> **RUTH ANN:** I think it was shared by different countries, like Spain—maybe France?

> **DANTE:** We got a lot of land from Mexico, now it's Texas.

JOHNSON: I agree with Jerome, I infer the lands were the Indians'—they lived there first.

ESTEPHANIA: Weren't they giving the land away? I thought people could have free land if they'd live there . . .

IVAN: But how did the government get the land, did they buy it?

Jerome's question "Whose land was it?" was the kind of thoughtful question that sparked a whole line of related questions that kids came up with and that centered on the concept of "land." Some of the students' questions were similar to the essential questions we teachers had identified ahead of time: How did the U.S. acquire so much land? How did settlers and pioneers come to own the land? How did the idea of "manifest destiny" drive exploration and settlement? In the end, whose land was it and what happened to those who had always lived on the land? Throughout the study, kids addressed these broader questions as well as their own questions, furthering their understanding of significant and controversial issues, some of which are still being debated today.

We believe historical thinking, for elementary kids, begins with kids' authentic questions. We doubt all these questions would have surfaced from a cursory reading of the textbook; kids' questions emerged because kids were immersed in rich, engaging picture books, trade books, articles, and visuals. When we honor kids' questions, they assume ownership of the process of learning about people, dilemmas, events, and experiences from far away and long ago. We added to the chart of questions as the study continued—and as kids investigated answers to their questions, we revisited our list to keep track of how our thinking changed over time.

Kids' Questions About Westward Expansion

The Native Americans were here first, so whose land was it?

I know the Indians followed the buffalo—did they own the land, or just hunt on it?

Did the government buy the land from the Native Americans, what about the treaties?

Could settlers just start to live on the land and then it was theirs?

What happened when the pioneers went west—did they meet the Indians?

Did people go west for religious freedom?

> Immersing children in authentic texts with rich images gives them the opportunity to develop a mental picture or map of what history is. So often the historical concepts we teach to children are very abstract and we assume they can follow. Why not spend the time to build background knowledge through the use of a myriad of materials that give them access to the time period? Helping build these images is of particular importance to students who are learning English as a new language because it gives them a framework from which they can base both their own background knowledge and the work ahead of developing new schema and working with new vocabulary.
>
> —Anne G.

Why did people go west if it was so dangerous?

Were some people forced to go west? Who? Why were they forced to go west?

Some Indians were forced onto reservations—how did they resist or fight back?

3. Merge Thinking with New Information

> *Purpose:* Create mind maps on which students merge their thinking with new information.

> *Practice:* Kids read a variety of sources and formed self-selected small groups to discuss, write, and draw their new learning on large posters.

Kids were choosing and reading books to build background on the topic, jostling to take home their favorites—particularly on outlaws or the Donner party. They needed a way to organize all their new learning and they loved the idea of "working big," so they created posters and mind maps to merge their thinking with new information. We called these "background knowledge mind maps" to emphasize that we were "building" background and "constructing" knowledge about the topic.

Kids chose the topics for the mind maps. For example, one small group focused on the transcontinental railroad. They decided together on a focus question, which they wrote in the middle of their poster: "How did the railroad affect the wild west?" (see Figure 2). When Joshua found a nineteenth-century painting of Native Americans tearing up what looked like newly laid railroad track, he suggested another question which he added to the mind map—"Who tried to stop them from building the railroad?"

Victoria, who had read the picture book *Coolies* (Yin 2001), was outraged that the Chinese workers who risked their lives dynamiting mountains and persevering through snowstorms received so little recognition for their labors and wondered why they were treated so unfairly. She added her thoughts to a section of the map, and later concluded:

> *My conclusion is that the railroad builders were unfair with the Chinese because they didn't give them credit for all the hard work and sometimes didn't even pay them because in the book Coolies, they had to protest about it. They even stopped working on the railroad*

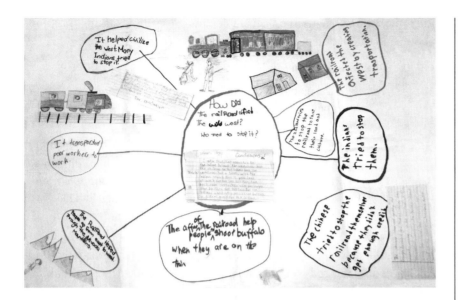

Figure 2 Mind Map: How did the railroad affect the wild west?

Every time I visit Brad's classroom, I am struck by how thoughtfully the kids can show their learning on large charts or murals. These formats allow children to work big, to co-author side by side, and are large enough to be used in whole-class presentations. The kids and teachers at Columbine (and in other comprehension-centered classrooms around the country) have invented a whole new genre: nonfiction posters!

—Smokey

because they were so upset. But then they had to go back to work because they took away their food.

Nicholas drew his own conclusions from his reading, and added these to the mind map:

I infer that it wasn't fair for the Indians because the Americans built the railroad on the Indians' land. There was a treaty with the Indians saying this is your land we won't bother you, but they took back that treaty. I feel grief for the Indians.

Giving the kids a choice in what they read and who they worked with to make the mind maps made a big difference in their enthusiasm. Adding drawings and illustrations heightened their interest in the process. Rather than wait until the end of a study to "do research," kids were engaged in investigating what they were interested in right from the start. With everyone's new learning visible on their mind maps, and kids adding information to each others' posters, kids created their own community of researchers (Harvey and Daniels 2009).

As kids delved into sources, we noticed that it was difficult to distinguish between more and less reliable sources of information. While this was understandable because the kids were just beginning to learn about the topic, we next focused on several lessons on reading, asking questions about, and evaluating different sources.

4. *Ask Questions for Different Purposes*

Purpose: Develop kids' awareness of the many types of questions they ask as they read a variety of sources.

Practice: We read a letter from a pioneer on the Oregon Trail (a primary source) paired with a magazine article (a secondary source) about this same pioneer woman to compare information across sources (Brown 1848; Wolfe 1954). We categorized the types of questions kids asked and discussed how each kind of question furthered historical understanding.

Together we read a letter from Tabitha Brown, a sixty-six-year-old grandmother who ventured west because she didn't want to be left behind—traveling with her adult children and her seventy-seven-year-old brother-in-law, Captain John, on a wagon train to Oregon. Tabitha's letters provide a remarkable account of her journey and her near-fatal experience losing her wagon and all of her belongings in a rushing river.

Reading Tabitha's letter was tough going due to the formal and "old-fashioned" language she used. We guided the kids through it and they were bursting with questions: Why did she go when she was so old? Didn't she know she'd be a burden on her family? How long did the journey take? But the kids stuck with it, and were eventually rewarded with a riveting account of the night she and Captain John spent alone in the wilderness, under a tarp in the pouring rain, and lived to tell about it.

Students then compared the information in Tabitha's letter with a 1954 *Reader's Digest* article about Tabitha's journey and her new (and successful) life in Oregon (Figure 3). As we discussed the differences between primary sources and secondary sources, one child astutely pointed out that someone probably used Tabitha's letters to write the magazine article. In this way, the kids began to grasp the idea that we learn history from the stories, accounts, journals, and letters of real people.

At the end of the lesson, we had a chart covered with a jumble of questions. To put some order to the chaos, we organized the questions, identifying several different types the kids had asked about each source. As the study continued, we used the chart as a reference, modeling how different kinds of questions inform and contribute to our understanding.

The Independence of Tabitha Brown

Condensed from
"Adventures on Horseback"   Louis Wolfe

TABITHA BROWN sat in her rocking chair beside the fireplace, her determined brain working as

I infer that Tabitha want all of the adventures she can take in before she dies

Oregon Territory was fit only for young men, they said, but this pioneer grandmother wouldn't believe it

she had taught school and raised and supported her children by herself — in Maryland, then in Virginia, later in Missouri. Now, in 1846, she was 66 years old and lame in one foot. And her son, Orus, was trying to persuade her not to go.

"The West is for young men," he had said. "It's 2000 miles to Oregon, and the journey will take eight or nine months. There are Indians, mountains and deserts. At your age, Maw, you'll never have a chance."

"Nonsense, son," she answered. "I'm younger in spirit than a lot of

<small>© by Louis Wolfe, is published at $2.75 by Dodd, Mead & Co., 432 Fourth Ave., New York 16, N. Y.</small>

you young folks. I'll take good care of myself and Captain John. We'll be no bother."

Captain John was her husband's brother, an old sea captain. He was 77 now; she had kept house for him since her husband died.

Tabitha's thin, strong face looked as if it had been carved from granite. "I'm going to stay with my children," she declared. "I'm going West."

Orus shrugged when she told him. He knew his mother. Once she made up her mind there was no use

I predict that Tabitha will be the only one left if she keeps on saying that she will never give up.

The first part ... smoothly. The Indians were friendly, the weather clear, the trails in good shape. As the wagon train snaked across the plains and over the hills of Nebraska and Wyoming, Captain John rode horseback and Tabitha not only took care of herself but

Why did they want to go to the Oregon country anyway?

and up into Oregon, skirting the desert, the Cascades and the Columbia Gorge. He would act as guide for the payment of $2 from each family.

Orus Brown and most of the other pioneers scorned the idea. The old route had been used several times and had proved successful. So they pushed on.

The Pringles and the men of several other wagons, however, voted to risk the short cut. Since Tabitha was traveling with her daughter, Pherne Pringle, she had no choice. Rolling out of Fort Hall, she sat glumly on the front seat of her wagon and stared straight ahead. "I don't like it," she snapped to Captain John, riding alongside. "I just don't like it."

The little party of 14 wagons and 62 pioneers was out of Fort Hall only a couple of weeks when they

Figure 3 Student responses to a magazine article about Tabitha Brown.

QUESTION TYPE	EXAMPLE	HOW IT INFORMS UNDERSTANDING
Information-seeking questions/ questions of clarification	Did Tabitha meet Native Americans on her journey west?	To fill in gaps in our information
Questions seeking explanations (Why? How?)	Why would someone this old go west?	These are often the most interesting questions
		We keep lingering questions in mind, although we can't always answer all our questions
Questions of empathy	I can't imagine losing all my belongings in a river—how did they keep going?	Encourage human interest and engagement
		Build awareness of other perspectives and points of view
Questions that encourage supposition	How might things have turned out differently if . . . ?	Focus on imaginative thinking
Questions that encourage historical investigation	Where else could we find out about her?	These questions help us to evaluate sources
Questions that challenge information	Her story was so amazing I wondered if she was telling the truth . . .	

Immersing kids in the study of history means teaching them to ask questions for many different purposes: for research and investigation, to fill in gaps in their knowledge, to think critically about information, and to grapple with significant human dilemmas and issues. As kids broadened their question-asking repertoire, they began to see the importance of asking many different kinds of questions, especially those that took a more critical and evaluative stance toward what they were reading (Busching and Slesinger 2002).

5. *Read and Discuss Different Kinds of Sources*

> *Purpose:* Understand that the disciplines of history and social studies are based on different kinds of sources, and that every source has an author, a purpose, and a perspective. Depending on their purpose, we read sources in different ways.

> *Practice:* We displayed examples of different sources (a page from a textbook, one of Tabitha Brown's letters, an article in a trade book, a copy of a nineteenth-century print, and so on) on a large chart to compare and contrast these different sources.

In a 24/7 media world, kids need to be aware of the fact that someone wrote or created all the information they're bombarded with each day. Some sources are dense with information and readers have to winnow the information down to what's important to remember. Others require us to draw inferences or conclusions based on evidence. Kids knew that every source they read or viewed had an author, a purpose, and often a definite perspective. But they needed a lot of practice building a context for the information they were learning. To teach kids the importance of "sourcing" (Juel et al. 2010) in learning history, we posted the different kinds of sources kids had been reading and discussed what we were learning from each of them.

Next we tackled online sources. As in most classrooms nowadays, the kids were constantly asking to "go online" and search for articles. While not wanting to discourage curious minds, we found that kids had difficulty distinguishing between more and less reliable sources of information. This was understandable because often kids' background knowledge wasn't sufficient to alert them to problematic or dubious information. We demonstrated how to take a more critical stance by reading what we told students was a "mystery source," which we posted on the board (see Figure 4).

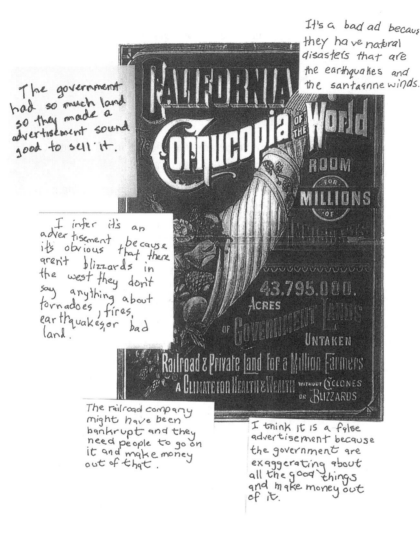

Figure 4 Students respond to an advertisement for land in California.

It's a bad ad becaus they have natural disasters that are the earthquakes and the santaanne winds.

The government had so much land so they made a advertisement sound good to sell it.

I infer it's an advertisement because it's obvious that there aren't blizzards in the west they don't say anything about tornadoes, fires, earthquakes, or bad land.

The railroad company might have been bankrupt and they need people to go on it and make money out of that.

I think it is a false advertisement because the government are exaggerating about all the good things and make money out of it.

ANNE: Remember how we discussed the idea that every text has a perspective and probably a message—and that our job as readers and historians is to figure out what these are? Let's read this source together, and we'll use evidence from this text to figure out who wrote it and why. You can code the text—jot down your questions, inferences, connections . . . whatever you're thinking as we read and we'll share out our thoughts as we go.

GREGORY: What does it mean—"Millions of Immigrants"? There weren't millions of immigrants, were there?

ALICIA: It said "government lands untaken"—they wanted people to know there was no one there so they could come live on the land.

JENNY: It says there are no blizzards, but what about earthquakes? I know there are earthquakes in California.

NAYELI: I think it's a false advertisement because the government's exaggerating about all the good things.

ALLAN: I was thinking that the government had nothing to do with it. Maybe somebody owned this land and wanted to sell it . . .

NICHOLAS: The railroad company might have been bankrupt and they need people to ride on it and make money.

Kids used their knowledge about California, settling the west, and the growth of the railroads to try to make sense of this source. The exaggerated claims led them to believe it was an advertisement, perhaps in the newspaper, to convince people to come to California. We discussed the idea that sources have a bias, and concluded that the half-truths and hype pegged this source as an example of what we might call "propaganda." Hoping to teach kids to be skeptical of sources found online (and everywhere else, for that matter), we shared several more modern examples of what can happen when mindless "googling" replaces thinking.

6. *Viewing and Responding to Works of Art*

> *Purpose:* Interpret prints to understand the artists' perspective and purpose.

> *Practice:* Students choose from a variety of nineteenth-century artwork on the theme of westward expansion and use questioning and inferring to interpret these sources (Chertok, Hirshfield, and Rosh 1998).

Historical prints provided yet another experience in "reading" and viewing to interpret a source. While kids had some experience viewing photographs as primary sources and sharing what they could learn from them, this time we asked them to make interpretations and inferences about several historical works of art. We posted the following questions on the board for kids to think about as they examined and responded to this art (Ritchhart 2002).

What do you see or notice about this work of art?

What questions do you have about this painting or print?

> Examining and questioning artwork is a great tool to give students so they learn about different ways of thinking about, discussing, and interpreting historical events.
>
> —

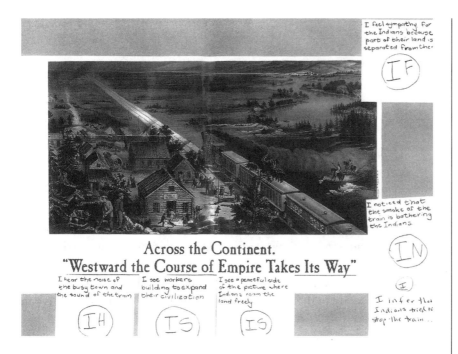

Across the Continent.
"Westward the Course of Empire Takes Its Way"

Handwritten student notes on the print:

I feel sympathy for the Indians because part of their land is separated from the [other] — (IF)

I noticed that the smoke of the train is bothering the Indians — (IN)

I infer that Indians tried to stop the train... — (I)

I hear the noise of the busy town and the sound of the train — (IH)

I see workers building to expand their civilization — (IS)

I see a peaceful side of the picture where Indians roam the land freely — (IS)

Figure 5 Students respond to a print by Ives and Palmer, 1868.

What's the message here?

What can you say about the artist? His or her perspective?

Reacting and responding to these visual images, kids put themselves right into the scene (Figure 5). As we listened in to pairs discuss the print (Chertok et al. 1998), Dante wondered what the word *empire* meant, while Najah was more analytical and drew inferences about the scenario: "I think the Indians were surprised by the train and the smoke that was bothering them. I got the feeling they didn't like it." Ruth Ann and Victoria observed that the artists had put the town and all the people on one side of the tracks—"with the train and cabins and people cutting down trees." On the other side, they noted, were "mountains and a lake and trees and grass with just the Indians, like it used to be. And the river is maybe the one Lewis and Clark went on." Some students felt that the artists were making a statement about "civilization"—"I see workers expanding their civilization—they are building houses and schools." We encouraged different interpretations and divergent thinking, but asked kids to tie these back to the print. Viewing and drawing inferences about the images supported kids to "see" and envision ideas about westward expansion in a way that words couldn't fully convey.

7. *Discover and Surface Themes by Reading the Narratives and Stories of Others*

> *Purpose:* Infer to surface themes and important ideas in historical fiction and nonfiction.
>
> *Practice:* We read aloud the historical fiction picture book *Cheyenne Again* by Eve Bunting (1995) and compared the information and themes with first-person accounts written by Native Americans who had attended Indian boarding schools.

When kids immerse themselves in historical fiction, they break out of their immediate frame of reference and gain a more complete understanding of past issues and dilemmas. Historical fiction can free kids to imagine, wonder about, and entertain many possibilities—and help them understand things that might not come across in more straightforward nonfiction sources. We tell kids that historical fiction may not have happened, but is often grounded in authentic information about peoples' lives or based on events that occurred. Levstik and Barton (2001) suggest that historical narratives support an "informed and disciplined imaginative entry into events" so that students can grapple with important moral and ethical issues themselves. The drama and power of these human experiences explains kids' intense interest and engagement as they gain insight into people whose lives were very different from their own.

In *Cheyenne Again* by Eve Bunting (1995) a child is taken from his family to an Indian boarding school in an attempt to transform him and bring him into the white man's world. We guided the students through an interactive read-aloud for the first few pages of the story, modeling how we used text evidence to come up with themes (Harvey and Goudvis 2005). Kids continued reading the story in small groups and, at the end of the lesson, came back together to share out their responses:

> NICHOLAS: I think the goal was to separate the Indian children from their culture. They were trying to teach them the ways of the white people, but Young Bull kept dreaming of his family and home, just like in *Thomas Blue Eagle* (referring to another book: *The Ledgerbook of Thomas Blue Eagle* Grutman and Matthai 1994). I have an evaluation—this is cruel and not fair—to take them away from their family. It's not fair at all . . .
>
> DEVANTE: I have very strong feelings, I'm comparing this to slavery— the white people thought the Native Americans were like animals

. . . they thought they were savages, like the saying said "From Savagery to Civilization" (this motto from the Carlisle Indian School was reported in the book's historical note). But we're all human beings—we all have human rights. They had to erase their culture and turn it into their own culture, but they should let them keep their culture.

RUTH ANN: The teacher in the story said, "Never forget you are Indian. Keep your memories . . . " That's an important part of the story, I think he would have forgotten who he was if it weren't for that teacher.

Students discussed and recorded many themes: racism, prejudice, determination to hold onto one's memories, pride in one's culture, kindness, injustice, and hope, among others. They practiced historical thinking as they surfaced themes and tied these to evidence—the words, events, illustrations, and actions in the text.

To demonstrate that historical fiction may be based on primary sources and accounts by real people, the kids next read first-person accounts written or told by adults who had been taken to boarding schools as children (Philip 2000). Comparing the perspectives, ideas, and information in these primary sources with the events and experiences described in *Cheyenne*

THE CUTTING OF MY LONG HAIR

Figure 6 Account of Gertrude Bonnin's childhood experience at an Indian school.

Again helped kids understand that historical fiction is based on what really happened.

8. *Interpreting Historical Fiction—Synthesizing Information Across Sources*

> *Purpose:* Use knowledge of historical events gained from different sources to synthesize the information and ideas in a picture book.

> *Practice:* Using the words from *Sitting Bull Remembers* (Turner 2007) by Ann Turner, kids work in book discussion groups with evidence from previously read sources to interpret, analyze, and understand the text.

The historical fiction picture book *Sitting Bull Remembers* tells the story of the famous chief Sitting Bull—from his early days as a young warrior, through the defeat of Custer and his army at Little Bighorn. He looks back on his life and adventures during his final years when he was living in isolation on a reservation. We read the book aloud to the children, and then they worked with a script of the picture book to annotate, elaborate on, and respond to the text. Before sending the small groups off, we created a chart of what to do in a book discussion group—listening topped the list—and the kind of language kids might use in their discussions. To disagree, one might say "That's a good idea, but I respectfully disagree. . . . " To bring someone else into the conversation, one could ask "What are you thinking, _____?" as a way of inviting someone else to speak.

In their small groups, students discussed and synthesized knowledge from several different sources. They referred to the picture book *A Boy Called Slow* (Bruchac 1994) and a variety of nonfiction articles about the Native American victory at Little Bighorn as well as what they knew about Sitting Bull's valiant efforts to keep his people free and his final, tragic years on a reservation. The kids remembered and brought in an astonishing amount of information prompted by the visual images and poetic language in *Sitting Bull Remembers.* They had learned about Sitting Bull and his people through several different lenses and were able to use these various perspectives to enrich their understanding far beyond what their interpretations would have been had they read just one account. As they engaged in deep discussions in their groups, they seemed to be piecing together a puzzle, a real-life puzzle with implications for the history and fate of a people.

At the end of the study, students used the knowledge they had gained about westward expansion to "critique" several articles and textbook excerpts (Zarnowski 2006). These junior James Loewens were fair in their criticisms, and took their charge quite seriously. They actively used the knowledge they'd gained from all their reading to identify what they thought was "missing" from the various accounts. They noted that in some textbooks Native Americans were barely mentioned in descriptions of the journey west. Kids wondered why the importance of Sacagawea's role in the Lewis and Clark expedition was often downplayed or why a photograph and caption of Chinese workers along railroad tracks said nothing about their contributions to the building of the transcontinental railroad. They had learned the real stories behind famous figures including Kit Carson, Wild Bill Hickok, and others who were hardly the frontier role models described in some sources (Paulsen 2006). Descriptions of the "wild west," they noticed, were far more likely to mention outlaws than courageous marshals such as the former slave Bass Reeves, who devoted a good part of his life to bringing law and order to Indian Territory (Nelson 2009). As a way to wrap up the unit, this critique provided another opportunity for students to put to use the knowledge they had gained over the course of the unit.

What We Learned from Our History Lessons

Over time, we noticed that kids began to

- develop the tools to read critically and think like historians;

- realize the importance of accurate information and getting the facts straight—not because they needed to memorize them, but because accurate information is important and furthers historical understanding;

- broaden their repertoire of comprehension strategies—especially their use of questioning as a historical tool and inferential thinking as a way to support their ideas and conclusions with evidence;

- take a more tentative and thoughtful stance—be open-minded, ready to listen to the ideas of others, suspend judgment, and change thinking in the face of new information or more convincing arguments; and

- understand that there are many different historical truths and that reading and learning from others provide ways to get at these truths.

Just as reading changes and shapes thinking, learning to read and think from a historical perspective can alter how we read and view the

> Anne and Brad provide vivid examples of the power of teaching strategic thinking, not as the end result of a unit of study, but as the vehicle propelling students to new learning. These fifth graders have actually transformed and integrated information into personal understanding. Now *they* are the experts as they spot author bias and missing information in published historical accounts. Bravo!
>
> —*Chryse*

world. As history enthusiasts, it was heartening to see kids so curious about people, places, and events that occurred long ago and far away. Students expanded their view of literacy to include ways to read, view, write, draw, talk, and think about history—connecting the past and present. These experiences encouraged them to think for themselves and make full use of their own minds. What better way to prepare them for their future role as engaged, thoughtful adult citizens?

References

Allington, Richard L., and Peter Johnston. 2002. *Reading to Learn: Lessons from Exemplary Fourth Grade Classrooms.* New York: Guilford.

Bain, Robert B. 2007. "'They Thought the World Was Flat?' Applying the Principles of How People Learn in Teaching High School History." In *How Students Learn: History in the Classroom,* edited by M. Suzanne Donovan and John D. Bransford. Washington, DC: National Academies Press.

Brown, Tabitha. 1848. Letters of Tabitha Brown. Private collection.

Busching, Beverly, and Betty Ann Slesinger. 2002. *"It's Our World, Too": Socially Responsive Learners in Middle School Language Arts.* Urbana, IL: National Council of Teachers of English.

Chertok, Bobbi, Goody Hirshfield, and Marilyn Rosh. 1998. *Teaching American History with Art Masterpieces.* New York: Scholastic.

Harvey, Stephanie, and Anne Goudvis. 2005. *The Comprehension Toolkit: Language and Lessons for Active Literacy.* Portsmouth, NH: Heinemann.

Harvey, Stephanie, and Anne Goudvis. 2007. *Strategies That Work: Teaching Comprehension for Understanding and Engagement,* 2d ed. Portland, ME: Stenhouse.

Harvey, Stephanie, and Harvey Daniels. 2009. *Comprehension and Collaboration.* Portsmouth, NH: Heinemann.

Juel, Connie, Heather Hebard, Julie Park Haubner, and Meredith Moran. 2010. "Reading Through a Disciplinary Lens." *Educational Leadership* (67) 6: 12–17.

Levstik, Linda S., and Keith C. Barton. 2001. *Doing History: Investigating with Children in Elementary and Middle Schools.* Mahwah, NJ: Lawrence Erlbaum.

Loewen, James W. 2007. *Lies My Teacher Told Me: Everything Your American History Textbook Got Wrong.* New York: Simon and Schuster.

Loewen, James W. 2010. *Teaching What Really Happened.* New York: Teachers College Press.

Pearson, P. David, Elizabeth Moje, and Cynthia Greenleaf. 2010. "Literacy and Science, Each in the Service of the Other." *Science* April 23 (328): 459–63.

Ritchhart, Ron. 2002. *Intellectual Character: What It Is, Why It Matters, and How to Get It.* San Francisco, CA: Jossey Bass.

Zarnowski, Myra. 2006. *Making Sense of History.* New York: Scholastic.

Selected Resources for Children

Bruchac, Joseph. 1994. *A Boy Called Slow.* New York: Putnam and Grosset.

Bunting, Eve. 1995. *Cheyenne Again.* New York: Clarion.

Eubank, Patricia Reeder. 2010. *Seaman's Journal: On the Trail with Lewis and Clark.* Nashville, TN: Ideals Publications.

Freedman, Russell. 1983. *Children of the Wild West.* New York: Clarion.

Grutman, Jewel H., and Gay Matthai. 1994. *The Ledgerbook of Thomas Blue Eagle.* Charlottesville, VA: Thomasson-Grant.

Nelson, Vaunda M. 2009. *Bad News for Outlaws: The Remarkable Life of Bass Reeves.* Minneapolis, MN: Carolrhoda Books.

Paulsen, Gary. 2006. *The Legend of Bass Reeves: Being the True Account of the Most Valiant Marshal in the West.* New York: Random House.

Philip, Neil. 2000. *A Braid of Lives: Native American Childhood.* New York: Clarion.

Turner, Ann. 2007. *Sitting Bull Remembers.* New York: HarperCollins.

Wolfe, Louis. 1954. "The Independence of Tabitha Brown." *Reader's Digest* (August): 73–78.

Yin. 2001. *Coolies.* New York: Philomel.

CHAPTER NINE

Comprehension in Science

Gina Cervetti

One year fourth grade teacher Phyllis Whitin found a bird feeder in her attic and decided to hang it on a crabapple tree outside her classroom window. Phyllis invited her students to take turns observing the birds during their writing time. Whitin and Whitin (1996) described what happened as the invitation to observe the birds that came to feed became extended investigations through which the students began to live the lives of scientists—recording their observations of the birds at the feeders, formulating questions about bird behavior, seeking out other experts, engaging in text-based research, and altering the food in the feeders in order to learn more about what the birds prefer to eat and what they need nutritionally.

Whitin and Whitin studied students' literacy practices during the investigations. They documented the role that talk, reading, and writing played in the students' bird investigations with special attention to how students' literacy practices were *shaped by their investigations*. The fourth graders developed sophisticated literacy strategies to meet their needs as inquirers. They began to think like scientists and to read, write, and talk like scientists because they encountered the same kinds of questions and dilemmas that scientists encounter as they engage in investigations. In one powerful example, the students found that they could not take notes quickly enough to fully describe the birds' behavior. They realized that they needed to find ways to record their observations quickly, so they could capture the maximum amount of information. So they began to develop note-taking strategies, including the use of abbreviations, and they set up cooperative observations—having figured out that two people writing concurrently can capture more than an individual observer. These strategies did not arise as part of a lesson on "how to take observational notes." Faced with an authentic problem, the students worked together to develop literacy practices that met the needs of the situation.

In the context of the bird investigations, reading and writing were not ends unto themselves; they were tools that students could use to answer their own questions. These may not be questions that the students brought to Phyllis Whitin's fourth grade classroom, but Phyllis had invited the students to wonder about the birds, and they were soon driven by curiosity and growing expertise to read to inform their investigations, to question and wonder about what they read and observed, and to read across different sources and their own experiences. When the students leveraged strategies, they did so in the interest of a purpose that transcended the simple recall of information. These are highly sophisticated practices in both literacy and science.

There is no question that attention to informational texts, including content-rich science books, is on the rise in elementary reading instruction. This is a hopeful change for those of us who have been concerned about opportunities for students to learn science and to learn to read science texts. However, as I think about the future of comprehension instruction (with a special focus on science reading), I want to suggest that we transition from the current concern with making sure that students read many different genres of text during English language arts instruction to a focus on the literacy practices that are part of disciplinary participation and learning. That is, rather than reading nonfiction science books as literature in the context of English language arts instruction, students should learn to comprehend science texts *in science*, and they should put reading and writing to work as they engage in investigations—just like Phyllis Whitin's fourth graders.

> Our overriding goal must be conceptual development and scientific understandings—by any means necessary. Of course literate behaviors facilitate the process and some are more efficient than others, but it is the engagement in the natural world that stimulates the learning.
>
> —*Nancy*

> Perhaps this kind of inquiry-based investigation provides a partial answer to the dilemma Steph Harvey poses—children come to school brimming with questions, but by later grades, seem to have lost that natural curiosity.
>
> —*Ellin*

The Genre Movement and Science Reading

Over the last two decades, many teachers and educational researchers have become concerned about the overwhelming emphasis on fictional literature—and relative absence of informational text—in the elementary grades. These educators are motivated in part by the understanding that reading practices are shaped by genre, but they're also concerned that literature-based programs are both failing to support vocabulary development and failing to prepare students for the texts and tests of later schooling. They suggest that the texts that students read in the elementary grades should reflect the range of texts that students will encounter as they continue in school and the texts that they will read in their lives outside of school—contexts that are filled with informational texts.

You might imagine that such impassioned interest in nonfiction text genres would mean that students are reading more science texts in school, and this appears to be the case. It seems that commercial reading programs (basals) are beginning to respond to the call for more diverse text genres; current basal programs incorporate a greater diversity of genres, including large quantities of informational text—and it seems that the inclusion of more informational text in basals has resulted in the inclusion of more science content. Norris et al. (2008) studied the degree to which current commercial reading programs in wide use in Canada include texts with scientific content. Not surprisingly, they found that basals included a substantial proportion of texts with science content and that the majority of these texts (55 percent) were expository in genre.

However, while students are likely reading more about science, the rise in the number of science texts in basal reading programs has coincided with a reduction in the amount of time that students are spending in actual science instruction. Time devoted to science teaching in elementary classrooms has been severely impacted by the renewed emphasis on language arts and mathematics and the onset of yearly testing in those subject areas. Even before changes to elementary classrooms prompted in part by No Child Left Behind (NCLB) legislation, elementary teachers devoted an average of less than two hours per week of instructional time to science (Fulp 2002)—and there are indications that time devoted to science is declining. In a recent study of teachers in northern California, Dorph, Goldstein, Lee, Lepori, Schneider, and Venkatesan (2007) found that 80 percent of the 923 elementary teachers surveyed reported that they spend *less than one hour per week* teaching science.

Moreover, while students are being exposed to more science content in basal texts, it appears that little attention is being paid to the development of science knowledge or to the reading practices of science. Instead, basal-based science texts are being treated instructionally like stories. In the Norris et al. (2008) study, the researchers found the instruction with science texts described in the commercial reading programs emphasized personal reflection and response, not an understanding of the science concepts presented in the texts. They provide the following example of instruction designed for a scientific text about magnets from a third grade teacher's guide:

> In small groups, discuss your experiences with magnets or compasses. What can magnets be used for? What tricks can you do with magnets? Have you ever used a compass to find your direction in an unfamiliar place? (Norris et al. 2008, 788)

Across the basal programs, the researchers found little attention to science concepts and scientific reasoning. The goal of including more science texts in basal programs seems to be focused on exposure to and experience with texts of different genres, not on the development of science reading practices or content knowledge. In addition, while 55 percent of the science selections in the Norris et al. (2008) study were expository, 45 percent were not; for example, 16 percent of the science texts were narrative or poetry. This matters, because stories do not support students' understanding and recall of science content as well as informational science texts (Cervetti et al. 2009). As a result, both the basal-based instruction and the texts themselves are working against the likelihood that students will develop either understandings about science text genres or coherent understandings about science. On a more positive note, in spite of the limitations of the basal instruction, recent studies have shown that elementary teachers are both providing exposure to nonfiction texts in their classrooms and using the texts to teach about the structures and features that distinguish nonfiction and literary genres (e.g., Maloch 2008).

Genre or Discipline?

One solution for the mismatch between the many different kinds of texts that teachers are now using in elementary reading instruction and the basal instruction that treats them all like stories would be to modify basal-based reading instruction to be more in line with the best practices of teachers

Connecting the new to the known is critical to reading and understanding scientific information. But as Gina points out, you have to know something for this strategy to be helpful. For too long, science in schools has been thought of as merely a "hands-on" endeavor. But kids need to *read*, *write*, and *talk* about science as well as do science in order to acquire scientific knowledge and understand it. So it really is "hands on and minds on" for science knowledge and understanding to flourish.

— *Stephanie*

who are increasingly teaching nonfiction reading comprehension. This would ensure, at least, that students are prepared to read and comprehend the many different kinds of texts that they will encounter in school and in life, including the text genres that they will encounter when they read about science. This would be a positive step in the right direction, given that one of the main differences between reading in science and reading in literary contexts—and other disciplinary contexts—*is* that the texts are different.

However, while teaching students about differences among texts would surely be an improvement over the current state of affairs, I want to propose a different solution. Rather than putting text genres at the center of reading comprehension instruction, I suggest that we put context and purpose—the how and why of reading—at the center. For science reading, this would mean that, rather than teaching students to read science texts using a smattering of different informational books and attention to the features and structures of these texts, we would teach students to read science texts as part of *participation in science*. This would involve more than an adjustment in the proportion of science texts that students read and the nature of comprehension instruction involving those texts; it would require that the reading of science texts be put to work in the context of conceptually coherent and, preferably, inquiry-oriented science instruction.

Reading is an authentic part of participation in science, but reading in science is shaped only in part by the unique features of science text. Both the text and reading practices of science are shaped by the goals of developing expertise about the natural world and engaging in investigations of natural phenomena. That is, reading in science is shaped by involvement in inquiry, and learning to comprehend science text should be shaped by inquiry, too.

The most obvious benefit of learning to read science texts in science is that it is more likely to support meaningful knowledge (and vocabulary) development. We should always be thinking about how reading can help students acquire information about the world—for its own sake and as a foundation for reading and writing in the future. Helping students build knowledge and vocabulary has been an important motive behind the genre movement, but reading in disciplinary contexts is more likely to accomplish this goal. I know of no research that documents students' construction of meaningful science knowledge from reading collections of thematically unrelated science texts.

In addition, given that knowledge is probably the most important influence on the comprehension of science text, it makes little sense to teach science reading comprehension without simultaneously building knowledge. To neglect the foundation of knowledge ultimately denies students access to a deep understanding of science texts, and it likely diminishes the potency of comprehension strategy instruction. Comprehension strategies are largely about using available resources to overcome hurdles in understanding; in science, the most valuable strategies are those that help students connect the resource of their current knowledge to the hurdle of new knowledge. Inviting students to leverage their background knowledge in order to surmount an obstacle to comprehension only works if the students have some knowledge to leverage.

Perhaps more importantly, science investigations invite students to read and apply strategies as they put reading to work in the interest of another (more meaningful) goal. We know that creating opportunities for students to read and write for real reasons (reasons other than practicing reading and writing) can have powerful effects on motivation and achievement. John Guthrie and colleagues found in a long series of studies on Concept-Oriented Reading Instruction (CORI) that participation in on-going science investigations made students more strategic readers. Involving students in extended science investigations involving firsthand experiences and reading increased students' use of reading strategies and improved their text comprehension compared with students doing separate science and literacy instruction (e.g., Guthrie et al. 1999; Guthrie and Ozgungor 2002). Importantly, it also increased their conceptual learning; think again of the fourth graders in Phyllis Whitin's class. The students read and wrote because they were motivated to learn about the birds they were observing, but the act of investigating also motivated them to be more strategic and focused in their reading and writing.

It shouldn't be a surprise to any of us that authenticity matters, but what does it look like? In science units that I've been involved in developing, we try to ensure that reading is led by genuine curiosity, associated with firsthand experiences, and put to work in the interest of answering questions or accomplishing a compelling task. In one unit, students use a scientist's notebook to figure out how the sand samples they are examining with magnifiers were formed. In another unit, students both observe earthworms and isopods firsthand and read about life under the soil as they grapple with how an organism's adaptations help it survive in its habitat. Using text in these ways can lend purpose to reading, and can involve students in reading science texts as scientists.

Perhaps most importantly for this chapter, reading in the context of participation in science provides a context in which students can employ

> I fully support inquiry-based approaches to science, but the lessons Gina describes here are fundamentally important to understanding science and are not likely to be student-generated. The balance between student-generated and teacher-generated questions will be key if students are to retain and reapply the most essential ideas underlying the discipline.
>
> —Ellin

comprehension strategies in order to overcome the kinds of challenges that are actually part of reading in science. In the next section, I will highlight several aspects of reading comprehension that, while not unique to science, have been identified as particularly important in science, and the role of comprehension instruction in helping students read science texts in science.

Comprehension Strategy Instruction for Science Reading

The RAND report Reading for Understanding (2002) identified four "urgent" questions in their "agenda for research on reading instruction," one of which was, "How can excellent, direct comprehension instruction be embedded into content instruction that uses inquiry-based methods and authentic reading materials?" In this section, I describe a set of characteristics of science reading along with ways that comprehension strategy instruction can be used to support students in understanding science texts in the context of science activities and investigations.

Reading Across Texts

The kinds of questions that science calls students to investigate generally can't be answered by reading a single article or book. How do humans impact life in the ocean? How do different organisms depend on one another for survival? What makes the weather? How does the Sun support life on Earth? In scientific practice and the best science instruction, participants wrestle with juicy scientific questions by "reading" across many different information sources—prior knowledge, firsthand experiences, and texts (Guthrie et al., 1999). Often this includes reading across multiple texts of different genres, and comparing artifacts and experiences in the physical world to those encountered in books. Because science texts are typically designed to be read in the context of extended investigations, bringing existing knowledge and experiences to the table may be particularly important. Yet there is a lot of evidence that students do not automatically make these links. Craig and Yore (1995) interviewed students in fourth through eighth grades to find out what students knew about science texts and science reading. The students regarded reading in science as a process of extracting and remembering information from the texts. In addition, the students did not think about their knowledge, experiences, or science explorations as resources for understanding texts they read.

The focus on bringing together information from different sources can be supported by comprehension instruction that emphasizes activating and leveraging prior knowledge (What do we already know about *X*?), making inferences across texts (How is this different from what we read/experienced yesterday?), and revising one's thinking based on the introduction of new information (What do we know now that we didn't know before? How does this change our ideas?).

Palincsar and Magnusson (2000) described how one teacher used reading in conjunction with firsthand investigations of light to invite third-grade students to not only engage in reading across text and experience, but also to bring their own evidence to bear on claims encountered in text. In one example, students had concluded from their firsthand investigations that light reflects off of all objects. When they encountered contradictory evidence as they read a fictional scientist's notebook, the students used their data to question the scientist's finding that light does not reflect off of black felt. They speculated about why their own data and the scientist's data were different. Later, the students were gratified to find that the scientist depicted in the notebook later revised her statement based on the introduction of new evidence.

Reading Selectively

When students read in science (rather than merely about science), the ideas that matter most from any particular text are those that inform some aspect of students' ongoing investigations. This means that student scientists might read texts selectively, using search features of the text—such as tables of contents, headings, and indices—to head straight to the most relevant information. In addition, it means that student scientists often use the lens of their investigations as a filter for selecting information to remember, reflect upon, and record. Reading *in science* is not driven by the culling out of main ideas in the same way that it might be when science texts are read in isolation. In fact, the most important ideas for a science investigation may not be those designed by the text's author to be the main ideas.

Comprehension instruction in strategies such as goal setting and question posing (How can this text help us with our investigations?) can be used to help students identify the ideas from a text that help them answer their own questions. Handbooks and field guides are terrific texts for

Gina's example re-
minds me of how
critical it is to provide
well-written, relevant
texts for students. I
still see science text-
books used as the
primary resource in
many schools. With
the abundance of
great resources
available in science
today, it is incum-
bent upon schools
and districts to invest
in the types of re-
sources Gina de-
scribes here.

—*Ellin*

teaching selective reading. In a science unit I helped to develop, we invite students to read from a handbook about everyday ingredients (baking soda, salt, flour, etc.) in order to inform their selection of ingredients that they will use to make the strongest, stickiest glue they can. We model how to find information about the ingredients the students have on their tables and how to hone in on information about the properties of these ingredients that might help them meet their design challenges. Together, we practice keeping *our* goals in mind as we read.

Evaluating Claims and Evidence

Another important marker of science reading comprehension is the ability to evaluate the relationship between evidence and claims and to decide whether the evidence is good enough. As Whitin and Whitin (1996) point out, nonfiction texts are often treated in schools as "repositories of definitive truths and unassailable facts," but inviting students to read as they live the lives of scientists calls them to understand that scientific facts and theories are always subject to revision based on the introduction of new evidence, evidence that they can participate in gathering (84). Students of science need to be able to evaluate evidence, apply scientific information from text to understanding issues and concepts, and to distinguish relevant evidence from irrelevant evidence. These are challenging comprehension tasks, but they are at the heart of science reading.

The challenging task of evaluating evidence is supported by a knowledge-enhancing context—like an in-depth unit of study—and by being taught as students pursue their own curiosities and questions. In the summer of 2009, I participated in a middle school summer science program where students studied ocean science as they learned to read, write, and talk science. One Friday, we took the sixth graders on a field trip to the California coast. They were surprised to see a dead sea lion on the beach and were disturbed to find out that there had been a rash of unexplained sea lion deaths in recent months. On the Monday following the field trip, a number of students told us that they were bothered by the sighting and wanted to learn more about what was happening to the sea lions. We invited the students to read several newspaper accounts about the rise in sea lion mortality along the California coast. We used the reading as an opportunity to teach and model how to evaluate the explanations from different scientists in light of the evidence that they provided. We modeled connecting evidence with claims. Then we asked a number of questions: Is this evidence convincing? Could this evidence support any other explanation? Does this new evidence change your thinking at all? How does the explanation offered by this scientist relate to other things that we have learned about life in the ocean? Students read about and discussed the explanations and, just as scientists had drawn different conclusions from the evidence, so did our students.

Navigating Complex Texts

While existing knowledge of concepts and vocabulary is the foundation for all reading comprehension, science reading often demands that students bring a great deal of specialized knowledge to a text. Spence, Yore, and Williams (1995) note that readers of science text "must have knowledge about the scientific enterprise, the concept under consideration, the scientific language, the patterns of argumentation, the canons of evidence, the science reading process, the science text, and the science reading strategies" (5). In addition, studies of naturally occurring science text have often characterized these texts as dense and poorly constructed.

Given these challenges, reading comprehension instruction in science should prepare student scientists to navigate the complexities of science text. In part, this involves leveraging existing knowledge and experiences from the text to clarify and make sense of science ideas (What do we know that can help us understand this?). It also involves identifying points of confusion and areas for further investigation or reading (What more do we need to know? What's confusing about this?). Comprehension monitoring and clarifying strategies that help students identify problems with meaning construction during reading are best combined with instruction aimed at supporting knowledge development. Students do not automatically leverage their knowledge when reading texts with new information, but the context of ongoing science investigations places a premium on connecting prior knowledge and new information—and they provide reasons to understand that go beyond getting through a text and answering questions about it.

Particularly at the middle and secondary levels, science texts tend to include challenging grammatical features—such as passive verbs and nominalizations, and connectives and prepositions that build long sequences of logic and relationships. It is with respect to the complexities of science text that a genre perspective on reading comprehension is particularly useful for understanding science reading comprehension. A

Understandings about the nature of academic language as discipline specific and the work that has been done by researchers and practitioners in the field of second language acquisition to uncover the language demands of science and other content areas adds much to this discussion. It can help all teachers begin to see increasing linguistic and cultural diversity as a gift and not a problem.

—Nancy

Representing thinking symbolically helps us understand new information and concepts. Sanctioning symbol systems other than print leads kids of all ages to create informational texts that we read and learn from. Think of John James Audubon!

—Anne & Brad

number of studies have demonstrated that readers' understandings about the features and structures of scientific text genres can support them in understanding and retaining science information. Romance and Vitale (2009) have developed particularly rich instructional routines for helping students pull apart complex science texts and understand how ideas are represented in science. In Romance and Vitale's IDEAS program, teachers focus reading comprehension instruction on identifying the features of science language (e.g., linking words, visual features, etc.) that signal relationships and on developing concept maps that rerepresent the ideas graphically.

Reading Across Representations

As Lemke (1998) pointed out, science does not communicate about the world in words alone; the language of science is a synergy of words and graphic representations—such as diagrams, pictures, graphs, and maps. In their study of the reading practices of experts in different disciplines, Shanahan and Shanahan (2008) found that the scientists' (in this case, chemists') reading involved a focus on the transformation of information between prose and visual and graphic forms. The researchers concluded that, in chemistry, graphical and pictorial representations are processed continually during reading and are necessary for understanding the science concepts. As such, another important aspect of scientific reading comprehension is the ability to interpret data presented in text and use multiple representations of information to further learning goals.

In science, creating a coherent representation of a text involves more than integration of sentences; students need to use information in images, charts, and tables to understand text. Comprehension instruction for science texts can support students in understanding pictures, diagrams, graphs, and maps—and to forming connections across text and graphics. Scientific investigations offer genuine opportunities for students to create the same kinds of graphic representations that they are learning to comprehend. In my experience, second graders find it thrilling to record their data—about, for example, the characteristics of their favorite sand samples or their snail's food preferences—on the very same table that a scientist uses in a book they are reading. And as they record their data and then compare it to the scientist's, they develop insider knowledge of graphical representations of science information.

Conclusion

In closing, I want to suggest that we have learned enough about the importance of knowledge and vocabulary development and informational literacy to establish broad consensus about the importance of content-rich instruction in the elementary grades. Situating reading comprehension instruction in science is good for both reading and science—reading deepens science investigations and supports better conceptual understanding in science when combined with firsthand investigations, and science puts reading to work in authentic and knowledge-enriching ways.

While I have suggested that "comprehension going forward" should involve a move toward a more disciplinary-contextual view of reading, I want to emphasize that the genre perspective on reading should not be left behind. It has invited the production of higher-quality informational books for elementary students, and it has urged us to address the complexities of comprehending texts with different features and structures. The genre movement has called us to better understand form-function relationships in text, addressing Louise Rosenblatt's (1980) discontent when encountering a third grade workbook with the following question preceding the poem that the student was about to read: "What facts does this poem teach you?" But we should extend the genre perspective to think more about authenticity of context and purpose, and about the development of coherent knowledge in disciplines. Currently, it is likely that students are learning to navigate informational text genres, but it is also likely that the focus of instruction is on the genre features and structures, rather than on meaningful knowledge development. Meanwhile, time devoted to science is shrinking under the assumption that reading instruction is both more important than and distinct from science. Given the importance of knowledge-building for reading, the continuation of these trends can only mean that reading instruction will ultimately suffer from its position of curricular prominence in isolation from subject matter instruction.

References

Cervetti, Gina N., Marco A. Bravo, Elfrieda H. Hiebert, P. David Pearson, and Carolyn Jaynes. 2009. "Text Genre and Science Content: Ease of Reading, Comprehension, and Reader Preferences." *Reading Psychology* 30: 1–26.

> Reading your chapter reminds me what Steph Harvey said about science and social studies on page 122: "It is the *content* that is seductive." In the many fields of science, we have the most delicious, fascinating, staggering, and sometimes mind-bending array of topics you could ever wish for. If we can't hook kids with invasive species, life on other planets, what happens in a car crash, or climate change—what's the matter with us?
>
> —Smokey

Craig, Madge T., and Larry D. Yore. 1995. "Middle School Students' Meta-cognitive Knowledge About Science Reading and Science Text: An Interview Study." *Reading Psychology* 16 (2): 169–213.

Dorph, Rena, David Goldstein, Shirley Lee, Kathleen Lepori, Steven Schneider, and S. Venkatesan. 2007. *The Status of Science Education in the Bay Area: Research Brief.* Berkeley, CA: University of California.

Fulp, Sherri L. 2002. *2000 National Survey of Science and Mathematics Education: Status of Elementary School Science Teaching.* Chapel Hill, NC: Horizon Research.

Guthrie, John T., Emily Anderson, Solomon Alao, and Jennifer Rinehart. 1999. "Influences of Concept-Oriented Reading Instruction on Strategy Use and Conceptual Learning from Text." *The Elementary School Journal* 99 (4): 343+.

Guthrie, John T., and Sevgi Ozgungor. 2002. "Instructional Contexts for Reading Engagement." In *Comprehension Instruction: Research-Based Best Practices*, edited by C. C. Block and M. Pressley, 275–88. New York: Guilford.

Lemke, Jay L. 1998. "Multiplying Meaning: Visual and Verbal Semiotics in Scientific Text." In *Reading Science*, edited by J. R. Martin and R. Veel, 87–113. London: Routledge.

Maloch, Beth. 2008. "Beyond Exposure: The Uses of Informational Texts in a Second Grade Classroom." *Research in the Teaching of English* 42 (3): 315–62.

Norris, Stephen P., Linda M. Phillips, Martha L. Smith, Sandra M. Guilbert, Donita M. Stange, Jeff J. Baker, and Andrea C. Webber. 2008. "Learning to Read Scientific Text: Do Elementary School Commercial Reading Programs Help?" *Science Education* 92 (5): 765–98.

Palincsar, Annemarie S., and Shirley J. Magnusson. 2000. *The Interplay of Firsthand and Text-Based Investigations in Science Education* (CIERA Report 2-007). Ann Arbor, MI: Center for the Improvement of Early Reading Achievement.

RAND Reading Study Group. 2002. *Reading for Understanding: Towards an R&D Program in Reading Comprehension.* Available at: www.rand.org/multi/achievementforall/reading/readreport.html.

Romance, Nancy R., and Michael R. Vitale. 2009. "Transfer Effects of a Reading Comprehension Strategy on Achievement and Teacher Judgments Across Grades 3–7." Paper presented at the annual meeting of the American Education Research Association, San Diego, CA.

Rosenblatt, Louise M. 1980. "What Facts Does This Poem Teach You?" *Language Arts* 57: 386–94.

Shanahan, Timothy, and Cynthia Shanahan. 2008. "Teaching Disciplinary Literacy to Adolescents: Rethinking Content-Area Literacy." *Harvard Educational Review* 78 (1): 40–59.

Spence, David J., Larry D. Yore, and Richard L. Williams. 1995. "Explicit Science Reading Instruction in Grade 7: Metacognitive Awareness, Meta-cognitive Self-Management and Science Reading Comprehension." Paper presented at the annual meeting of the National Association for Research in Science Teaching, San Francisco, CA.

Whitin, David J., and Phyllis E. Whitin. 1996. "Inquiry at the Window: The Year of the Birds." *Language Arts* 73: 82–87.

CHAPTER TEN

What High School Students Remember About Strategy Instruction

Marjorie Larner

> *I teach because I search.*
>
> —PAOLO FREIRE

"This too shall pass." I've heard this common refrain from teachers for years as yet another directive from above shifts the direction of curriculum or instruction. With each new approach and the increasing urgency to "fix" our schools, my search for what is essential to guide us through the next new approach grows more urgent.

For me, there has been a staying power in the foundation provided by what we've called cognitive or comprehension strategy instruction. This approach to teaching has reverberated through all the years of my work as a coach and consultant, since the days I first sought to bring cognitive strategies and the workshop model to teachers in their classrooms.

Cognitive strategies to teach for understanding have endured for me through all the fads and trends because they offer tools and language that give readers the power to unlock essential mysteries of text and media—as well as hidden aspects of events, ourselves, and other people in the world. I would argue that one of the most important gifts we can offer our students is a capacity to think about what matters in their lives.

The value of this approach has been brought home to me most significantly in my recent work at the Denver Center for International Studies (DCIS), a 6–12 small urban public school serving a linguistically, ethnically (45 percent Latino American, 38 percent European American, 9 percent Asian American, 7 percent African American, 1 percent Native American), economically (50 percent free and reduced lunch), and academically diverse population.

I realized there was a potential wealth of anecdotal data here related to the classroom implementation from instructional coaching provided by Public Education and Business Coalition (PEBC) staff developers in the Denver area when many of these students were in elementary school. Having been explicitly taught to think about and find meaning in their reading text, what was most essential to them? What did they even remember? What endured?

I knew that I had a particularly promising opportunity to learn from students at DCIS, where they are used to voicing their opinions and thoughts on everything from school operations to world events. While the population of students reflects the diversity of Denver and the school is required to comply with district assessments, standards, and curricula, the mission is not typical—it includes preparing students to be "interculturally competent citizens who are actively involved in our rapidly changing world." The school community's core values—integrity, high expectations, diversity, collaboration, and reflection—not only line the hallways on blue banners but also guide classroom routines and the school's daily schedule. Over the course of their years at DCIS, students develop perspectives through their project-based and service learning experiences that often include a real-world purpose.

Walking through the hallways of DCIS, I hear kids more than teachers in nearly every classroom. I see adolescents seeking teachers to talk with during unscheduled times. International and local issues that need attention are posted by kids on walls, lockers, and outside classroom doors—alongside opportunities for service-oriented travel and ongoing

> Hats off to you, Marjorie, for this wonderful paragraph about why we all continue to believe in the power of this work! When kids have repeated chances to grab hold of their reading, the energy for learning empowers them to unlock all that reading holds.
>
> —*Chryse*

fund-raisers to support that travel. They are constantly reminded that what goes on in the world affects us and we can affect what goes on in the world. The hallways are crowded; the kids can be loud. Their liveliness and high spirits are contagious.

When I began a series of conversations with DCIS juniors and seniors to find out if they remembered and used what they'd learned from explicit reading comprehension strategy instruction, I hoped I'd gain new insights to refine my own instructional practice. I was not disappointed. They helped me think about what is essential in teaching kids to think and read so they find meaning and engage in reading in a way that helps them grow as people.

I started each of many conversations by asking students if they remembered learning about reading comprehension strategies and usually found that I needed to prompt their memories with examples. Once they heard specific words or phrases like *making connections, schema, questioning,* and *inferring* many of them not only remembered strategies, but had vivid memories of stopping to track their thinking while reading with sticky notes, reading logs, and discussions. The language of meta-cognition that they had learned was evident in their articulation of memories. Many of them first mentioned and described predicting— though most often the students' memories were evoked if I mentioned text-to-text, text-to-self, and text-to-world connections.

Sapphire and Emma, two girls in their junior year who describe themselves as "not the very best students," got particularly engaged in reminiscing.

Sapphire said, "I like the connection piece of it—some teachers know how to do that for us. A teacher can bring out the best of the book. We read some boring stuff but [our teacher] would explain it. She would act it out. She would tell us her personal experience, real-life situations and relate it to the reading. And you start to question your mentality and your thoughts and think this is how *I* could relate to the book." She took a breath and added, "I think the teacher has to be passionate in the way they want to teach. It's a give-and-take relationship."

This was more than merely modeling a thinking process. Sapphire was talking about the power of making connections at two different and inter-secting levels. By sharing personal experiences, the teacher also established relationships that in turn led the students to be more interested in and attentive to the teacher's thinking when she modeled. Olive, another student, said in a different conversation, "If you are having a personal connection with the teacher, then the teacher can help you make connections." The teacher was not only providing a model but *being* a role model.

Brooke added, "If the teacher gave us an event it related to then I would get it—or an activity—interacting with the text. When I just have to listen with no emphasis on how to make a connection, I'm lost."

While they recalled making connections with some enthusiasm, they also grimaced at the memory of constantly having to stop reading to talk about what they were thinking. "We just wanted to read the book," Emma said.

I told them they were touching on one of our most significant topics for ongoing debate and something I continually watched in my own practice. I recalled years of trying to find a rhythm to my think-aloud interruptions so that I didn't ruin the excitement and connection to the joy of reading. Once that became my clearly defined central purpose, I was able to distinguish a few of the most powerful examples for thinking aloud from all the connections (or questions or images) I could identify. Then I could sustain the group's engagement in the intrinsic enjoyment and value in the act of reading with some powerful instruction included.

Working with high school students who are developmentally quicker to grasp abstract thinking than their younger counterparts made it even more crucial to increase sensitivity to timing—when to continue modeling and knowing when to let go because they're flying on their own.

If our ultimate goal is that students naturally engage in thinking for understanding and to find meaning, as we'd learned naturally proficient readers do, then it is essential to discern when to release them to practice on their own, without intrusion. As Olive said, "Part of reading is creating this world in your mind. [Sometimes] we don't want anything interrupting the creative process that comes naturally."

When asked to recall learning about specific ways to think about reading, Sapphire said, "It was pushed in my mind and my mentality when I was little. I don't remember when I didn't know it. It's like you can't explain breathing. We as human beings would have figured it out anyway. We do it naturally."

However, many students recalled how this once seemingly tedious instruction turned out to help them. They suggested maybe it was necessary to stop and consciously notice their thinking while reading so they'd know how to find their way through when they didn't automatically get it, especially with textbooks in content areas. Bella summed up the general consensus that "Those strategies that you're taught with reading need to be taught with other subjects—make it clear. We use them if we learned them well enough but we don't always know we're doing it, we need to be taught to do it."

They continually returned to making connections, which led to talking about why they read. "I don't think I would have learned to read if it wasn't for the books I read—that's what helped me get reading. I read books about kids who had problems. I could relate to the drama and passion and compassion."

Emma is "fascinated" by World War II and the Holocaust. "I like to think how it [what happened then] is close to our time now—how much we've grown since then. In history, we talked about how this happened. It could happen again. It's people's stories. A lot of people don't know personal stories about other people. I've read about it from the German point of view. I read a book about a Nazi prisoner of war. Another story explained how they [Germans] had to go by the orders to protect their families. There are two sides to a story and to who is a victim. There are victims on both sides."

Sapphire added, "Reading helps you see there are multiple ways to look at something—more than movies, which are about one person—books give you a variety of different subjects."

When students identified the connection with reading texts and thinking about the world, I was reminded of Paulo Freire and shared this quote with them: "We cannot ask children to remain isolated, as though in a glass capsule, while learning to read and write, and only later require them to begin to 'read' the world around them" (Freire 1998).

Students were quick to tell stories and weave hypothetical examples about how they read the world. Sapphire said, "Reading people and emotions—that's why we communicate better as people or why we don't."

Emma said that "especially as children from the Latino culture in the U.S., we make connections with things you know and look around to see what other people are doing . . . with what you see around and other people. Reading people and emotions—that's why we communicate better as people or why we don't."

Sapphire added, "Yeah, we look for context clues all the time—if you don't know what to do, look around you."

Interestingly, it was when talking about reading the world that anyone first talked directly about inferring.

As Emma said, "We use inferences and predict what's in people's heads. I'll be thinking, 'I wonder if she thinks . . . ' Trying to understand

---

Hmmm. I wonder if their continual return to connections stems from their teachers' emphasis on connections over the years? Sometimes we think aloud most about the strategies *we're* most comfortable with . . .

—Debbie

I have witnessed the staying power of the comprehension strategies in myself, yes—but also in the students with whom I've worked over the past decade. I first taught a particular group of kids as primary students, but now work at the secondary level with many of them. I hear language of the strategies when they talk about text, and notice the participatory, investigative manner in which they read. It is fulfilling to see.

—Tanny

reactions of people, their body language, means different things in different cultures. We need to keep an open mind because it could mean something different than it would mean for us in our culture."

Bella had offered specific examples of looking beneath the surface to understand what you see: "When you're reading, you have to pick apart the plot to infer the themes; in a different culture, observe the culture—making inferences about the reason or meaning behind what people do. I have a Mongolian student staying with me. When something drops on our floor she throws it away. Food dropped on her napkin and she threw it away. Then I learned their floors are not clean. They are paranoid about getting sick— won't go outside with her hair wet. It's like when I lived in Bosnia for a month. Because of war when there was pollution from bombs and stuff in the air, they think a breeze will get you sick—they assume bad stuff is in the air."

What the students retained and engaged most in was making sense of what was around them, often beneath the visible surface. Whether it was print, media, or life experience, they want to understand what they need to know—and what, if anything, it suggests for how they should act.

And so, with my next opportunity to work with a teacher and her students in the classroom, I focused on the intersection of reading and understanding text with "reading" and understanding students' experiences in their lives and in the world.

When Susan Marion told me she had a sizable group of students in her English class of twenty-eight who were reading literally while not getting underlying themes and symbolism, I saw an opportunity to explore new possibilities of a classic comprehension strategy lesson in making inferences, which required the use of other strategies (particularly making connections)—and which in turn supported synthesizing.

We started the lesson with an overview of what we were going to do and why we were doing it. I introduced the students to the idea of learning ways we could get more meaning out of our reading. I didn't identify what we were doing as learning comprehension strategies but rather I explained inferring—how it is necessary for us to understand more in a text and that there is a simple process that includes drawing on clues in the text and on what we already know. I invited them to join me in unraveling the mystery of a book that would probably be confusing at first, but we'd look for clues along the way to help us figure out what it was about.

As further context, Susan talked with the kids about understanding what a text is about in the literal sense (such as characters, events, and actions) and what the text is *about* in the bigger sense—in terms of the meaning we take from the theme and message. The students loved her physical gesture as she raises her hands over her head in a small circle for what the book is "about" in the first sense and then in a circle stretching her arms as wide as they will go for what the book is *about* in terms of meaning, themes, and messages. It was touching that these juniors and seniors relied on the anchor of a physical gesture just as the first graders I used to work with had. As we talked, they used the gesture to distinguish the level of understanding they were getting—details and the big picture.

We had realized we'd need a text with a plot and theme that connected to students' personal and school knowledge without being too obvious. We used *Encounter*, a picture book by Jane Yolen, which describes the first meeting between Columbus and the indigenous people of San Salvador (the Taino) through the eyes of a young native boy in the beginning and through his life. Yolen never names the narrator, any other characters, or the setting—though she provides many clues along the way. The narrator begins with an ominous dream that strangers are coming who will bring trouble. The boy tries to warn his people but is ignored as they offer their customary generous welcome with feasts and gifts. The strangers bring trinkets and eventually abduct many of the young natives, including the narrator. He escapes and slowly makes his way home, still trying to convince people along the way of the threat posed by these strangers. In the end he is a defeated old man with a sad story: "May it be a warning to all of the children and all the people in every land."

We distributed the text for each student with the title and pictures hidden so they would have only clues in the text and their own background knowledge to make inferences. We began with the concrete questions about the basic story elements to practice inferring with questions that could be concretely answered—such as "Who are the characters?" and "Where is this taking place?" to get us oriented in the reading as well as in the process of inferring. After the first reading and identification of those basic facts, we planned to go back through those facts to discuss deeper thematic elements.

I read the first two pages before pausing to share a question about the setting and a couple clues as we began to orient ourselves in the story ("I left my hammock and walked to the beach" and "three great-sailed canoes floating in the bay"). On pages 5 and 6, there were many clues about who the strangers might be but I read on, letting the clues linger until page 7 ("Our chief said, 'We must see if they are true men.' The hand felt like flesh and blood, but the skin was moon to my sun"). With this clue, the students started predicting who the natives and newcomers might be. After stopping to share my thinking two times, the students started identifying clues that led to inferences about who and what this story was about.

When the book described the feasting fire, pepper pot, yams, and cassava, Alex's hand shot up: "I think they are Aztecs." From then on, he kept insisting, hopefully, that the book was about the Aztecs. He was particularly convinced when the native's gold nose rings and armbands were described. He brought personal knowledge of Aztecs from his own ancestral background as well as stories and readings in previous years. He tried to match the information in the book to his background knowledge of Aztecs. We could see the expectancy that perhaps this was a book about his people and their culture. He shared so much of his knowledge about Aztecs as he kept finding clues that matched what he knew. As the story unfolded, it became harder for him to hold onto the hope that the people in Yolen's book were Aztecs, when he had to concede that these people lived on an island in the ocean, and he knew the Aztecs did not. In the end, he acknowledged that even though the story wasn't about the Aztecs, it was about people who had a similar story of being conquered and having their culture suppressed.

When we had finished the story, everyone was pretty certain of surface content like place and characters—that it was on an island and the strange newcomers were European explorers or conquerors. We then directed the students to look back through the book for further clues as to what the story was *about*. We added a prompt of looking for repeated symbols of which there are many in this narrative. When Sophia said, "There are lots of threes of things. Three birds. Three men. Three great-sailed canoes." Several students shouted, "It's Columbus! The three ships!" This insight provided a historical context that supported their thinking about an underlying theme. As Ric explained, "The people in one culture, it was their home and they had a strong tradition, really a rule, about welcoming strangers. The new people . . . they were just interested in money. They kind of didn't even notice how the native people acted so nice to them. It made it possible for the strangers to take over." To put it in Alysha's words: "It's about two different cultures meeting and what happens. How one gets taken over by the other." We thought it was time for them to hear the title, and Josh responded, "Oh, it's an encounter between two different ways and which one gets power."

Andrea, who until then had sat relatively quietly by my side, spoke. "This is reminding me," she said, "about how my grandfather from Mexico always said to me over and over, 'Never give up your culture. Hold on to our ways and our language.'" She spoke at length to this group of classmates (whose families have come, many quite recently, from every continent) with a deeper understanding of the relevance and empathy for the urgency of the narrator's message to her: "I think I know more what he's saying now. How he feels."

We showed them the picture of the narrator at the end of the book. Everyone could connect to the sadness and isolation of the indigenous narrator at the end of the story shown in the picture sitting alone on a rock. Even those who didn't have direct experience in their own lives could feel the pain of losing your familiar culture.

The shared emotion evoked by the picture as well as Andrea's story of her grandfather prompted more kids to talk about their own experience, particularly as immigrants to this country, how they navigate through and adapt to values of a dominant culture "different than our own." In many different ways, students said, "That's like my family. It's still happening here." We paused to let students whose families had emigrated from every continent reflect on the experience of encountering a culture overtaking what was familiar in their homes.

As they thought about their own lives, each student had accessed and also expanded their schema for thinking about first contact between indigenous peoples and explorers, between invaders/colonizers and those who already reside on a land, between cultures with different ways of meeting strangers—as well as for the process of finding meaning through the systematic process of analytical thinking. They were exposed to language used when analyzing a text. They had been able to identify character, setting, story arc, and tension as a foundation for a discussion of the possible import of repeated symbols, lingering mysteries, the author's message, and themes.

They were able to transfer their expanded background knowledge and increased capacity for thinking to analyzing Chief Seattle's (purported) letter to Congress, which is one of the essays in the collection used for AP Language exam preparation. Students were more ready to break down this longer, denser, and more complex (though similarly themed) text using the same process of connecting to background knowledge and experience in order to articulate theme and meaning.

When I walked away that day, my excitement as a teacher came not just from the fact that students learned how to use a strategy, but from the lively and confident engagement in conversation that strategy had allowed all students—even those who were not often sure of themselves. Through

> Now we're really teaching! You don't have to fight for kids' "engagement" when you anchor the learning in their own experiences, family, and community. Our ongoing job is to figure out how to find these anchors in all kinds of subject matter.
>
> —Smokey

reading, struggling readers found their way to explore multiple aspects of a significant conflict that impacted their own lives and the world.

Ultimately the results we see and value inspire us to believe and persevere. When we use strategies that lead students to come up with satisfying insights, themes, and messages that matter to how they live—they want to continue. We are engaged when there is something touched inside of us—our common human creativity, the capacity to articulate deeply resonant themes and emotions of life, and an appreciation that is bigger than the sum of our words and our thinking. In an era when many educators are expected to accept prescribed curricula, data-driven instruction, and increasingly lean budgets, it is doubly important to focus on thinking that matters to our students' development as human beings and citizens.

My conversations with students show me that in these rapidly changing times they are capable of thinking and conceptualizing in ways that can leave us, with our old perspectives, in the dust. As Emma said, "We grow up differently now." Yet we grow together in our understanding of the human experience; of the world; of our students' capacity to learn, think, and contribute to the beautiful and seemingly threatened world we inhabit.

> *It is the same for us—whether we are Latin American school-children, students in Asia or university teachers in Europe or America: friend, please never lose your capacity for wonder and astonishment in the world which you regard and in which you live.*
>
> —Paolo Freire

References

Freire, Paolo. 1998. *Pedagogy of Freedom: Ethics, Democracy, and Civic Courage*. Latham, MD: Rowman and Littlefield.

Yolen, Jane, and David Shannon. 1996. *Encounter*. Boston, MA: Houghton Mifflin Harcourt/Sandpiper.

CHAPTER ELEVEN

It's Not Too Late to Be Smart

The Hope and How of Secondary Strategies Instruction

Cris Tovani

Hustling down the hall, with fifteen teachers in tow, I enter an eighth grade reading support class. My job is to demonstrate a thinking strategy so that the students can see how I make sense of an obscure short story. Some observers are more focused on how I'll cover Standard 4 ("Students can compare literature to other works") than how I will teach comprehension. Among the fifteen teachers watching, I know that there are at least four who are pretty sure that eighth graders no longer need reading support— and if they do, too bad because teaching reading isn't their job. There are also a few in the group who seem to think that writing connections on sticky notes is synonymous with strategy instruction. Fortunately, the majority of teachers participating are curious to learn how to better serve their students when it comes to reading instruction. Like the students I'm about to teach, I know that each teacher observing will need something different. I take a deep breath and enter the classroom.

The first time I work with a class I try to discover as quickly as possible what the students already know about constructing meaning. It's been my experience that many kids aren't sure how to use strategies to make sense of text. For them, comprehension is pretty black or white—they read the words and if they get it they move on. If they don't get it, they quit. When I ask students what they do when they get stuck, they usually say that they "Reread or sound it out." Unfortunately, the few who actually do reread don't change how they read. For example, a student may read a page thinking about his soccer game after school. He recognizes that he didn't remember anything so he goes back to reread. Not knowing how to reread differently, his eyes glide over the page—this time instead of thinking about the soccer game, he thinks about the test he's going to have next period. This reader gives up because for him, he knows no other way to help himself.

In order to figure out what kids do when they read, I typically start every first demo the same way. On the board I write *What do you do when you get stuck?* I ask the kids to jot down on a yellow sticky note any strategies or plans they use when their reading doesn't make sense. I model a few responses and say, "If you quit when you get stuck, it is okay to write that. If you ask a question to isolate your confusion, I want to know that too. Anything counts," I say. "Just be honest, because I want to show you new ways to think when you read."

Each time I release students to do this, heads bend down and usually every kid in the room starts to write. Walking around, I peak over their shoulders and I notice that Miguel is staring out the window. He is finished; on his sticky note he has written *I quit.* At the next table a girl named Sienna has written *I think hard and try to focus.* Leonard writes *I look for metaphor.* Before I head back to the front of the room, I notice the kid to my left has written the good old standby *I sound it out.* I am not surprised by their responses. Strangely, these are the very same initial responses I see in almost every school I've worked in.

Recognizing confusion is vital when it comes to monitoring comprehension. Equally important is knowing what to do when confusion sets in. Early in my career I read Frank Smith's seminal work *Understanding Reading*, and remember being struck by the line "Readers hear voices." My life as a student would have been dramatically different had I known that I had the power to control those voices.

> Cris, this is exactly what first graders say, too!
>
> —Debbie

Like the struggling readers I get to teach, when I was a student the voices in my head would stray from the text, especially when the reading was difficult or uninteresting. My mind wandered and it wasn't until someone asked me to do something with the information that I recognized I didn't comprehend it. Rereading didn't help because I didn't change the way I read. I didn't know about thinking strategies, so I had no way to turn off the voices that distracted me. My eyes moved down the page but my mind was nowhere close to thinking about the ideas it held. The process made me feel like I was reading but unfortunately I couldn't remember a thing I read.

Many adolescent readers know when they aren't comprehending. What they don't know is how to help themselves. They believe the label they've been assigned and accept being branded as a struggling reader. They lose hope that they will improve because they have no idea how to read differently. Twenty years ago when I started learning about thinking strategies a whole new world opened up. For the first time I had specific ways to teach my students how to reread and think about text. Once students have an idea how to help themselves, they can begin to reread and think about text in more complex ways. Often I start off modeling how to ask a question to isolate confusion. Sometimes I share how a connection I've made between the book and a life experience helps me to infer the motivation behind a character's action. When my mind wanders or I become confused, I can consciously apply a thinking strategy to dig deeper into the text. Strategies allow me to not only hear the voices in my head but they also empower me to interact with them to construct meaning.

My understanding of what good readers did began with the research synthesis of P. David Pearson and Janice A. Dole et al. Twenty-five-plus years ago, these visionaries made a huge contribution to the reading community by publishing what we fondly referred to in Denver as Chapter 7 (*Developing Expertise in Reading Comprehension*). Their work synthesized years of comprehension research and brought to light a finite list of comprehension strategies used by proficient readers. We started referring to the work as the "Proficient Reader Research." I was intrigued by this synthesis because it focused on strategies used by successful readers. I thought to myself, "If this is what good readers do, then this is what I should be teaching my students." Following is the anchor chart of strategies that I've adapted from Pearson and Dole's research synthesis. I post it in my classroom so that students can see different ways they can think about text.

> **Thinking Strategies Used by Proficient Readers**
>
> A strategy is an intentional plan that is flexible and can be adapted to meet the demands of the situation.
>
> Proficient readers:
>
> - **activate background knowledge** and make connections between new and known information
>
> - **question the text** in order to clarify ambiguity and deepen understanding
>
> - **draw inferences** using background knowledge and clues from the text
>
> - **determine importance** in order to distinguish details from main ideas
>
> - **monitor comprehension** in order to make sure meaning is being constructed
>
> - **reread and employ fix-up strategies** to repair confusion
>
> - **use sensory images** to enhance comprehension and visualize the reading
>
> - **synthesize** and extend thinking

Readers may notice that the above list contains eight strategies whereas other authors in this book may name a different number. No matter how we categorize them, we are all trying to name the same skills.

Thinking Strategies Give Readers a Way to Interact with Text

When reading material is difficult and ideas are complex, strategies give readers a way to interact with text. Too often secondary students surrender when meaning doesn't magically arrive. They write their lack of comprehension off to being a poor reader or they blame it on boring text. All readers, regardless of age or ability, need to know how to proceed when meaning breaks down. Strategy instruction affords them an opportunity to engage deeply with sophisticated content. AP students as well as struggling fifth graders need to know how to talk back to text.

Unlike a scope and sequence, the list of thinking strategies used by proficient readers doesn't change as students progress through the grade

> Since I work with kids at both the primary and secondary levels, I think about this as I plan. Like Cris says, my students need much the same thing, regardless of how many birthdays they've had. They need explicit comprehension instruction and time to practice the strategies—so each reader can learn to hear that inner voice.
>
> —Tanny

levels. What does change is the difficulty and sophistication of the text. For example, all readers need to infer—it doesn't matter if the reader is a first grader trying to make sense of a picture book or a senior trying to make sense of *Anna Karenina*. Strategies are also necessary when readers encounter nonfiction. Chemistry students who are expected to read data must know how to determine importance just as prealgebra students do when reading a graph. As students get older, the texts they read change. However, the need to know how to determine importance or infer meaning while reading doesn't. Knowing that the strategies remain constant is comforting. Every year students are expected to read faster and better. Their reading load increases and so does its difficulty. For this reason it is imperative that each grade level gives students the means and the time to use strategies to engage in complex thought.

When the text is easy and enjoyable, readers construct meaning so quickly that they are often unaware of the strategies they've used. Invariably, however, there comes a time when the reading material becomes difficult or uninteresting and comprehending isn't so easy. It is beneficial in these instances to have an awareness of how thinking strategies are used to enhance meaning. Unfortunately, a lot of students are completely unaware of how strategies can help them.

Some in the field have argued that thinking strategies can actually interfere with reading comprehension. They make a case that there comes a time when they are no long useful to students. I contend that this is a misconception of the work. Here's why. When students are reading at their comfort and interest level, they automatically use thinking strategies to access text. Often the strategies have been internalized and the reader is unaware of how meaning is being constructed. In this case, stopping to apply a thinking strategy would be interference. Unfortunately, most readers don't always get to read at their comfort and interest level, especially during the school day. So knowing when it is time to teach a strategy or let the kids read is tricky. Thankfully a group of fifth graders helped me sort this out.

Years ago, I visited a fifth grade classroom in an affluent part of town. Coauthor Chryse Hutchins was serving as the literacy trainer for the building. She was trying to figure out how to support the fifth grade team who claimed that their students no longer needed strategies. Students kept telling their teachers that they didn't want to record their thinking and complained that it wrecked the reading.

Goodness knows the last thing any teacher wants to do is wreck students' reading. So Chryse dug in and starting conferring with students to

For students learning English as a new language, this time to think about a text and engage in meaningful conversations is a scaffold that helps them more deeply understand what they are reading and writing.

see if she could figure out when the strategies were necessary and when they weren't. She soon discovered that the teachers and kids in these classes were right. They didn't need to stop and consciously apply reading strategies. The students' texts were so easy for them that they were seamlessly incorporating strategies as they read. Stopping to write a sticky note felt like an interruption instead of a tool to deepen thinking. The teachers seemed surprised when Chryse pointed this out. They wondered, "Do kids eventually grow out of needing strategies?" Reading in the comfort zone is extremely important. However, in addition to reading text quickly and effortlessly, students must also be able to make sense of complex, challenging, and sometimes uninteresting material. The fifth graders hadn't grown out of using strategies, but they needed to spend part of each day wrestling with challenging text that would require a more conscious use of strategies. Their thinking needed to be pushed so their endurance could increase.

Chryse explained that strategies weren't really connected to a grade or age but rather to the difficulty of the text. She suggested that the teachers present their students with a more difficult piece of text. If meaning broke down, perhaps the strategies the students had learned how to use would now become useful as they worked to construct meaning. Sure enough— when the difficulty of the text increased, strategies were once again useful. Students and teachers alike stopped complaining.

Thinking Strategies Are Not Activities or Study Skills

Over the last two decades, strategy instruction has become a staple of many language arts curriculums. The comprehension work pioneered in Denver years ago has received both acclaim and criticism. Much of the criticism that our work drew came from outsiders who tried to translate strategy instruction into a program or a formula. When we set out to understand how to teach comprehension, we quickly discovered just how complex the work was. We knew no two readers were alike and therefore no single solution, technique, or strategy could meet the needs of all students. Teaching readers *how* to comprehend, versus *what* to comprehend, is multifaceted. Those who tried to simplify the strategy work and make it formulaic underestimated its complexity.

Those of us who were there in the beginning, many of whom are co-authors of this compendium, know that we've come a long way since those

So true, Cris. Teachers and students will only experience the utility of comprehension strategies if the strategies are put to work in genuine problem-solving situations, as when students encounter truly challenging texts.

— Gina

This happens again and again! Don't you think our work begs the question, "Are children's texts *worthy* of what it is we're asking them to do?"

— Debbie

Why wouldn't Vygotsky's "Zone of Proximal Development" apply equally to older readers? They need to be stretched, off balance a bit in some of their reading and it's under those circumstances that strategy instruction continues to be relevant.

— Ellin

early days. We boldly went into classrooms at all grade levels and tried to "figure out" how research translated into practice. We discovered the importance of modeling our thinking using a variety of text structures. We also learned that if we didn't give students ample opportunities to read and respond to text, the comprehension strategies we modeled would be forgotten the second students left their classroom. Most importantly, we learned that there were no tricks or shortcuts. We needed to find out what expert readers in each subject did when it came to constructing meaning, and to teach those "moves" directly to kids.

When I first encountered Pearson and Dole's synthesis of the comprehension research I remember being stumped by the meaning of the word *metacognitive*. I knew that it was something good readers did but I wasn't exactly sure what it was. I joined a few book clubs and began watching how expert readers constructed meaning. I quickly discovered that teaching students to be metacognitive wasn't about planning fancy activities or using the latest study skills program. It was about showing kids how real readers "collaborate" with the writer in order to construct meaning.

Thinking strategies are not about using sticky notes and highlighters. And they aren't something that just the "low-level" kids need. Strategies are intentional plans that readers use to construct independent thought. It is important that I help my students see that strategies aren't something they just "do" for my class. I want them to see how empowering they can be. I simply define a strategy as a plan that helps people negotiate difficulty and achieve success. I relate the word to something they are familiar with. I mention that they use strategies when they play video games. I give them examples of offensive and defensive strategies used by professional athletes. I point out that they use strategies when they set up their Facebook page so that people will want to read it. I suggest that many of them are even pretty good when it comes to using strategies—as is evidenced by all the different ways they have figured out how to avoid reading. People who are strategic know that the more tools they have at their disposal, the more successful they will be when negotiating difficulty.

> I would add here that strategies aren't just useful in nonfiction text, as some writers have suggested. Strategies enhance meaning across the genre spectrum.
>
> —*Ellin*

Strategists also know that some plans of attack work better than others depending on the situation. "My job as your teacher," I tell them, "is to show you lots of different ways to construct and repair meaning when you are reading and writing." The best strategies, I tell them, are the ones that help readers "talk back to the text." Strategies breed independence because they give readers a way to interact with the words and ideas on the page rather than passively absorbing them. Successful communicators, for example, know that they don't talk to their boss the same way they talk to their child. Likewise, successful readers know they read a novel very differently than they do a word problem. Different text structures require readers to have different conversations. Strategies make those conversations possible.

Knowing how to use strategies to "talk" back to different kinds of text is crucial for older readers. As a secondary teacher and staff developer, I quickly discovered that I couldn't have the same conversation with a textbook as I did with a novel. I remember the science teacher who told me he couldn't afford to "waste" a day of instruction watching me do a reading lesson. He said, "If you are going to come into my room and do this reading strategy business, you better be able to do it with the chemistry book." While trying to read and make sense of that text, I became excruciatingly aware of just how deficient my science reading comprehension skills were. I quickly discovered that the way I "conversed" with fiction wasn't going to help me when it came to "conversing" with a chemistry book. I was in a foreign territory.

Choosing the Right Lens

So to be able to help that chemistry teacher, and improve my work as a staff developer, I've needed to immerse myself in all kinds of text structures that I wouldn't normally choose to read on my own. Over the last several years, I've read chemistry textbooks, electronic manuals, and online instructions. I've read Victorian novels, primary documents, blogs, and political cartoons. I knew from the preparation I was doing for demos that students were encountering unfamiliar text structures and subjects they knew little about. For me there was a bright side to this dilemma. Every day, I got to see what it felt like to be a struggling reader. The challenge I faced was discovering how content-specific teachers used strategies to talk back to their specialized text. I knew for sure that the way I read fiction was only going to carry me so far. If I were going to figure out how to help kids, I needed to seek out my colleagues to learn how they read their social studies, science, math, and technology texts.

Preparing for demos, I frequently struggle right along with the students when it comes to initial reads. However, I differ from them in that I have the ability to help myself when meaning breaks down. I am also constantly improving as a reader, because every chance I get I ask expert readers how they do it. At first colleagues think I'm crazy—"What do you mean, how do I read?" they ask. I explain that I want to know how they

> We so rarely get to struggle as readers and doing so forces us to analyze and more clearly articulate our reading process for students. I think all teachers should put themselves into very challenging reading contexts occasionally. It may be one of the most direct ways to improve our instruction!
>
> —*Ellin*

181

decide what is important. What do they do when they have to read something and they lack background knowledge? I ask them how they know where to start and why they read the diagrams before the words. These questions help me to "see" how they think. I want to know what they understand and why they make the cognitive moves they do.

For example, Lynn (an AP science teacher) spends a good deal of her time reading the graphics in her biology text. She studies the arrows in the diagrams and makes sure that she knows the why and how of each process. If there is something in the diagram that is confusing, she asks a question to isolate her confusion. She uses the question to help her sift and sort important information. Lynn's purpose for reading is to build background knowledge so that she can find an answer to her question.

Merle, an electronics teacher from British Columbia, reads texts that are often blueprints or schematics that describe how to assemble something. He knows that he will have to read a short bit of text and then check his model. He sometimes reads out of order and may have to read one section many times. He says he is a "staccato reader" because he knows he will have to read back and forth between the blueprint and the circuit board many times in order to successfully connect his circuits.

Listening to my colleagues, it didn't take long to notice how differently we all read specific content. Each of us automatically and efficiently knew how to read in our subject area. Since the majority of the reading my colleagues did was in the area they taught, they had internalized strategies that made them unbelievably effective readers. They didn't use a different set of strategies, they had just fine-tuned them. For example, math teachers used inferring when reading data to make predictions about trends. Language arts teachers inferred traits of a character through dialogue. Each teacher knew what to pay attention to and how to locate the important information. The math teacher didn't always start at the beginning like the English teacher did. He knew there were different places to enter a word problem, unlike a novel where starting at the beginning was incumbent upon understanding the plot.

It was fascinating to watch expert readers use their finely tuned knowledge of strategies. They not only comprehended, they also read efficiently. I realized that many teachers weren't aware of how skillful they were as readers. Often secondary teachers tell me that they can't teach reading because they don't know how. I am baffled that they don't consider sharing what they do as readers with their students as reading instruction. This is the most authentic reading instruction there is. Did they think that they needed to make time for "tips and tricks"? Were they so comfortable with their own reading that they forgot what it felt like on a first read? Or were they just unaware of the strategies they used to construct meaning?

The longer I taught secondary students the more I realized that readers at all levels of instruction could benefit from strategy instruction. However, simply "covering" the comprehension strategies isn't enough. The cold, hard truth is that explicit strategy instruction needs to take place at every grade level because each year students are expected to read more and more difficult text. As students progress through the grades not only do they have to read better, they also have to read faster. Knowing how to use strategies flexibly to meet the demands of the reading allows students to not only recognize and repair confusion, it also helps them think more critically about content.

I wanted students in my reading class to take strategies outside of my classroom to help them be more effective readers in their other classes. To do this they needed to "tweak" the strategies like their content-area teachers did. Could they change their reading lenses when they moved from class to class or did they read everything the same way?

Choosing the right lens to view a thinking strategy helps readers engage with unfamiliar text structures. It gives them a way to think intensively about the reading. Sometimes strategies will clear up confusion. Sometimes they provide a way to think beyond the plot or factual information. Strategies help readers create new thinking. When readers are armed with a variety of strategies, they are able to read and think about complex texts with sophistication. The best part about strategy instruction is that readers who have strategies have a plan to construct meaning—so they don't have to wait for someone else to explain what the reading is about. Strategies allow readers to take responsibility for their own meaning making. It is exhilarating for the kid who has labeled himself a "bad reader" to know how to help himself reengage when reading words alone doesn't produce meaning.

Thinking Strategies Offer Hope to Those Who Struggle

I remember having coffee with Stephanie Harvey right before I started teaching high school. I had been an elementary teacher for ten years and worked as a staff developer for the last five. Steph wanted me to be successful—and

> Cris, I'm overwhelmed when I think of the vast number of kids you've helped to make the transition from thinking of themselves as "bad readers" to leading intellectually engaged lives. It makes all that reading of chemistry texts worth it, doesn't it?
> —*Ellin*

also, since she had two high school students at home at the time, she wanted me to do the best job I could. She cautioned me that going to high school meant that I had a responsibility to teach content as well as process. Steph said, "Remember, Cris, you can't think about nothing. The content is the *something* and the strategies are tools that help readers understand. Readers need both—content and ways to access it." For the students who struggle, strategies are a way to get back in the game. They give hope that meaning can be constructed and that it's not too late to be smart, to learn what good readers do. After *Do I Really Have to Teach Reading?* was published, I received an email from a teacher whose words stayed with me long after I deleted her message. She thanked me for my work and then made a request. She was worried and unhappy about the way I referred to strategies as "something good readers did." She feared this phrase undermined students' confidence. She was concerned that if struggling readers knew they were struggling, they would give up. I took her words to heart and at the end of first quarter I shared the email with my students and asked them if they were bothered by the use of my words *good readers*.

CJ looked up from his desk and said, "No. I know what you mean. It's not like you are dissin' us or anything. I just have to keep working on using these strategies to remember what I read because I know I'll need that when I have a job."

Michael chimed in, "I know my reading sucks. Why else would I be in a reading class? At least here I'm learning something besides how to sound out words."

I nodded and waited for more responses. Chris then said, "Yeah, when you never get to take an elective, it's a sure sign that you're not a good reader. Maybe next year, I'll get to take something fun."

Kylie agreed, "Some teachers might think we don't know that we are bad readers, but we do. We see our test scores. I want to get better test scores. Maybe this year I will."

Quietly from the corner come Daniel's words, the most profound of all, "I just wish someone before now would have shown me what good readers did."

Regardless of age or ability, all readers deserve to know how to think when reading words alone doesn't produce meaning. AP students as well as struggling freshmen need strategies to bring them back to the text when their minds start to wander. They need to know how to build background knowledge when they are given a text for which they have none. They need

This story reminds me of the sixteen-year-old boy who said to me one day when I was visiting your room, "Miss, did you know there are books about EVERYTHING?" He just couldn't believe his luck at this discovery after years of being a nonreader.

—*Sam*

to know how to read data so they can draw a conclusion or figure out a theme so they can argue a thesis. Students deserve to be taught what expert readers do.

At the end of the school year, students in my building have an opportunity to express gratitude to their teachers on special cards. Often I would get short notes from students thanking me for showing them how to "get unstuck." Some would write, "I wish I learned how to read like this sooner but at least I will know how to do it next year."

The Equity Issue

Unfortunately, struggling readers aren't given the same opportunities to get smarter as their counterparts in higher tracks are when it comes to engaging with text. Often struggling readers are grouped together and are asked to read texts with controlled vocabulary and watered-down plots. The nonfiction they are given isn't much better. Typically it is an oversimplified version of complex concepts. Sometimes the text is taken away altogether and students have to rely on lectures and note taking in order to get their information. It is evident that the underlying assumption is that thinking critically about difficult text is not something these students are capable of doing.

For teachers who have given up hope that they can teach all students, strategy instruction offers *them* a way to get back in the game, too. Knowing one's content is not enough when it comes to being an effective teacher. Successful educators know that they have to show readers how to interact with their text so they can continue to get smarter about the content when the teacher isn't around to tell them what to think. When teachers are able to weave strategy instruction into their lesson plans to show students how to make sense of the reading, they not only show how smart they are but also how smart their students can be.

When teachers refuse to give time to strategy instruction for fear of not covering all the content, they handicap their students and end up doing all the work themselves. They talk as fast as they can to cover content and then assign reading in hopes that kids will learn the rest. This is frustrating for teachers and students alike because kids don't often learn or retain the material. Teachers complain that students won't or can't read, and students think the reading is a waste of time. Students aren't reading because they have no strategies to interact with text so they don't remember what they've read. Eventually they stop trying altogether.

Thinking Strategies Afford Equity in a Democratic Society

Teaching *all* students how to think critically is an issue of equity. Providing rich text, strategic instruction, and opportunities for all kids to read, write, and discuss has as much to do with equity as does race, gender, or economic class.

I've noticed that the most proficient readers in schools are shown a great deal of courtesy when it comes to instruction. They are usually the ones who get to read and make sense of the best texts. Notes are provided online in case they miss a class or want to review. They get to write about complex ideas and take stances on issues. Class sizes are usually smaller, the texts are usually newer, and because their teachers trust them to think they are given class time to have rich discussions. And because these students often know how to make sense of "grade-level" text, the seasoned veterans clamor to teach them.

The world severely penalizes those who haven't been taught to think for themselves. Giving up on readers who struggle is not an option. "Dumbing down" text and defaulting reading instruction to phonics work-sheets is not an option either. Students whose reading skills begin and end with decoding find themselves at the mercy of others when it comes to constructing meaning. Readers who are armed with thinking strategies are more independent because they know how to help themselves and are therefore more likely to build knowledge and think critically about the world around them.

When students are forced to rely on someone else to tell them what to think, they lose their autonomy. Those who hold the power keep readers who haven't learned multiple ways to construct meaning at bay. Herein lies the inequity. In a democratic society this is not the way schools should be run. All over the country districts are doing "equity work" in an attempt to close the achievement gap. Equity is about giving all learners a way to access information. Regardless of race, gender, or socioeconomic status every student deserves the opportunity to be shown how to make sense of complex text.

Of course, all teachers want their students to be able to think critically when they read. Unfortunately, not all teachers assume responsibility for teaching their students how to do this. For students who have never been given an opportunity to read and wrestle with rich complex text, thinking

> When trusted to connect and react to compelling text, all kids have smart thinking to add to the words on the page. However, after watching a comprehension demonstration lesson, teachers often report, "I never thought they could do that." As Cris points out, our job is to have faith in these readers, surround them with worthy text, model how to help themselves when the reading gets tough, and expect that they can do the hard work of constructing meaning.
>
> —*Chryse*

in sophisticated ways is difficult to do. Critics of strategy instruction posit that consciously applying strategies can inadvertently pull students away from authentic reading. They assume that all readers have been given the gift of strategy instruction and therefore can choose to read strategically. It is not only unreasonable but it is also naive to ask students to construct meaning when they've only been taught how to sound out words. Struggling readers aren't aware that when they don't read actively, they give up their right to think independently and are therefore forced to accept the interpretations of others.

We can't lose faith in our students' abilities to think. All readers, no matter how old, will encounter text sometime in their life that is "above their reading level." It may be a loan agreement or directions on how to use the latest piece of technology. Providing opportunities and time to wrestle with rich text for only some students is an issue of equity. Some kids go all through school never getting the chance to read great works because someone along the way decided they didn't need it or couldn't do it.

Recently, I was signing books after a workshop and I overheard a snippet of conversation from a teacher who was waiting in line. She was bragging that she let her "low students" read best sellers. When she stepped up to the table and handed me her book, I asked her name and what her ninth graders were reading. I was curious to know if in between the best sellers they had an opportunity to read other ninth grade works like *To Kill a Mockingbird* or *Romeo and Juliet*.

The best seller fan said, "No, they won't read that stuff."

"Why not?" I asked.

She looked confused and said, "Well, those books are too hard for my students. They could never read something like *Romeo and Juliet* and understand it. They're not going to need it. They aren't going to college. Most likely they'll go straight into the workforce after high school. It's not like the welders and the mechanics of the future are going to need Shakespeare."

Too stunned to respond, I finished signing her book and wondered how she got to be the one who decided what her kids were going to be when they grew up. I remember my algebra teacher deciding that I wasn't going to need higher-level math. He gave up on me. He decided that carefully scaffolded instruction wouldn't improve my knowledge and abilities, so he gave his time to someone else.

Lack of success doesn't always reflect one's level of cognition. Sometimes students get stuck and they need to be shown other ways to negotiate difficulty. They need a teacher who believes that equity crosses boundaries

If there is a crisis in American schools it is a crisis of low expectations. Cris is right on when she says this is an equity issue. Kids who pass the test get text they can sink their teeth into. Kids who don't get pablum. And then we blame them for not growing as readers. High time that all kids have access to the most compelling texts available and the strategies to understand them.

— *Stephanie*

of race and socioeconomics by giving all kids access to strategic thinking. At fourteen, my life as a mathematician ended. At the time, I was relieved my math teacher recognized that "I couldn't do math." Once I knew that he had given up on me I didn't have to try. Unfortunately, neither did he. Each time I write my quarterly check to my accountant, I curse my high school math teachers. I think about all the money I would be saving if there had been equity of instruction. I would have tried harder if only someone had shown me how to think more strategically.

Not a Fad: It's What Good Readers and Writers Do

Years ago, while attending a summer writing workshop that featured Donald Graves, I discovered that the work we were trying to do in Denver with reading strategies was very similar to the work Don and his colleagues were doing with writing at the University of New Hampshire (UNH). We were both trying to figure out how real readers and writers constructed meaning. Pearson and Dole's synthesis informed us of strategies used by real readers. Don's work taught us about the work of real writers.

- Real writers write. We learned that in order to be a good writer we too had to write—and our students learned the same.

- Real writers need time to draft. We learned that we needed to carve out blocks of time during the day so students had time to write.

- Real writers crave useful feedback. We learned that we needed to collaborate with our students by showing them our writing and giving them opportunities to share their writing with peers.

- Real writers have mentors. We learned that we could use our writing and our thinking process to mentor our students. We also learned that we could find mentors in published works and that we could study what published authors did in order to improve our own craft.

As a young teacher I was surprised by how simple this way of teaching writing sounded. I couldn't believe how freeing it was—no grammar sheets for me to design, no gimmicky prompts like "Describe your life as a pencil" to come up with. Basically all I had to do was teach kids what real writers did. It seemed too simple to work. Little did I know I had confused simplicity with authenticity.

Over the years, I had the privilege of getting to know Donald Graves on a more personal level. Often we spoke at the same conferences, so naturally I took every opportunity I could to learn from him. One afternoon, sitting in a deli waiting for our sandwiches to arrive, I told Don that I was making the move from elementary to high school. I was worried that this grade change would prevent me from using what I had learned from the "Proficient Reader Research." I handed him the list of strategies and asked him point blank how I might incorporate them in with my new teaching assignment. Don perused the sheet and quickly recognized that the list of strategies were things he himself did as a reader. He compared it to the writing work being done at UNH. He smiled and said "I think this research will fit nicely with your new job."

I don't know if impatience or panic took over, but I abruptly asked "How?"

Don smiled and said, "It seems to me that there isn't one thing on this list that a reader could do without learning or at least thinking about the reading material."

"What do you mean?" I asked.

"Well, a reader can't ask a question if he hasn't thought about the content. He can't make a connection or synthesize a new idea either if he hasn't thought about material. It seems to me that even if the text doesn't make complete sense to students, they will at least have a strategy to think about the reading."

I knew from my own history as a fake reader he was right. In the past when I had encountered difficult text, I would read the words and think about something unrelated to the text. I needed a way to bring my mind back to the page I was reading. A strategy would have done this for me. I could have said, "OK, brain, you might not get this whole thing—but at least you can ask a question or make a connection." Knowing how to use those simple strategies would have forced me to interact with text. I might not have completely comprehended what I was reading but at least I would have been on the road to constructing meaning.

After talking to Don, I realized that this simple list of comprehension strategies could be the crux of my reading curriculum. In content-area classes the strategies would be a way for me to show students how to access challenging text. I knew as a high school teacher I would be expected to not only cover content but also raise reading scores. Showing students how to use the "Proficient Reader Research" was a way for me to teach kids how to be better readers so teachers could cover more of their content.

> Cris, thanks for reminding me of how much we all owe Don Graves, and how we miss his patience and wisdom. You were so lucky to be mentored by him face-to-face; but he also guided thousands of others almost as powerfully in his books, speeches, and simply by his way of being in the world.
> —Smokey

Being able to "talk back to the text" empowers readers beyond the school day. When I began teaching adolescent readers, I discovered a lot more students than I expected who didn't know how to help themselves. Often their confusion caused them to stop reading altogether. Sadly, many report this happening as early as fourth grade—and interestingly enough it coincides with the last book they admit to having read. Students who don't know how to help themselves quickly learn how to fake their way through text by listening to class discussions, finding other students who actually read and understand, or simply accessing *SparkNotes* online. Struggling readers "fake read" just long enough for the teacher to move on to something else, hoping all the while that the next assignment they get will be easier to read. They do it to survive.

What a Long, Strange Journey It Has Been

For the last decade, I've been a hired gun, paid to convince and show secondary teachers that their students can benefit from strategy instruction. For many, seeing is believing. This is why I frequently find myself in content-area classrooms, demonstrating how to read difficult text in front of skeptical teachers and eye-rolling teenagers. The bottom line is that our last chance rests with the critical readers we grow today. If we truly want all students to pursue a rigorous course of study, then it's up to us to show them how to access challenging text. We must show them different ways to think when they read—and be willing to sacrifice some content so they have time to read, write, and think.

Constructing meaning requires more of readers than simply reading with expression. It also takes time, effort, and knowing how to think strategically. All over the country I've met defeated middle school and high school readers. For this reason, I've staked my teaching reputation on strategy instruction. The "Proficient Reader Research" demonstrates to these readers that it isn't too late for them to become better comprehenders.

It pains me when students tell me they have never known what it feels like to be lost in a book. Lacking confidence, they fear to venture outside their area of interest or read above "their grade level." I am equally sorry for the readers who travel through the grades never challenged to read, discuss, and critically think about challenging text. For these students, thinking strategies can be a downright nuisance. I am concerned for those who are always told what to read. These students are lulled into thinking that they can read everything comfortably unaware that strategies could open up new doors to more sophisticated text.

Knowing how to get unstuck is empowering. When a reader has the agency to construct meaning they don't have to wait for someone to tell them how to think. Comprehension strategies are plans that readers have at their disposal so that they can access and acquire knowledge. They are not simply a set of study skills reserved for the kids who will "never go to college," nor are they to be reserved for students reading sophisticated texts in honors classes. They are for everyone.

When I left first grade to teach high school, people asked me what the biggest difference was between primary kids and high schoolers. At first, I thought it was strange to reply that the two age groups had so much in common. Both needed strategy instruction. Both needed time and opportunity to construct meaning. Choice drove their engagement, and both age groups craved opportunities to respond to their reading and share thinking. One day the real difference finally dawned on me. Older readers need hope.

Access to meaning is at the heart of equity. Teachers have the potential to be "gatekeepers, gate-closers, or gate-openers." Each one gets to decide who they will be. Too many adolescent readers are defeated. They are the ones who never got a chance to read in the comfort zone. As a matter of fact, I've never met a struggling high schooler yet who actually wanted to read. At the beginning of the year, I can tell these kids are dramatically different from the first graders I used to teach. They have lost their confidence and their desire to read. Looking into their eyes I ask myself, "What happened to those first graders who were once 'chompin' at the bit' to make sense of text?" Somewhere in those lanky teenage bodies I know there lives a bit of that little kid who knew reading well would mean having power and access to the world.

I smile when I think of those eager first graders. They *all* wanted to learn to read and they trusted their teacher to show them how. With a little strategy instruction—who knows, maybe that first grader in each of our students will reemerge.

> Yes! And young readers need hope, too. Can you believe that even some six- and seven-year-olds believe they'll never learn how to read? Yikes, huh?
>
> —Debbie

CHAPTER TWELVE

Meaning Is Everything

Comprehension Work with English Language Learners

Nancy Commins

It is not news to anyone reading this chapter that the linguistic diversity in U.S. classrooms is increasing. As demographics shift and the pressure to raise performance scores rises, providing high-quality and appropriate instruction to second language learners becomes increasingly important. The vast majority of English language learners (ELLs) in this country are Spanish speakers, though they also come from dozens of other languages and cultures. These students represent a wide range of linguistic, cultural, and socioeconomic profiles with varying levels of bilingualism and prior academic experience. Some are already literate, and a very small percentage will receive literacy instruction in school in their primary language. For most ELLs in this country, initial literacy instruction will be through English—a language they do not yet understand or speak well.

The current understandings surrounding literacy development in most classrooms are based largely on how native English speakers learn to read in English. This is not surprising since, until very recently (and-still today), most teachers are prepared as if they are going to work exclusively with native English speakers (Commins and Miramontes 2006). Addressing the needs of ELLs has been an afterthought and mainly addressed in additional endorsement programs. Especially when teachers have experienced success working with native speakers, they can easily feel that they just need to slightly adjust what they are doing to work with second language learners.

There are many resources that provide excellent guidance regarding best literacy practices for ELLs.[1] Though these texts have been aimed at and pitched to mainstream classroom teachers, in my experience they are read mainly by ELL and bilingual specialists. In the absence of deeper understandings of second language development, classroom teachers are usually encouraged to focus on the similarities and gloss over the differences between literacy development in first and second languages. When this happens, critical aspects of what second language readers need are missed.

Too often, little thought is given to how approaches to reading (and comprehension strategies in particular) depend on certain funds of ideas, words, and even grammatical structures to express them. Even though second language readers might be able to decode English text, they might not have sufficient knowledge of English to bring meaning to it or cannot connect the words on the page with the knowledge they do have. Especially for students learning to read solely through their second language, different approaches are needed and additional steps taken before students can handle (and benefit from) text in the same way as native speakers.

Over the years, I have been guided by Spindler and Spindler's (1988) advice to educational ethnographers to try to "make the familiar strange." The intent of this chapter is to do just that—to try to uncover what we take for granted when we work with second language learners based on our knowledge of students becoming literate through English as their primary language.

I don't pretend to be an expert in the area of literacy instruction or comprehension strategies per se. It is humbling to find myself in the company of so many of the leading experts in this area who have contributed to this volume. The reading methods course I took as a teacher candidate consisted mainly of how to make the best use of the teacher's guide for the basal reading series currently in vogue at the time. But my thirty years of working with ELLs and preparing their teachers has provided

---

[1] See for example Cappellini (2005), Escamilla and Hopewell (2009), Freeman and Freeman (2008), Gibbons (2002, 2009), Cloud, Genesee, and Hamayan (2009), and Peregoy and Boyle (2005).

me with many insights into what works and what doesn't. During this time, I have read extensively, watched and learned from teachers, and listened to my colleagues.

I have also successfully taught many children to read with meaning— almost all of whom were learning to read through their second language, many of whom were refugee students with no prior literacy experiences. What I have come to believe is that regardless of theoretical orientation, if instruction for second language learners is based on what works for native English speakers with either slight adjustments or no thought at all to the fact that the task might need to be approached differently, ELLs are unlikely to make the kind of intellectual and academic progress we would hope for. The difference can be summed up as follows: when students are reading in their primary language, text acts as a doorway to meaning and new information; however, for students learning to read in a second language, meaning is the key that unlocks the door to comprehending the text.

Some of the fundamental aspects of good literacy instruction do hold true across languages. It is important that the learner knows and can make use of the different cueing systems, reads for meaning rather than decoding alone, and experiences a gradual release of responsibility (Pearson and Gallagher 1983). But the ultimate goal of all this instruction is for students to access and express meaning and deepen thinking (Goudvis and Harvey 2005; Harvey and Goudvis 2000; Perkins 1993). Every comprehension strategy depends on a fund of concepts, as well as vocabulary and grammatical knowledge that readers rely on to make sense of the text in front of them.

It is especially important that literacy instruction for students learning through their second language be based on the understanding that "meaning is everything." Second language students will require much more extensive attention to language development than is required for native speakers. In order to comprehend text, they will need to have a strong command of the concepts, words, and language structures utilized in the reading material. It will be easier to learn to read and derive meaning when students already have had practice in talking about and understanding the big ideas and vocabulary represented in the text.

> This entire chapter screams out equity to me. Good instruction involves responding to individual student needs and designing instruction that targets those needs. But over and over, kids who score below grade level on standardized tests are forced to sit in their seats, listen to a teacher and fill in bubbles and blanks. While kids who score high are sent off to read, write, question, discuss, inquire, and research, all acts that lead to diverse, flexible thinking, deeper understanding, knowledge acquisition, and ultimately power. Every child deserves this.
>
> — *Stephanie*

Creating the Appropriate Mind-set: Combating a Deficit Perspective

ELLs are too often characterized for what they can't do rather than for what they can. I despair when I hear teachers say that second language learners don't know anything because they can't yet express what they do know in English. I shudder every morning when the underwriting announcement on my public radio station reminds me that children need to be reading by third grade. I know that many of those not at grade level are ELLs who are actually making appropriate growth for their level of English proficiency, but all anyone cares about is that their scores are low and (worse) they are making the school look bad. It is the children who are stigmatized and not the kind of instruction they have received. What we most need are teachers, at every grade level, who can work on cognitive development and teach important concepts whether or not their students can already read well—or do so in English.

Political debates surrounding the education of language minority students often center on the efficacy of bilingual education and which language should be used in instruction to assure that students can succeed academically. While I am a staunch advocate for primary language instruction, it is not a question of which language is better, but rather what opportunities are provided and what strategies are most appropriate given the language of instruction. The public—including many teachers—sees English as the only important vehicle for learning and expressing knowledge. They generally devalue, minimize, and dismiss what children bring with them in their primary language.

An asset orientation recognizes that second language learners arrive at school with the essential fund of language that English speakers come with, encoded in their primary language (Miramontes, Nadeau, and Commins 2011). It values students' language and culture as a foundation upon which to develop concepts, literacy, and higher-order thinking skills and affirms that students actually do know a lot. In every type of program or approach to literacy instruction, teachers can honor and build on what students bring with them in their first language and find ways to tap into and strengthen their conceptual development through both languages. This means viewing students' families and communities as resources for deepening conceptual development, regardless of the level of literacy in the home.

Because ELLs must comprehend new material and master a new linguistic code, simple exposure to the target language is not enough to guarantee success. Second language learners require many, many hours of exposure to both oral and written input that is meaningful to them and that they can comprehend. Without special attention to making things understandable, an all-English environment can be nothing more than incomprehensible sound. Because second language development in schools is a multidimensional process, a broad range of experiences and

> We must move away from this mind-set and find ways that allow our students who are learning English to express what they do know, because their minds are full of exciting, interesting, and dynamic information that we won't be privy to if we don't invite them to share it!
>
> — *Anne H.*

opportunities is required to gain full academic and social proficiency (Gibbons 2002, 2009).

CONCEPTUAL RESERVOIR

To better understand the nature of learning through two languages, it can be helpful to think of the brain as a kind of "conceptual reservoir" as represented in the figure below. This conceptual reservoir can be accessed and added to through any language a person knows. Monolingual speakers will always add to their conceptual reservoir and represent what they know through their one and only language. The pathways in are receptive—listening, observing, exploring, reading, and imitating. The pathways out are the productive representations of thought and ideas—speaking, writing, artistic expression, and physical movement. In Figure 1 the arrows labeled *L1* (primary language) show these pathways going in and out of the reservoir. People can develop a shallow or a deep reservoir. As we learn more, the pathways in and out grow stronger. As the pathways strengthen, the ability to take in and represent more information increases.

As educators, our job is not just to teach students to read and write well, but rather to fill the conceptual reservoir as deeply as possible whether students can read and write—or not. Reading and writing are simply a means to the end of conceptual development. They are among the ways of accessing and adding to the reservoir, but they do not constitute the reservoir itself. Decoding is on the pathway; understanding an author's intent is in the reservoir. Comprehension is not about the text itself—the words on the paper or screen—but more importantly how students are given

Figure 1 Conceptual Reservoir

Using both languages

Conceptual Reservoir

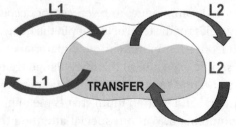

From *Restructuring Schools for Linguistic Diversity, 2nd Edition* by Ofelia B. Miramontes, Adel Nadeau, and Nancy L. Commins. Copyright © 2011 by Teachers College Press, Columbia University. Published by Teachers College Press. Reprinted by permission of the publisher.

access to the *ideas* represented in the print. This is a critical understanding if we are to move forward with work on comprehension with English language learners. Conceptual development is greatly facilitated by literate behaviors, but it can also be developed when students interact with concepts orally and physically, mediated by visual images, models, diagrams, charts, and pictures. Every important cognitive skill can be worked on, deepened, and extended *without text*—it just takes careful planning on the part of the teachers.

When people begin to learn a second language, they don't start a new reservoir—rather, they begin to express what they already know and understand through the new language. In Figure 1, on page 196, this is the arrow coming out of the reservoir labeled *L2* (second language) at the top of the figure. It is also possible to learn new information through a language you do not yet speak well, as is represented by the arrow labeled *L2* going into the reservoir at the bottom of the figure. To successfully add to the conceptual reservoir through a second language takes the combined effort of learner and teacher. Teaching on the second language pathway begins with the concepts students have to learn and not what they will read to learn them.

The Conceptual Reservoir and Full Academic Proficiency

Unfortunately we live in an era when mandated accountability measures equate academic success with a single score on a high-stakes test. The emphasis on test scores causes the public and many educators to lose sight of the fact that our goal should be to prepare children to become independently functioning adults, and only a narrow portion of this goal is currently tested.

Consider the kinds of tasks successful students in schools and capable adults must be able to accomplish: handle topics at a conversational level that are contextually supported; state positions and explain and defend them simply and clearly; articulate and develop subtle and complex ideas orally and in writing; answer questions and engage in spontaneous interchanges about a variety of technical and nontechnical topics, and so on (Commins and Miramontes 2005). For most of us, just dealing with a fully familiar topic in a second language is a challenge. To be successful in school and beyond, individuals must be able to operate in settings where the cognitive demand is high and the language requirements are complex. In order to have full opportunities to succeed, ELLs must develop linguistic and sociolinguistic competence similar to that of native speakers at the same time that they are acquiring academic skills and learning the content of the curriculum.

In response to the narrowing of the curriculum and overemphasis on test scores, I have surveyed hundreds of educators about what it means to be academically competent and literate in the world. The responses provide a detailed picture of what we would hope all of our students accomplish and can be thought of as constituting the conceptual reservoir and its pathways in and out. The responses invariably fall into the five categories presented below. Included are some of the descriptors from the many people surveyed.

- **Academic Skills:** read and comprehend a variety of materials; write for a variety of purposes and audiences; is technologically competent and demonstrates knowledge of the big ideas and enduring understandings of science, math, social studies, and beyond; fill out a job application; get into college

- **Higher-Order Thinking Skills:** think critically; solve problems, express opinions, and persuade others; infer and predict; analyze, explain, interpret, process, synthesize, apply, and reformulate information

- **Self-Efficacy:** ferocious curiosity; know where to go for help or to find needed information; high expectations of self; desire to achieve; advocate for oneself, have ambition; live independently; be flexible in new situations; anticipate future needs; be a lifelong learner

- **Civic Participation:** effective citizenship; responsible; keep up with political and technical changes in the world; be a productive member of society; go back and make a difference in the community; help change the world for the better; understand that actions have consequences

- **Intercultural Competence:** confidence to go forth into a diverse and changing society; can function anywhere and work cooperatively with others; bilingual and bicultural; has the social skills to work and live with, care about, and learn from people different from oneself; understand and respect cultural differences; see from multiple perspectives

These descriptors go far beyond the ability to "read and write." Yet in so many classrooms, literacy instruction has been narrowed to the first

> We have a parallel conversation when we talk about native English speakers learning another language. It is not just learning vocabulary and how to use the past tense but also about the particulars of how and what that language leads you to see and express your thoughts and feelings.
>
> —*Mayra*

descriptor and is measured by the ability to read and answer questions about previously unseen text, usually at the most superficial level. Teachers, whose performance increasingly is being measured by how students do on the tests, tend to reduce their instruction to similar kinds of activities. Ravitch (2010) has suggested that

> instead of the current wave of so-called reforms, we should ask our-selves how to deliver on our belief that every student in this nation should learn not only basic skills, but should have a curriculum that includes the arts, history, geography, civics, foreign languages, math-ematics, science, physical education, and health. But instead of this kind of rich curriculum, all they are getting is a heavy dose of high-stakes testing and endless test preparation. And as the stakes in-crease for teachers and schools, there will be more emphasis on test prep and not what children need (6).

This narrowing of the curriculum ignores the broader and more important conceptualization of comprehension as an aspect of thinking and not a reading strategy.

Learning in Linguistically Diverse Settings: Understanding the Different Pathways

Figure 2 is another way of representing the construct of the conceptual reservoir. The person at the end of the road embodies all the characteristics and skills of the academically literate person described on page 198. The arrows have become pathways with the intent of portraying what happens when students are learning through more than one language. The pathway on the left is the road taken by native speakers learning in their first lan-guage and represents the typical practice for native English speakers in schools today. It is also the pathway for ELLs in bilingual programs when they are learning in their primary language. The second language pathway on the right, which also leads to academic competence, constitutes best practice for second language learners—strategies and approaches that from the outset account for language proficiency and cultural diversity. Students who are able to receive quality instruction in school through both their pri-mary and second languages have a good chance of becoming academically bilingual. This can enhance their cognitive functioning (Diaz 1983; Grosjean 1989; Hakuta 1986) and put them at a distinct advantage over monolingual English speakers, no matter how well educated they are.

Figure 2

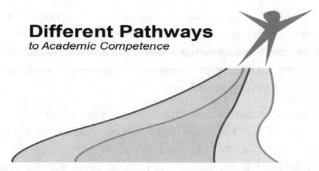

Different Pathways
to Academic Competence

From *Restructuring Schools for Linguistic Diversity, 2nd Edition* by Ofelia B. Miramontes, Adel Nadeau, and Nancy L. Commins. Copyright © 2011 by Teachers College Press, Columbia University. Published by Teachers College Press. Reprinted by permission of the publisher.

It is easy for teachers to overlook the fact that, even if instruction is only in English (as is the case for most ELLs in this country), second language learners are traveling with feet on both roads. Students will always be attempting to make sense of the content through any language they know. To improve literacy instruction (and specifically comprehension) means building on this understanding and seeing the relationship between the two languages as a springboard, not a deterrent. In linguistically diverse settings it should be our goal and intent to help students learn to deepen and express what they know through any language they can speak.

Particularly in the upper grades, teaching methods appropriate for native speakers such as reading textbooks and listening to lectures are still the main ways that students are expected to gain knowledge. This works for literate, motivated speakers of the language of instruction. But if you don't read well, or fluently speak the language of the text, your level of language and literacy skills act as a barrier to the information. Too often, when students are unable to make sense of the text on their own, they are not provided opportunities to work on the concepts that are represented in print or strengthen the schema upon which they can draw. Instead they are treated to remediation—focused on the discrete aspects of print, often in front of a computer with little or no adult interaction. In this way, the text acts as a limiting factor and keeps students from working at their level of cognitive understanding.

We often describe academic work as falling into the categories of oral language, literacy, and content-area knowledge. I have found it more useful to view every academic task or moment as having three intertwining aspects—the conceptual understandings of the activity, the ways in which we talk about those ideas and concepts, and the interactions students will have with the ideas and concepts in print. Appropriate instruction on the second language pathway can be summed up as follows: beginning with the ideas and conceptual understandings, make intentional connections regarding how we talk about them and the text we use to represent them through the use of visual images, movement, modeling, and demonstration.

Best practice for second language learners requires that teachers do whatever is necessary to make the content accessible and comprehensible while providing students the opportunity to interact with, connect to, act on, talk about, read about, and write about important ideas and information. To teach on the second language pathway is not to dumb down or reduce expectations or teach what is easy. Rather it requires differentiation along multiple dimensions, having determined how to make understandable for the students what is deemed most important for them to learn.

Of course the two pathways overlap—but for the second language pathway, planning must begin with the conceptual understandings students are to acquire *and* the language used to talk about them within a culturally affirming context. Teachers then can choose a variety of activities and texts to convey those ideas and practice the language. They should plan for and link a variety of meaning-enriched opportunities to use language and learn concepts throughout the school day (Miramontes, Nadeau, and Commins 2011).

Especially in all-English settings, it is incumbent upon teachers to encourage students to take what they know in one language and express it through the other. All educators must affirm the importance of the primary language for learning regardless of program type—and recognize that learning through the primary language will strengthen learning through the second. This will require advocating that family and community members continue to use their strongest language with their children—usually the primary language—to deepen understandings and help build schema.

Teaching well through a second language coincides with what we know about multiple modalities and intelligences (Gardner 1993) and the need to work on thinking. According to Harvey and Goudvis (2005),

> like writing, reading is an act of composition. When we write, we compose thoughts on paper. When we read, we compose meaning in our minds. Thoughtful, active readers use the text to stimulate their own thinking and to engage with the mind of the writer. . . . Comprehension strategies . . . serve to help readers construct their own

> Building conceptual understandings while simultaneously teaching language structures provides students who are learning English the tools to actively participate in discussions about content and share their own background knowledge around the subject.
> — *Anne H.*

> meaning and interact with the text to enhance understanding and acquire and use knowledge. (14)

According to David Perkins (1993), "Understanding a topic of study is a matter of being able to perform in a variety of thought-demanding ways with the topic, for instance to: explain, muster evidence, find examples, generalize, apply concepts, analogize, represent in a new way and so on."

These same understandings guide the work with ELLs—however, on the second language pathway, words alone are not sufficient to represent the thinking and understanding. All these authors encourage teachers "to make thinking visible" but visibility must go beyond the written or spoken word. The concepts need to be formulated through images and movement as well.

It takes a different approach to adequately prepare second language learners to work on the ideas and understandings in the text. Pictures may first need to be the vehicle for introducing words and even concepts they have never used before. It may take multiple exposures for second language learners to activate the necessary background knowledge and be able to express their understandings through English. If they haven't heard and spoken the words many times before, they will have no idea if something "sounds right" or be able to connect the words to the understandings that are in their conceptual reservoir.

While some think that to modify instruction to account for understandings of language acquisition is an additional burden, in reality adaptations intended for second language learners will enhance instruction for all students (though not necessarily the other way around). The key in a linguistically diverse environment is that teachers always mediate understanding by building the conceptual understandings in the text through visual imagery and oral discussion, not just the written word.

Making the Familiar Strange: Teaching on the Second Language Pathway

The examples below are intended to help you examine how your assumptions about what works for native speakers apply or don't to second language learners. One of the reasons it is hard for teachers to understand the challenges faced by second language learners is that once we can read, it is nearly impossible not to make sense of the print placed before us if it is in a language we understand.

Example One

To illustrate, look at but *do not read* the two indented lines below. *Put your eyes on the words for only three seconds, but do not read them. Then cover them up right away and keep them covered as you read on.*

> Every afternoon, Mary comes home from work,
> sits on her front porch and eats chocolate

Now, with the words covered and without having "read" the lines, think about what you gleaned in those three seconds. My guess is that you can answer the questions "Who?" "What?" "Where?" "When?"—and even predict "Why?" The point is that once we can make sense of text, it is literally impossible not to do so and thus we become blind to the process many of our students are going through.

Example Two

Many teachers try to organize the print in their room to make it more accessible to students, often using word walls organized in alphabetical order. The question is, will this be sufficient if students can decode—but don't yet understand and speak the language well?

A mini–word wall such as this short list of simple words in Hebrew (see Figure 3) may be used.

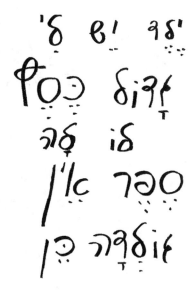

Figure 3

Figure 4

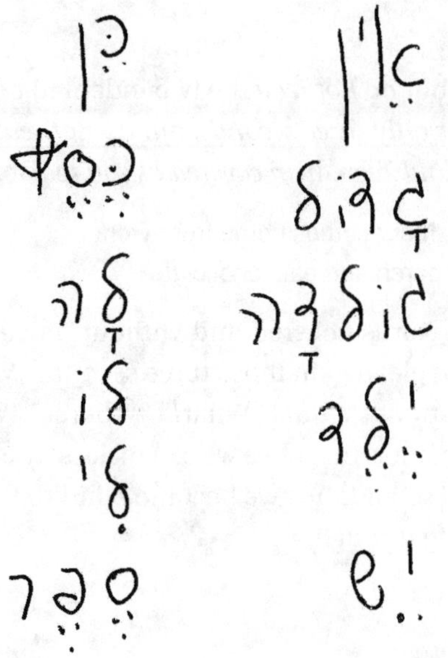

In the second list (Figure 4) they are in alphabetical order—does that help you make sense of the text?

Now see if you can make sense of the same text with visual clues in Figure 5.

Figure 5

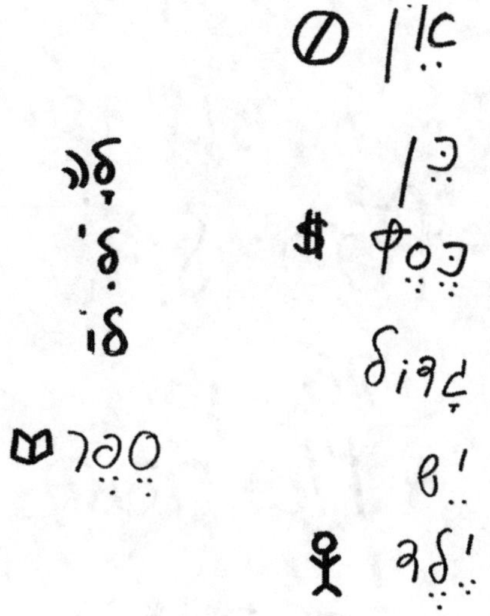

Example Three

What follows is transliterated Hebrew (including some of the same words as on the previous page) to demonstrate what happens when second language learners who can decode try to comprehend text in English. Read the sentences below and see what sense you can make of them.

> Yaish lee kesef, ayn lee sefer
> Yaish lee sefer, ayn lee kesef

People like me, who were raised having to learn Hebrew for religious purposes, may recognize some of the words when they are pronounced. But because the words are not from the prayers so many of us learned by rote, there are few clues to their meaning. Yet a native Hebrew speaking kindergartener would likely have little difficulty decoding or comprehending the same words in Hebrew in Figure 6. Think about what kind of support you would need to comprehend them on your own.

Many teachers say they do make adjustments to account for the needs of second language learners. For example, they tell me that during guided reading, when they do a "picture walk," they extend it by naming more of the objects in the pictures. Talking about the pictures before reading is intended to stimulate connections and preview what students are likely to encounter in the text. Native speakers, for the most part, will meet words,

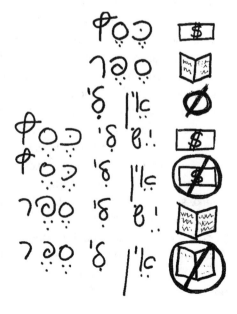

Figure 6

Nancy, the Hebrew examples totally knocked me out! Definitely one of those laugh-or-cry insights. We teachers, full of sincerity and good intent, try to do the right thing. But if we don't deeply understand the challenges language learners actually face, we aren't helping, and may even make things worse. Thanks for the wake-up call.

—Smokey

language functions, and grammatical structures they already have in their linguistic repertoire. The picture walk activates schema and brings to mind words that may not be in the text but that add cohesion to the ideas. This is happening to varying degrees with the second language learner as well, but not necessarily in English.

If there are only one or two unfamiliar words in the whole text, a small adjustment may be effective. However, when each page represents several new words and possibly an unfamiliar—even if simple—grammatical convention (possessive pronouns, irregular plurals), spending just a few extra minutes extending the picture walk may not be sufficient to tap into what students do know but are not yet able to talk about in English. This minor adjustment does not allow students sufficient time to generate the language used to represent the ideas and build the vocabulary, concepts, and schema needed to successfully comprehend the text in English. While short texts may seem like they should be simpler, in fact the lowest-level books may be the most challenging to second language learners because they don't provide enough natural language to be comprehensible and the students can't automatically supply it on their own.

In my experience, most teachers rely on leveled books to organize and drive guided reading, without giving thought to what separates different levels of text. They accept that the leveling means something because an "expert" has said so. Generally, the leveling has less to do with the ideas in the book than the features of the text itself. What makes a Level D different from a Level K is related to graphophonic regularity, how many syllables the words contain, how long the sentences are, the types of clauses, and so on.

For a second language learner, the levels are not reliable indicators of their ability to read and comprehend text—knowing the content makes all the difference. Their literacy instruction needs to account for a spiral and not a linear growth pattern. Depending on background experience, a second language learner may know what a multisyllable word means (*umbrella, super soaker, vacation*) but not a phonically regular one syllable word (*wax, skim, peep*). ELLs may be able to understand and read fluently a Level P book about a familiar topic, but when a new topic is introduced may only initially be able to make sense of Level J. They may be able to discuss the ideas of a chapter book read to them, but not comprehend the text on their own. The more experience students have talking about the content of what they are going to read and interacting with the concepts physically and visually before they set their eyes on the text, the more likely they will be able to comprehend it.

I am a strong advocate of proficiency level differentiation (Gottlieb, Katz, and Ernst-Slavit 2009; Miramontes, Nadeau, and Commins 2011), creating a time for all students to work at their level of literacy (and language) on aspects of text (and features of language) as a part of an overall instructional plan. It is critical, though, that this not become a way to separate students onto different thinking and conceptual paths. An unintended consequence of organizing substantial portions of literacy instruction according to reading levels and not around a cohesive set of ideas represented in the different levels of text is the disruption of the sense of community in the classroom. Proficiency level differentiation that is anchored in a thematic approach to instruction allows students with different levels of literacy and language proficiency to communicate about important ideas and see each other as knowledgeable supports. One way to accomplish this is to have common culminating activities for the units and themes that tie the students together as a community of learners.

Often teachers and administrators reject recommendations to implement strategies that are appropriate for second language learners. The most disturbing reason classroom teachers give is that it is too much trouble for just a few students. Usually, though, classroom teachers say they can't take a thematic approach because guided reading, the core of their literacy block, is driven exclusively by their leveled book collections and it is not possible to coordinate the topics.

Others tell me that while they might like to increase the links, they have been informed by the reading specialist in their building not to muddy language arts with content. They worry that if the focus is on *content* it will take away from *literacy*—with the result that students won't become writers or learn to appreciate good literature. To link instruction would violate the integrity of language arts, and prevent the teachers from sharing their favorite authors. In many cases "balanced literacy" has evolved into "balanced literature." Reading is equated with fiction, and writing is mainly personal and narrative expression.

I am also told that providing a common topic for writing for the whole class during writers workshop—or co-constructing joint texts and having students copy them into a journal, or using framed paragraphs—will take away students' ability to develop their "voice." Voice, however, is almost exclusively interpreted to mean a writer's literary voice. My response has generally been, "If they don't have any words they don't have a voice either, so why not provide them words and ideas to use until they are more fluent?" I do agree that we owe students a voice, but it is not necessarily a literary one. What we owe our students are literacy skills that allow them to express their identity, make their way in the world, demand their rights, fight oppression, or better their communities.

I have often asked myself why there is such a strong emphasis on literary voice, when to be academically successful and able to move into the larger society, students must read and create far more expository text than narrative. I have concluded that the resonance with the written word is characteristic of many people who go into teaching—especially literacy and language arts teachers—but it is not representative of the broader population.

This was exemplified for me in a seminar I attended some years ago hosted by a group of Ph.D. candidates in writing. The talk centered on what one of the students described, and all agreed, was that uncontainable feeling one gets when a piece of writing is in progress and the ideas just must get down on the paper. They carried notebooks with them everywhere, and had paper by the bedside and in the car in order to capture that joyous moment when their ideas (in the perfect wording) came to mind or popped out. (These days, like-minded students must sleep with their iPads.)

> *For me, joy does not come from producing the written word—not ever.*

Having written a dissertation, two books, and many chapters and articles, I have never felt that way about a piece of writing. Yes, I can write well when I have something to say; and yes, I am happy when my work is recognized. And I am a voracious reader of fiction. But for me, that sense of joy does not come from producing the written word—not ever. It comes from interpersonal interaction—classes well taught or good conversations are the highlights of my days.

Following the seminar, I asked the students in one of my own graduate education classes how many kept a personal journal and felt the need to write daily. About fifteen of thirty raised their hands. I then asked the same question of a close friend who was studying for his third master's degree—computer science, preceded by water quality engineering and geography. I asked him to estimate how many students in any of his classes he thought kept a personal journal. In all seriousness he responded, "What is a personal journal?" When I explained, he said, "I'd guess none, why waste the time?" This was from someone who is articulate and able to express himself very clearly in writing.

A lightbulb went on. My friend, like so many others, resonates with ideas and concepts on a different plane than the written word. That feeling of joy and fulfillment that writing gives so many of you reading this book is achieved by others through solving a mathematical equation, caring for another person, throwing a no-hitter, creating a stronger bridge support, finding new ways to test a hypothesis, playing or creating a musical score, or any other type of artistic or physical expression. I may offend some of you by saying we can all draw, we just weren't all born to be artists. We should expect that all our students can "write well," but not that they will be published authors. There are as many budding computer scientists, or welders, or physicians as there are novelists among our students.

We do owe our students nonfiction and expository text—crafting an argument, distinguishing fact from opinion, synthesizing and succinctly organizing their thoughts for a multitude of reasons (filling out a job application or preparing a report to a supervisor, writing a letter of appreciation for a favor done, or creating an editorial in the newspaper for the betterment of the community). Indeed, some of our students may be the next Edwidge Danticat or Junot Diaz and we are certainly graced by their presence among us. There is no question that their talents deserve to be cultivated in school—just not them exclusively.

You may be wondering how this relates to comprehension work with second language learners. Students who are learning to read and write through their second language often flounder when the focus is on character, plot, voice, "small moments," or using their imagination—when there is little concrete to hang onto. They struggle when the intent of reading instruction is mainly to uncover what it teaches the learner about being a writer, and not the ideas and conceptual understandings contained in the text. Teachers must act intentionally to help ELLs make the links and connect the abstractions to what is in their conceptual reservoir.

Initial literacy instruction for second language learners is much more likely to be successful when it is centered around nonfiction (do not read textbooks). The goal is not to learn and memorize facts, but to begin to engage with ideas and to use resources where the concepts are easily represented visually and graphically so that meaning can be attached to the text. Of course students should be continually exposed to fiction, but wherever possible it should connect directly to their lives, allowing them to see their own experiences reflected or linked (even loosely) to topics they are studying.

Students can experience the satisfaction of having enjoyed a story well told, whether through listening, watching, or reading it themselves. To deepen the conceptual reservoir and build schema, teachers should provide an overview, organize the plot and characters visually, and even give a detailed preview of what will happen. They may need to read stories to or with students or show them the movie first. We will not be denying them the eventual pleasure of making those discoveries on their own, but rather strengthening the conceptual framework needed to do the kind of cognitive and thinking work we want for all our students.

ELLs have the greatest success in settings where they can meet concepts and vocabulary repeatedly throughout their school day. Ideally, literacy instruction helps students make sense of and perfect what they will need to read and write to be successful in the rest of their day. This means thinking throughout the day or working in collaboration with other teachers to connect what students are reading and writing about during language arts, and the important concepts from other areas of the curriculum (social studies, math, science, and the arts).

Literacy as a Public Act: Using the Physical Environment to Support Conceptual Development

A successful teacher of second language learners purposefully plans to incorporate both linguistic and conceptual aspects of instruction. The aim is to create independent learners who can function in the disembedded, cognitively demanding environment that characterizes high-level academic work. If all students are to thrive, every aspect of classroom design, including the content covered, ways of grouping and regrouping students, and strategies for instructional delivery must be intentionally designed.

Learners need be able to use every resource that can be made available to them to connect to and engage in the important ideas and activities of the curriculum. Especially in a linguistically diverse setting, the physical environment is a key factor in supporting meaning-based instruction. It should be apparent to students from the physical environment what the topics they are learning about are, the expectations for their behavior, and the main guidelines for how to accomplish their work independently. In addition, abundant examples of student work—and invitations to interact with one another around important ideas—should be incorporated.

Many teachers embrace the understanding that students thrive in a "print-rich" environment. In these classrooms, good readers of the language are able to make use of the print that surrounds them to know what to do.

"Print-rich," however, does not equate to "meaningful" if students can't understand what the print says. Even if second language learners are able to decode, they still may not be able to derive any meaning from what is posted.

Unfortunately, too often I see what I think of as "word wallpaper." The standards are up, the steps in the writing process are on the wall next to a list of potential story starters, and a description of strategies good readers use are nearby. In the science center the steps in the scientific method are delineated, and the math center lists how to solve a word problem. But there are no exemplars, no student work, and no visual rubrics to help bring the print to life.

Take a moment and visualize your classroom and imagine that all the text is in a script you can't read—Hebrew, Lao, or Hindi. Is there any meaning that can be derived from the print? Could you locate the math center or the books related to the oceans unit students are studying, or what the steps of the writing process look like? It is not simply a matter of attaching pictures. The organization of the physical space should be guided by the intent to connect the concepts being studied, the way we talk about them, and how they are represented in print. This needs to happen in the classroom and any public spaces—hallways, offices, the cafeteria, the playground—where students may find themselves.

Over the past ten years I have come to believe that to meet the needs of a linguistically diverse population we need to view literacy as a public act, not simply a private interaction between the reader and the page (though that is an important part of the act of reading). Nowhere have I seen this better exemplified than at Columbine Elementary in Boulder, Colorado, where the physical environment plays a key role in building connections among students and a sense of community across the school (Buhrow and Garcia 2006; Goudvis and Harvey 2005; Harvey and Goudvis 2005).

Every time I visit Columbine—a school where the vast majority of students are low-income, second language learners of English—I can't help but stop and engage in the dialogue. I find evidence that all students, regardless of background or language proficiency, are immersed in a world of ideas and concepts. And I am constantly learning something. Students at every grade level and language background represent their thinking through words and pictures—as well as posing questions and responding to each other's ideas in the hallways, the classrooms, and even on the bathroom stalls. All of the work, both cognitive and physical, is authentically by and for students and is centered on the major themes of the content areas. This is unlike most other schools where the halls may be nicely decorated, but there is no indication of what the learning is about or how students' thinking has evolved.

The presence of increasing numbers of second language learners in our schools is a gift. They provide us with the impetus to rethink our theories and examine our practices in a new light. I am confident that any teacher willing to uncover hidden assumptions about language and literacy will find new ways to reach not just the second language learners, but all of their students.

Meaning Is Everything: A Summary

- Think first about thinking and then about text.
- All students have something to say and something to offer—even if it isn't through the written word, or in English.
- Every important comprehension (thinking) strategy can be worked on through the use of pictures, models, and physical interaction.
- Use text to represent ideas and concepts that students understand and can talk about.
- To increase comprehension, meaning needs to take precedence over the features of the text itself.
- Students' primary language is a resource to build thinking and literacy skills regardless of the language of instruction.
- Become acquainted with the ways literacy is used daily in the homes of your students.
- Make conscious connections between the big ideas from the content areas and the things that students will read and write.
- Seek materials on every topic at a range of reading levels and complexity.
- Let ELLs know from the beginning—everyone is a reader and writer, just not solely of fiction.

References

Buhrow, Brad, and Anne Upczak Garcia. 2006. *Ladybugs, Tornadoes and Swirling Galaxies.* Portland, ME: Stenhouse.

Cappellini, Mary. 2005. *Balancing Reading and Language Learning: A Resource for Teaching English Language Learners, K–5.* Portland, ME: Stenhouse.

Cloud, Nancy, Fred Genesee, and Else Hamayan. 2009. *Literacy Instruction for English Language Learners: A Teacher's Guide to Research-Based Practices.* Portsmouth, NH: Heinemann.

Commins, Nancy L., and Ofelia B. Miramontes. 2005. *Linguistic Diversity and Teaching: Reflective Teaching and the Social Conditions of Schooling.* Mahwah, NJ: Lawrence Erlbaum.

Commins, Nancy L., and Ofelia B. Miramontes. 2006. "Addressing Linguistic Diversity from the Outset." *Journal of Teacher Education* (57) 3: 240–46.

Diaz, Rafael. 1983. "Thought and Two Languages: The Impact of Bilingualism on Cognitive Development." *Review of Research in Education* 10: 23–54.

Escamilla, Kathy, and Susan Hopewell. 2009. "Transitions to Biliteracy: Creating Positive Academic Trajectories for Emerging Bilinguals in the United States." In *International Perspectives on Bilingual Education: Policy, Practice, and Controversy,* edited by J. E. Petrovic, 65–90. Charlotte, NC: Information Age Publishing.

Freeman, Yvonne S., and David E. Freeman. 2008. *Academic Language for English Language Learners and Struggling Readers: How to Help Students Succeed Across Content Areas.* Portsmouth, NH: Heinemann.

Gardner, Howard. 1993. *Multiple Intelligences.* New York: Basic Books.

Gibbons, Pauline. 2002. *Scaffolding Language, Scaffolding Learning: Teaching Second Language Learners in the Mainstream Classroom.* Portsmouth, NH: Heinemann.

Gibbons, Pauline. 2009. *English Learners, Academic Literacy, and Thinking: Learning in the Challenge Zone.* Portsmouth, NH: Heinemann.

Gottlieb, Margo, Anne Katz, and Gisela Ernst-Slavit. 2009. *Paper to Practice: Using the TESOL English Language Proficiency Standards in Pre-12 Classrooms.* Alexandria, VA: TESOL.

Goudvis, Anne, and Stephanie Harvey. 2005. *Reading the World: Content Comprehension with Linguistically Diverse Learners.* Portland, ME: Stenhouse.

Grosjean, François. 1989. "Neurolinguists, Beware! The Bilingual Is Not Two Monolinguals in One Person." *Brain and Language* (36) 1: 3–15.

Hakuta, Kenji. 1986. *Mirror of Language: The Debate on Bilingualism.* New York: Basic Books.

Harvey, Stephanie, and Anne Goudvis. 2000. *Strategies That Work: Teaching Comprehension for Understanding and Engagement.* Portland, ME: Stenhouse.

Harvey, Stephanie, and Anne Goudvis. 2005. *The Comprehension Toolkit: Grades 3–6.* Portsmouth, NH: Heinemann.

Miramontes, Ofelia B., Adel Nadeau, and Nancy L. Commins. 2011. *Restructuring Schools for Linguistic Diversity: Linking Decision Making to Effective Programs.* 2d ed. New York: Teachers College Press.

Pearson, P. David, and Margaret C. Gallagher. 1983. "The Instruction of Reading Comprehension." *Contemporary Educational Psychology* (8): 317–44.

Peregoy, Suzanne F., and Owen F. Boyle. 2005. *Reading, Writing, and Learning in ESL.* 4th ed. Boston, MA: Pearson.

Perkins, David. 1993. "Teaching for Understanding." *American Educator: The Professional Journal of the American Federation of Teachers* (17) 3: 8, 28–35. Retrieved on July 22, 2010, from: http://exploratorium.edu/IFI/resources/workshops/teachingforunderstanding.html.

Ravitch, Diane. 2010. Friend of Education. Excerpt from speech presented at the Representative Assembly of the National Education Association, New Orleans. Retrieved on July 15, 2010, from http://www.nea.org/grants/40246.htm.

Spindler, George D., and Louise Spindler. 1988. "Roger Harker and Schonhausen: From the Familiar to the Strange and Back Again." In *Doing the Ethnography of Schooling: Educational Anthropology in Action,* edited by G. D. Spindler, 20–46. Prospect Heights, IL: Waveland Press.

CHAPTER THIRTEEN

Comprehension Strategy Instruction for Culturally and Linguistically Diverse Learners

Anne Upczak Garcia

It's May in Colorado and spring is supposed to be flourishing, but instead when I roll out of bed at 5:45 to start my day, a freezing mist is trying to penetrate my windows. The snow is refusing to leave. It feels like February, which is probably why I'm unconsciously repeating "it's May, it's May, don't worry it's May," in my mind.

I work in a school that serves 88 percent English language learners (ELL) and we are under a microscope. It is my job to ensure that my students not only learn to read, write, and think—but that they do it in eloquent, thoughtful English. Every single step we take is also about comprehension. From the first day a child walks through the door until they are finally considered a fluent bilingual child, we focus on going in-depth into content and language to make sure children develop solid understandings about every subject we study.

As I walk through the front door of my aging school building I begin to realize why I'm tired: "Did you hear about the teacher tenure bill? It passed!" "Now they want to tie our pay to test scores." "They'll shut us down if we don't close that achievement gap!" "The board is going to cut our pay." Over and over again, we are bombarded with snippets of bad news that sucks a small bit of hope from our hearts. We are told that we need to be pretesting and posttesting in every subject several times a week. We need to administer reading tests in two languages, writing tests, math tests—tests, tests, tests! It's enough to literally drive any creative-minded, well-intentioned, intelligent person insane. I ask myself, "When do I get to *teach*?" I realize that my stress comes from outside my school building. The challenges we face are enormous and the stress intense. We are all under a lot of pressure, but the ultimate truth is that each and every day my students rise to the occasion.

Comprehension Starts with Fostering Connections and Developing Thinking Routines

Working with culturally and linguistically diverse students has allowed me to learn about the amazingly rich cultures in which my students live and how they contribute to society. I have come to realize the importance of starting out by truly respecting their individual cultural schema. By doing this, I have been able to foster ways in which they can make connections to their learning in my classroom. As Leslie sits in a brown wicker chair in the reading corner, her legs crossed and her writer's notebook on her lap, I sneak a peek over her shoulder. She is writing about her *abuelita*. We have just read *Abuelita's Gift*, which explores the relationship between a grandmother and granddaughter. It also addresses issues of death and the afterlife. Leslie is writing about her own grandmother, who lives in Mexico and has taught Leslie about altars and the Day of the Dead. She is making connections between her own life and the story. Later she adds an exquisite drawing of an altar she and her mother have created in their house in the U.S., which includes images of her *abuelita*. Leslie is using her cultural schema to understand the text.

I constantly find myself reflecting on both my teaching and the state of education today when working with my students. My students are predominately children from immigrant families who struggle between choosing acculturation and assimilation as they work their ways through the American school system. Assimilation expects immigrant and bicultural children to abandon important cultural elements of their ancestors and fully, unconditionally adopt the new culture. I, on the other hand, believe that acculturation is a better, more additive approach to American culture and to student learning.

These days political rhetoric suggests that new immigrants in our country should just quietly assimilate. But acculturation allows for children to maintain important elements from their heritage cultures, while adopting new cultural schema from their new country. It implies the contribution of one's pride in and love for one's culture to people and systems of one's new country. When one assimilates, these beautiful, rich cultural experiences are lost. To me, acculturation brings a wonderful infusion of background knowledge and varied life experiences to classrooms. It fills notebooks with narratives of *quinceñeras* or making *albondiga* soup. It enriches conversations about geography, history, science, music, and art. It boils over with stories of familiar struggles like immigration crossings, babies' births, and grandmas' deaths. It helps children make connections with each other and in the end broadens their own personal growth as learners.

Schema theory not only focuses on building background knowledge, but also suggests that students' experiences and knowledge of the world contribute to their everyday English language proficiency (Scarcella 2003). Students' comprehension or background knowledge of a subject helps them interact with different kinds of text. This process allows students to bring new knowledge and blend it with what they already know and understand. Let's take it that much further and acknowledge the background knowledge our culturally and linguistically diverse learners bring to our classes. How can we access that knowledge to enhance the community of learners? If we are aware of what children know, we should include that knowledge in conversations to help them make connections in order to understand. Lisa Delpit notes that being able to function in academic circles doesn't mean one has to give up one's home identity, language, or values (1996).

Victor: Giving Space for Reflection

I remember Victor staring sadly out the window one morning after we had been analyzing a text of immigration stories from people of European descent. He normally is a talkative child, eager to share, telling stories and making connections—but this morning he is quiet and pensive. I approach Victor and ask him if he is OK. He answers yes, but he is thinking of his own crossing. He begins to tell me the story of how he, his ten-year-old brother, and his mother had been dropped off in an alley by a *coyote* (a human smuggler). They began running through backyards in the middle of the night. As they were running through one yard, his mother saw a police car coming up the road. They hid in the bushes. Moments after the patrol car had turned the corner he saw the barrel of a shotgun against his mother's head. Victor was four at the time.

He stops for a minute, almost not breathing. "She stood up," he said. "She stood up and said in not-very-good English, 'Shoot me, but let them go.'" He couldn't remember what the man looked like, or sounded like. He said he just remembers a big shadow that began yelling something he couldn't understand. His mother pushed him and his brother and they ran. They ran down the street and around the corner and hid behind a trash dumpster. "Mamá found us in the morning. She had a black eye, but wasn't dead." We talk for a long time about his crossing. He writes a book and gives it to his mom. The last page says, "Thank you mamá, we know what you've done for us." During this time Victor asks me if I think other people are scared, too. He wants to know if people from other places have so much trouble coming here. Victor's cultural schema led him to explore and wonder about more than just his world. By giving him the space to do this I allow him to understand that he is not alone, that he is part of a broader community, and that he is safe. This builds bridges for him to continue his work at school. Having the courage to let our ELL students take their own paths and explore topics that are uncomfortable for us is very important because it sets up an environment where stories and ideas are valued.

I read Victor's moving account and it makes me realize how important our work is as teachers to give students a voice and a way to share their experiences. Our country is doomed if we fail to recognize the importance of educating newly arrived immigrants. Instead of marginalizing their humanness, we must use what they bring to empower their independence in this country.

— Cris

Working with and for English Language Learners

Developing an interactive learning environment that includes scaffolded conversations and critical dialogue can also be very important to ELL students. Providing explicit practice in how to deconstruct, analyze, and question texts helps children grow in both language development and overall academic stimulation. An active literacy component where children interact with each other and with texts provides ELL students the opportunity to examine ideas and concepts at a deeper level, while presenting material that can be culturally relevant to a child's home culture and new school/country culture. This kind of environment supports individualized teaching and learning and reinforces participant structures that many ELL students are more accustomed to, such as group work or collaborative structures (Genesee et al. 2006). Many children who are coming from other countries are accustomed to working together to solve problems and need time to adjust to the American way, which often promotes independence and competition over collaboration. Additionally, it is important to recognize that reading, writing, and responding to each other's thinking contributes to a greater culture of literacy (Hudelson 1994)—and in the case of ELL students, to a broader culture in general. Literacy is not only about what we read and write within the constraints of the classroom walls. Literacy is a form of expression that links our ideas to the world around us. It helps us develop our own worldviews and be active participants in society. For ELL students it is also a path to understanding a new culture in which they should be empowered to fully function and succeed.

As we proceed with this work we also begin emphasizing thinking routines, which give the children opportunities to interact with me and with each other in constructive, productive, and positive ways. With what I know about my students I know that no matter what I am teaching, the children need tools to be able to construct their own knowledge. Once ELL students develop the inclination and ability to take risks, follow their curiosities, clearly communicate their understanding of learning, participate in an intellectual community, be thoughtful, and develop a sense of critical thinking is when I feel I am doing my job. It is through building background knowledge and working with students to be active in their own learning that leads them into being able to use this new knowledge.

> I hope we can remember that ultimately our job is not merely to teach children how to read and write so they can do well in school—we are teaching them to read and write as a way to learn about and make sense of their experiences in the world.
>
> —*Maryann*

Integrating Content Throughout the Day

Designing units that integrate content is interesting, exciting, and at times challenging. I often hear people say, "But I need to teach English during ESL, not content" or "Language arts curriculum shouldn't be muddled with science." But the idea of integrated thematic units isn't to compromise the core of a subject area, but to enhance it. If we can keep this in mind, it is easy to do both. Weaving content into language arts and ESL augments the culturally and linguistically diverse learners' experiences and increases the exposure to content that ELL students receive. Planning units and lessons within a framework of integrated thematic units supports children's learning. A thematic curriculum helps provide conceptual structures that support learning (Kucer, Silva, and Delgado-Larocco 1995). By doing this, teachers can help students make connections between content, the activities they are asked to do, and their own life experiences. This in turn creates an environment of collaboration in which the students are given opportunities to present varying perspectives and co-construct meaning.

When planning units, I start with enduring understandings, which are the bigger-picture ideas that link the entire unit together. Along with these are essential questions that children examine. These questions guide discussions, help children focus on specific ideas and concepts within the unit, and lead to more critical examinations of the topic. I also set process goals that focus on problem solving, inquiry, and self-instruction. This is where the comprehension piece comes in. What will we work on? I identify several explicit strategies that I can teach within the context of the unit and design lessons around them. By doing it this way it makes the learning more authentic. We're not teaching comprehension in isolation, but for a purpose, which is to understand what we want to learn and apply the strategies to our daily work.

Throughout this process I keep in mind the range in which ELL students are working with regard to their sociolinguistic language, the sophistication of their academic discourse, the level at which they synthesize or evaluate information, and the amount of metalinguistic awareness they bring to their language learning. While children may know how to use questioning as a tool to gain understanding, they may or may not be correctly forming questions orally or in written form. This is the additional piece that teachers of ELL students need to incorporate to help their students become more articulate in English.

There are a plethora of units that lend themselves well to integration, but a particularly valuable one is *weather*. Weather is exciting, weather is interesting, and weather is wild! It is a topic that children become naturally engaged in. We all have background knowledge about weather, wherever we come from. Enduring understandings need to be broad based and all encompassing, yet allow for room to explore the subject matter. For instance, an enduring understanding for a unit on weather for second graders might read something like "Weather impacts how people live and work." The enduring questions to accompany this enduring understanding might be phrased "How does weather affect people?" With these two basic pieces I can set the framework for further inquiry that encompasses questioning, monitoring comprehension, determining importance, synthesizing/summarizing, reflection, and more.

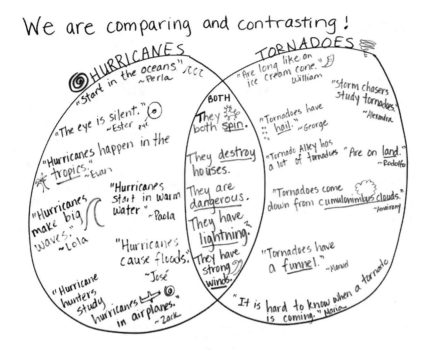

We are comparing and contrasting!

HURRICANES — TORNADOES

HURRICANES
"Start in the oceans." ~Perla
"The eye is silent." ~Ester
"Hurricanes happen in the tropics." ~Evan
"Hurricanes make big waves." ~Lola
"Hurricanes start in warm water." ~Paola
"Hurricanes cause floods." ~José
"Hurricane hunters study hurricanes in airplanes." ~Zack

BOTH
They both spin.
They destroy houses.
They are dangerous.
They have lightning.
They have strong winds.

TORNADOES
"Are long like an ice cream cone." ~William
"Storm chasers study tornadoes." ~Alexandra
"Tornadoes have hail." ~George
"Tornado Alley has a lot of tornadoes."   "Are on land." ~Rodolfo
"Tornadoes come down from cumulonimbus clouds." ~Amairany
"Tornadoes have a funnel." ~Manuel
"It is hard to know when a tornado is coming." ~Maria

Figure 1 This Venn diagram was co-constructed with the whole group through a guided conversation about the similarities and differences between hurricanes and tornadoes. The idea is for students to begin thinking about comparative language and how it is applied to the real world.

I can also design literacy-based ESL lessons that practice specific structures to give the students the language skills they need to discuss the content further. We might practice comparing and contrasting using a Venn diagram and language structures that scaffold their speaking and writing (see Figure 1). The language frames might be "Hurricanes (are more dangerous than) tornadoes" or "Blizzards (are colder than) sand storms." By practicing comparative adjectives the students are explicitly practicing how to discuss differences and similarities between different kinds of storms, which in the long run is a skill that they will use across the curriculum and in a myriad of situations (see Figure 2).

If I am teaching a lesson on how to read for meaning, why not do it using a text about weather? With my ELL students I may have to preview vocabulary, use images to support ideas and language, provide them with language frames to structure their answers both orally and in writing—but I am still teaching how to read for meaning. The difference is that in a content-rich environment they are learning about weather *and* how to use an important comprehension strategy in their interaction with texts.

Figure 2 This anchor chart is part of an Oracy lesson where ELL students are practicing how to use comparative adjectives to describe hurricanes and tornadoes. We try to integrate the content into our Oracy goals to make the activities pertinent to what we are currently studying and give children the opportunity to explicitly rehearse language structures.

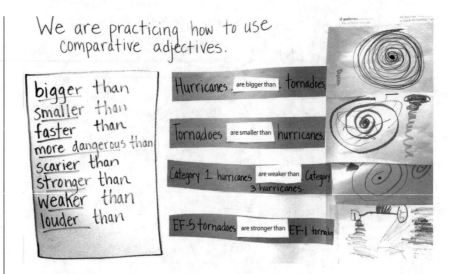

The content comes alive in my classroom because this supports culturally and linguistically diverse learners. We build tornadoes and swirling hurricanes that hang from the ceiling. We practice using nonfiction text features such as labels and writing captions by adding them to our artwork. We hang research posters and anchor charts about scientific experiments we've done. We develop content-based word walls that students illustrate, and I find as many books in both Spanish and English about the content that the children can read at any time. This life gives meaning to the children and gives them a reason to learn new vocabulary and new concepts because they are excited to learn and want to discover more, read more, write more, and talk more about the world's amazing weather.

As part of my weather unit I do ongoing writing assessments to help me work with the students in developing their ability to communicate what they've learned in written format. One of my students had a difficult time getting all of his thinking down on paper within the time frame that he had—so much so that when we had a conference about what he had written he blurted out "I just wish I could research lightning storms and do a huge poster so I could show you everything I really know and more that I will learn!" This was a good lesson for me, because he was able to communicate much more information through his poster than in the limited format I had provided for him. I helped him begin a research project on storms as an extension to his normal workload. His own curiosity and drive led him into an in-depth inquiry project of storms, where he not only applied his new schema, but gathered more information to fuel the fire in his mind. At every stage we conference about what he is doing. Can he add any nonfiction features to his poster? "Yeah!" Daniel says. "I should label all the parts of my storm so everyone knows what they are!" I guide him, "What about adding captions to these images we printed out from the computer?" Even though Daniel chose to express himself through art, I was able to guide him and work with him to add important information that he has learned through reading nonfiction books, magazines, and online sources to the poster—as well as teaching him to use text features that he often finds in the informational texts he reads.

Keeping in mind that there are many options to help students express their thinking broadens our ability to gather information about what children know. Consider using mediums such as mind maps, posters, poetry, and more. Transmediation—moving thinking from one mode of expression to another—helps ELL students in their quest to effectively communicate what they already know and what they have learned. Transmediation promotes language development by providing students with context cues that are not language based to understand the oral and written language used in the classroom (Freeman and Freeman 1994). In what ways can students express understanding that is not in pencil and paper form? Is there a way to integrate music and art into the classroom? What about movement? Can we be more flexible and creative in our teaching and still show student learning? We have to if we consider that the students have information to share and it is our job to help them communicate it.

According to my district curriculum, in second grade the culturally and linguistically diverse student is to be able to respond to complex and content-related questions about newly learned information through the use of comparing and contrasting as well as descriptions. They also need to be able to access content-area discussions in small groups by summarizing, defining, and explaining through the use of simple sentences as well as gathering, reading, organizing, and interpreting information related to academic content areas. This is a lot to process as a teacher; imagine what it must be like as a student learning English as a new language! What I do is try to translate the information given to me—and the tasks expected of the students—into meaningful, interesting lessons that help them meet these goals.

For example, as I plan a series of lessons on making connections, using inferences, and comparing and contrasting, I base my decisions on language and content goals around the idea that I want my students to become more critical readers of text. I decide to incorporate the social studies content, India, and target the similarities and differences in experiences my students have regarding schooling to those that children in India have. I use a series of short films, which are accompanied by several short texts. The books are accessible to young readers in that they have age-appropriate text and dynamic images to accompany the information presented. The DVDs are beneficial in providing repetition about what we read in the text and giving the children a more vivid sense of what life and school in India are like. They also give us more opportunities to practice viewing instructional materials in a different media format, writing inferences, and documenting new information as we watch the films and then stop to take notes. Giving them several chances in varying settings, yet with similar topics, allows my students to practice the different strategies I am teaching.

Later we use the text to read and discuss further similarities and differences and chart our thinking. Throughout this process I again support my ELL students with additional visuals, a preview of vocabulary and ideas (which I am able to do in Spanish), language frames to support their writing, and a review of the lesson in a small group. I also remind them to use the environmental print such as the content word wall when they are writing.

Scaffolding both language and content can be challenging, but I keep in mind that the more explicit I can be, the easier it is for my students to understand and learn.

The Linguistic Piece

No matter how well we scaffold lessons, provide additional support, and guide our young ELL students, the basic fact of the matter is that they still need specific English language instruction. Over the years strategies and instruction have grown and changed, and the importance of building schema, developing strategies to understand texts, and expressing this thinking is all part of acquiring English.

According to a 2006 report done by researchers at the Center for Research on Education, Diversity, and Excellence (CREDE), students who are at the beginning stages of English acquisition make what appears to be quick progress, but then slow down once reaching intermediate proficiency (Genesee et al. 2006). Students learning English as a new language need explicit instruction in the intricacies of the English language itself (nouns, verbs, adjectives, etc.) as well as explicit Oracy instruction. Oracy is defined

> Anne, having visited your school, I've seen your first grade English language learners joining in full-on inquiry work. It succeeds because of all the support that you teachers provide—and that you are describing in this chapter. Anyone who thinks that kids who are learning English can't fully participate in a progressive, engaging, inquiry-based curriculum needs to make the trip to Columbine. There are *no excuses* for this not happening everywhere.
>
> —Smokey

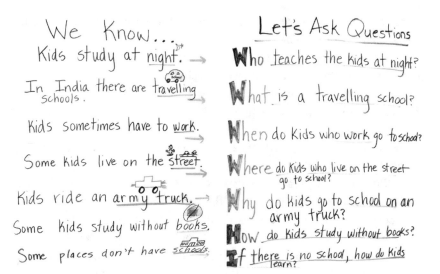

We Know...
Kids study at night.
In India there are travelling schools.
Kids sometimes have to work.
Some kids live on the street.
Kids ride an army truck.
Some kids study without books.
Some places don't have schools.

Let's Ask Questions
Who teaches the kids at night?
What is a travelling school?
When do kids who work go to school?
Where do kids who live on the street go to school?
Why do kids go to school on an army truck?
How do kids study without books?
If there is no school, how do kids learn?

Figure 3 While studying India we were asking a lot of questions. In order to provide the students with more tools and to practice standard adult English, we had to practice how to properly construct questions based on our current knowledge about school children in India attending classes. These statement and questions anchor charts show how the children transformed their thinking into questions.

as language that allows students to successfully engage in complex literacy tasks (Escamilla et al. 2009). In essence, providing lessons in which children can repeatedly practice the language structures and vocabulary that give them access to more complex ideas and information will help them grow as English speakers, readers, and writers.

Designing lessons to practice Oracy within a framework that includes the content supports both content comprehension and language development. Activities that practice Oracy out of context can be useful, but when they are within the context of the content being taught they provide ELL students with the tools to be able to talk about what they are learning and participate in the class as a whole in the present. This helps students make connections between learning about literature, poetry, science, social studies, or math and the acquisition of the English language. I am fortunate enough to be the English Language Development Instructor for my children, but in situations where the ESL teacher is different, the classroom teacher can plan with the ESL teacher to integrate content into the language instruction.

One example of an Oracy lesson might be how to transform questions into statements (see Figure 3). If a student has read in a text "Children in India sometimes ride in army trucks to school," and they want to know why but don't know how to construct that sentence, they will either be perceived as not being able to ask questions or not understanding the text. Taking the time to give students the tools to be able to write "Why do children in India ride in army trucks to school?" empowers a child to share their curiosities with the group and teacher.

Another example might be how to use comparative language. Design lessons around the content that gives the children opportunities to practice how to compare and contrast ideas—for instance, "Hurricanes happen in the ocean, while tornadoes happen on land." A lesson focusing on how to use words like *while, rather, instead, as well*, and *however* (and what these words mean) gives ELL students a boost in terms of the sophistication in which they will be able to communicate their thinking (see Figure 4).

Not only do new English speakers have to work hard to acquire basic communicative competence, but they must also learn the academic language or high-utility words that allow them to participate in more complex activities. So what is this "academic" vocabulary? For this discussion it is the language students need to comprehend and interact with more complex concepts and texts in a classroom setting. The language and strategies students need to learn and be comfortable using range from metacognitive strategies (such as identifying and marking important information, paraphrasing, monitoring comprehension, listening to one's inner voice, and planning) to oral discussion strategies (such as posing questions, answering those questions, and defending the answers). This can

> Have you read "The Words Students Need" in the October 2010 *Ed Leadership*? It focuses on middle school children, but it supports your thinking around "academic vocabulary" for younger readers, too.
>
> —Debbie

Figure 4 This image was generated by an ELL student as part of an Oracy lesson where the students are rehearsing comparative language and learning how it applies to our studies about tornadoes and hurricanes.

Meteorologists follow hurricanes **as well as** tornadoes.

seem like a daunting amount of instruction, but I like to tackle it in pieces throughout the day, with the content being the vehicle.

In the end learning is really about being able to engage in meaningful and interesting activities that teach children content, math, reading, writing, or the English language. Children deserve to become well-rounded, thoughtful adults with the desire to learn more about the world around them and engage in whatever activities they deem exciting, important, and undisputedly interesting. Skill and drill just won't get them there, nor will it create generations of learners who are curious and active in society. If I have learned anything over time it is that arguing over which curriculum is best and who is right has not benefited teachers, students, or the educational system in general. It has caused deep divides and cost a lot of money. Thoughtful discussions and a solid pedagogical base are what teachers and students need. It falls on teachers again to do what we know is best, to stand up and speak out when we see injustices, and to keep the wolves at bay. Joan Wink reminds us, "Daily, I feel the pull of courage and the counter-pull of patience. Oftentimes we need to be as courageous as the context will allow. At other times, patience is our greatest ally: patience with ourselves, our colleagues, our context" (2004). I try to keep this in my heart.

References

August, Diane, and Timothy Shannahan, eds. 2006. *Developing Literacy in Second Language Learners: Report of the National Literacy Panel on Language-Minority Children and Youth.* Mahway, NJ: Lawrence Erlbaum.

Cappellini, Mary. 2005. *Balancing Reading and Language Learning.* Portland, ME: Stenhouse.

Commins, Nancy. 2005. *Linguistic Diversity and Teaching (Reflective Teaching and the Social Conditions of Schooling).* Mahwah, NJ: Lawrence Erlbaum.

Delpit, Lisa. 1996. *Other People's Children: Cultural Conflict in the Classroom.* 2d ed. New York: New Press.

Escamilla, Kathy, Olivia Ruiz-Figueroa, Susan Hopewell, Sandra Butvilofsky, and Wendy Sparrow. 2009. "Transitions to Biliteracy: Literacy Squared." Boulder, CO: University of Colorado BUENO Center.

Freeman, David E., and Yvonne S. Freeman. 2004. *Essential Linguistics: What You Need to Know to Teach Reading, ESL, Spelling, Phonics, and Grammar.* Portsmouth, NH: Heinemann.

Wow, Anne. Our children need us to be more courageous—to stand up and speak out more often—not to defend our practices, but to articulate them. As Debbie Miller says in *Reading with Meaning* (2002), "...spend time defining your beliefs and aligning your practices. Once you've found what's true for you, stand up for what you know is right...be confident and clear about why you believe as you do. People will listen" (7). I'm listening, Anne. Thanks for speaking out.

Freeman, David E., and Yvonne S. Freeman. 2000. *Teaching Reading in Multilingual Classrooms.* Portsmouth, NH: Heinemann.

Freeman, David E., and Yvonne S. Freeman. 1994. *Between Worlds. Access to Second Language Acquisition.* Portsmouth, NH: Heinemann.

Garan, Elaine. 2004. *In Defense of Our Children.* Heinemann. Portsmouth, NH.

Genesee, Fred, Kathryn Lindholm-Leary, William Saunders, and Donna Christian, eds. 2006. *Educating English Language Learners: A Synthesis of Research Evidence.* New York: Cambridge University Press.

Gentile, Lance. 2003. *The Oracy Instructional Guide, Linking Research and Theory to Assessment and Instruction.* Carlsbad, CA: Dominie.

Goldenberg, Claude. 2008. "Teaching English Language Learners: What the Research Does—and Does Not—Say." *American Educator* (32) 2.

Harvey, Stephanie, and Anne Goudvis. 2007. *Strategies That Work: Teaching Comprehension for Understanding and Engagement.* 2d ed. Portland, ME: Stenhouse.

Harvey, Stephanie, and Anne Goudvis. 2008. *The Primary Comprehension Toolkit: Language and Lessons for Active Literacy.* Portsmouth, NH: Heinemann.

Hudelson, Sarah. 1994. "Literacy Development of Second Language Children." In *Educating Second Language Children,* edited by Fred Genesee. New York: Cambridge University Press.

Kucer, Stephen B., Cecilia Silva, and Esther Delgado-Larocco. 1995. *Curricular Conversations, Themes in Multilingual and Monolingual Classrooms.* Portland, ME: Stenhouse.

Perry, Theresa, and Lisa Delpit, eds. 1998. *The Real Ebonics Debate: Power, Language, and the Education of African-American Children.* Boston, MA: Beacon Press.

Ritchhart, Ron. 2002. *Intellectual Character: What It Is, Why It Matters, and How to Get It.* San Francisco, CA: Jossey Bass.

Scarcella, Robin. 2003. "Academic English: A Conceptual Framework." Irvine, CA: University of California.

Taberski, Sharon. 2000. *On Solid Ground.* Portsmouth, NH: Heinemann.

Wink, Joan. 2004. *Critical Pedagogy: Notes from the Real World.* 3d ed. New York: Addison Wesley Longman.

Thinking Through the Day

Tanny McGregor

Tanny mcgregor

Over the past decade, I and thousands of my colleagues around the country devoured everything we could about reading comprehension. We read P. David Pearson, Ellin Oliver Keene, and Susan Zimmermann; Stephanie Harvey and Anne Goudvis; Debbie Miller; and Cris Tovani. The proficient reader research opened our eyes. The ideas for strategy instruction energized us. Constant conversation and the sharing of ideas about comprehension gave us the kind of classrooms we'd dreamed of. We lived and breathed comprehension instruction every day, and lovingly placed it right in the center of our literacy block. A good chunk of our language arts time was allocated to building a foundation of comprehension. Never before had we felt so invigorated by research and professional reading.

But with the advent of No Child Left Behind, the unadulterated time and freedom we once had for comprehension instruction and independent reading dwindled away—and fast. Federal, state, and district mandates forced us to do things differently. It was easier to measure quantities like reading rate and accuracy instead of concepts. As a result, new programs bullied the time away, right out from under our noses.

But my colleagues and I aren't the kind to make excuses. So we used our energies to think about why we believed in the power of comprehension instruction in the first place. Why? Because of an indisputable research base. Why? Because we had witnessed the evolution from a culture of assigning and assessing to a culture of thinking, leaving an abundance of readers and writers in its wake. In theory and in practice, explicit comprehension strategy instruction deserved a prominent place in the lives of teachers and children, then *and now.*

Without meaning to, we had unwisely restricted the thinking strategies to one narrow part of the school day. We had tucked them away nicely in the confines of the language arts block, providing what we thought was a permanent home. How limiting—for our students and ourselves. For so many reasons, we should have infused strategy instruction through science, social studies, and all the places in between. Opportunities for thinking belong everywhere. The all-day, everyday kind of everywhere.

We started to include explicit strategy instruction in social studies and science with content-area text—better late than never. It amazed us how the explicit teaching of the proficient reader strategies in social studies and science helped make the content more accessible. Once-unfriendly nonfiction text seemed more inviting when strategic thinking was applied. Even textbook reading became a bit less daunting when approached through the lens of the proficient reader, especially when the reading was immersed in rich conversation. Strategy instruction across the day was the missing link for our students. It helped them make sense of all of the fragmented pieces of their daily academic lives, with thinking as the unifier. It primed our students to receive the important content that might otherwise go unlearned.

Thinking ties it together for all of us, just like the "red thread" that Ron Ritchhart taught us about in *Intellectual Character* (2002). In many cultures the red thread symbolizes connection and unity. That's exactly what thinking does for us in the classroom. It's the mostly invisible connection that amalgamates all learning. Your daily schedule is the skeletal structure, and the thinking strategies are the musculature. Without the thinking, everything's just a pile of bones.

SOMETIMES WE . . .	BUT WE CAN . . .
• relegate thinking strategies to reading workshop, strategy lessons, or mini-lessons	• notice, name, and practice thinking strategies in all subjects, across all texts, in every part of the school day
• divide the learning lexicon into subjects or content areas	• purposely unite areas of study by making ubiquitous the language of the strategies
• define thinking strategies as something to be taught and tested	• redefine thinking as a metacognitive disposition that is constantly seeking meaning
• ask questions like "When should I teach the strategies?" and "How long should I spend on each one?"	• ask questions like "How can I design each day so that students have ample opportunities to think, reflect, and talk?"
• take responsibility for teaching students to think	• provide endless opportunities for students to practice *sapere aude*: daring to think on their own

If you'll indulge me, I have a metaphor to share before moving on to the more practical realities of spreading thinking across the day. Compare the following two paragraphs. It's the best way I can think of to show the importance of the thinking strategies in everyday instruction.

> I have two teenage daughters. Of course what I want most is for them to have a healthy self-esteem. I know that if they love themselves, they can be and do anything. Even though I teach them how to organize term papers, sort laundry, practice Internet safety, and style their hair, what's really important is that they believe in themselves. I teach them through everything I do, every day. Not just in what I say to them. I try to live right before their eyes so they see a woman who is confident, strong, and believes she can do anything—even when I don't always feel that way inside.

Now here's a parallel paragraph, with just a few changes.

> I have a classroom of students. Of course what I want most is for them to be thinkers. I know that if they think, they can be and do

Tanny, I love how you show us how your thinking about strategies has evolved. There are so many applications and places where the work can empower not only students in their learning, but also teachers in their practice.

—Cris

I get it! And don't you think that the more we live this philosophy—showing kids how being thoughtful, reflective, and smart looks and sounds—the more it defines us, and becomes who we really are, outside *and* inside?

—Debbie

anything. Even though I teach them math, social studies, science, and reading, what's really important is that they are reflective thinkers. I teach them the value of thinking through everything I do, every day. Not just in how I teach the curriculum. I try to live this philosophy right before their eyes so they can see a teacher who is thoughtful, reflective, and smart—even when I don't always feel that way inside.

We need to concatenate all of the pieces of the instructional day with strands of thinking, or as Robert J. Swartz calls it, thinking-based learning (2008). I'm on the lookout for it. In some schools where I work, it's an endangered species. But more and more, I notice glimmers of hope as I see teachers and students valuing the making of meaning in what they do across the school day. I hear the language of and see visual representations of schema, questioning, determining importance, visualizing, inferring, and synthesizing. This chapter is the ideal place to share some of the things I've used and observed in the schools where I work. Of course there is so much more to learn about infusing social studies and science with thinking strategies. I'll leave that to the expertise of my colleagues in this volume. But how about the seemingly insignificant moments in a typical day that can get lost in the shuffle—moments that can add up to something extraordinary if we build in opportunities for thinking?

The following ideas may seem small individually, but sometimes the most simple things can make a big difference over time. Try to think of these ideas as echoes of the minilessons you're teaching in the literacy block, or snapshot opportunities to foster curiosity and questioning. In these minutes of transition, minutes that every teacher manages every day, the language of the strategies can be used. Since little or no text is involved, every student can focus on meaningful connections, inferences, and important ideas. When used consistently over weeks and months, the number of times that students hear and use the thinking lexicon multiplies greatly, and all the while students are engaged in tasks where everyone is practicing the proficient reader strategies. We can move closer to the ideal where strategic thinking is present in the literacy block, social studies, science, and throughout the day.

Thoughtful Beginnings

Students step into the world of school as they join us each morning, a world comprised of routines, procedures, and rituals. These structures don't have to be solely managerial. They can just as easily provide a practice field for strategy use. Here are a couple of ideas to consider that emphasize thinking, right at the onset of the day.

Thinking Taglines

Organizations and individuals have used taglines for decades. A tagline is a phrase that sums up what a company stands for or what an individual believes in—and often sticks with us for a long while. The repetition and brevity of taglines contributes to their stickiness. We remember products, movies, and people from the taglines we hear and read, and some have stayed with us for decades. From "all the news that's fit to print" (*The New York Times*) to "a really big show" (Ed Sullivan) to "a long time ago in a galaxy far, far away" (*Star Wars*), taglines help us attach meaning to people and things. Most of the television newscasters in my city use a personal tagline to end a broadcast. And my friend Nancy ends every email with this personal tagline: "Enjoy every day." Anyone who knows Nancy associates this simple phrase with her calm, positive manner.

Consider creating your own beginning-of-the-day tagline about thinking. Talk to your students about how you consider what's important to you and how you synthesize many ideas when creating a tagline. You'll soon become known for what you repeat at the start of your morning together. Seize the opportunity to let your students know what you believe. Here are some examples of morning taglines I've used and heard:

- You're welcome here! And your thinking matters to me.
- Our time together is valuable. Let's think deeply and learn from each other.
- It's my honor to think and learn alongside you today.

Add another layer of depth by encouraging your students to create their own morning taglines. While eavesdropping in the schools where I work, I've collected the following examples from students at various grade levels:

- My friends and I will talk, play, and think today!
- I don't give up. I think and think.
- I want to learn something new before I go home today.

During morning meeting or greeting time, feature a particular student's tagline as the day begins. Use it as a way to notice and name metacognition. Create a "verbatim wall" filled with various thinking taglines. Possibilities abound.

Focused Visualization

Kids spill off the buses and fill the room, or walk the neighborhood streets to join you. Sometimes they leave behind rushed mornings of day care, babysitters, and last-minute homework. As my own daughters would attest, mornings are often chaotic. Not much thinking is required to navigate the before-school rush; it's more a matter of survival. This is all the more reason to consider beginning the day as my colleague Ben does—with focused visualization. I've included this morning ritual across grade levels with great results. Perhaps you've noticed professional actors, athletes, and musicians as they quietly focus before an event or game. Performers I know visualize or meditate simply because they know it enhances their abilities. Research overwhelmingly shows its effectiveness—increased concentration, greater stamina, and decreased tension. The body and mind can perform at higher levels when treated to moments of calm focus. Now there's nothing complicated about what Ben does with his fourth graders each morning. The difficult part is to make the time commitment and to make it a priority each day. It only takes a couple of minutes, but students enjoy it and feel the benefits just as Ben does. Guiding students through these imagery exercises allows them to practice being metacognitive, the great underpinning of the use of reading strategies. Here's one sequence with which you might begin. Ben helps students center and reflect in only a couple of minutes.

> Tanny is making such an important point here: the need to slow down and give students time to get centered and reflective. This meditation doesn't take much time, but helps kids focus for the whole day. Perfect!
>
> —*Aaron*

- After the students are settled in, ask them to get quiet and ready to think.

- Have your students think about one thing they do well. It can be anything—understanding math, getting along with others, text messaging, doing gymnastics.

- Ask them to consider why they are successful. Is it something they enjoy doing? Or maybe something that their parents think is important and taught them to do? Or maybe they have practiced this behavior, skill, or strategy often?

- Then ask kids to think about an area where they want to grow, and consider what they might do today to make this a reality. Give a little time for reflection.

- End this reflection session with a turn-and-talk. Students can share new learning and listen to their classmates.

This is just one way to facilitate thoughtful, focused visualization. Ben mixes it up with a variety of prompts. Sometimes he reads a meaningful quote aloud and asks kids to think about how it applies to their lives at school. On other days he shares a painting or other visual image and guides students through moments of reflection. My favorite kind of morning visualization, however, is when Ben poses the question, "How can you make your life or someone else's life a little bit better today?" I've heard a variety of responses to this prompt, including:

- I'll sit with Evan today at lunch. Since it is his first week at our school I want to make him feel welcome.

- On the math test today I'm going to take my time like my mom said.

- I will try to be a peacemaker on the playground.

At the very beginning of the day, students have already spent time being metacognitive. They have had a moment where their own thinking is what matters most, and have had the opportunity to listen to the thinking of others. When kids get a chance to settle down, think, and share, the stage is set for a day filled with amazing possibilities.

Thinking Together in the Opening Meeting

In preschool through high school, many of my colleagues build morning (or beginning of class) routines that foster a sense of togetherness and thinking. Take Andrea and Meredith, for instance. One is a primary teacher, the other intermediate. They teach in different schools, and have students with different needs. But they share a commitment to a thoughtful meeting time, before the demanding rush of the day sets in. For Andrea, there's a place for the calendar, the weather, and a brief discussion of the day ahead. For Meredith, there's attendance and homework to tend to. But both Andrea and Meredith give thinking strategies a prominent place in the opening moments with their students. It's simple—and powerful.

A painting, photograph, or calendar picture is posted near the group meeting area or projected on a screen. Beside the image, thinking stems are available for use: *I think, I wonder, I infer, I see, I feel.* Students are asked to observe the image and reflect. They are prompted to think about what is "behind" the picture, and not to spend too much time on what can be seen with the eyes. And then all that's needed is an opportunity to think aloud, a brief turn-and-talk. With the use of this simple, social, image-based thinking practice, day in and day out, kids become more observant—and inferential, curious, and thoughtful. And the learning travels into their reading and writing, which is exactly what we want.

Today's young people never need to create an image in their own minds, since these are constantly supplied by movies, video games, and even on phones. These kids need remedial visualization! Plus, such sensory meditation is also one of the greatest "prewriting" tools ever devised—the ability to do "internal research" in your own mind and memory.
—Smokey

I can't wait to try this! I love its simplicity, and how it gets children in the "thinking mode" right away!
—Debbie

235

Note: Want to extend your knowledge about the power of thinking with images? Visit www.vtshome.org. The former director of education at New York City's Museum of Modern Art (MoMA), Philip Yenawine, and his colleagues research and teach about visual literacy and how to teach thinking strategies with art.

Transitions: Moving Right Along

Our schedules are peppered with transitions: students moving from one classroom to another, to and from special or encore classes, from subject to subject in our own classrooms, and of course to and from lunch. A couple of extra minutes here and there can be most difficult to manage, for novice and veteran teachers alike. Granted, often it doesn't seem we have *enough* time to accomplish our daily plans, but inevitably we find ourselves with awkward bits of time to manage. I used to dread when this would happen, but now I expect and take advantage of it! I can see these transitions as opportunities to echo the language of the thinking strategies, to foster curiosity about the world around us, and to support kids as they make inferences about what they read and hear. I've used these ideas at a variety of times: when kids are lining up to leave the classroom, when we have a couple of minutes before the bell rings for a class change, while kids are cleaning up after a project. The most amazing thinking can happen beyond the categories and compartments—maybe especially there.

Fact React

No word in the English language rhymes with *month*.

A sneeze travels out of your nose at one hundred miles per hour.

Jack is the most common name in nursery rhymes.

The typical school day is often so structured that a dose of randomness can seem like a treat or, as Snapple calls it, "chance discovery and momentary amusement." There are plenty of places where you can get your hands on random facts that will spur kids' thinking, but Snapple Iced Tea lids are my pipeline to the random and interesting little tidbits that I might never otherwise know. For years, the lids on glass bottles of Snapple delighted my students and me. The first 675 facts are now retired from circulation and are archived at www.snapple.com/retired-facts. Or you can access the new facts that are found in the lids at www.snapple.com/real-facts. Better yet, drink up and save the lids for your classroom collection.

- Have a student draw a lid from the stash and read the random fact aloud.

- Students turn-and-talk, reacting to the fact they've heard.

- Encourage students to make connections, ask questions, and draw inferences.

Even a minute of Fact React will give your students an opportunity to think, talk, and listen. If you don't have access to Snapple bottles or you don't want to drink a lot of tea, get your random facts from online fact generators like www.randomfunfacts.com, www.mentalfloss.com/amazingfactgenerator/, or www.learnsomethingeveryday.co.uk. Note: You will want to pick and choose the facts from these sites to be shared with students, as some facts might only be appropriate for more mature audiences.

Think About Things

No doubt about it, concrete objects can transport us into the realm of strategic thinking. Deep thinking can be launched with a common, everyday physical object. I've seen it happen before my eyes hundreds of times, across the grade levels, across the curriculum. Besides common sense and experience, however, I trust in the power of concrete objects to teach thinking strategies because of the time-trusted, reliable work of Harvard's Project Zero. Shari Tishman, named project director in 2009, has expertise in instructional approaches that help people learn to think. Tishman states, "Closely examining everyday objects sparks students' curiosity and leads to increasingly complex thinking." She believes, as I do, that student thinking can be motivated and strengthened through the observation of, and discussion about, a simple object. Many kinds of learners benefit, the experience is easy and inexpensive to prepare, and the discussion can last anywhere from a few minutes to, well, who knows? In her article entitled "The Object of Their Attention" (2008), Tishman guides the reader through examples of content-area object-based lessons. Let's think here, however, about how to use objects as quick, easy transitions that transform small bits of time into rich conversation.

Collect random objects from your garage, kitchen, the antique store, yard sales—anywhere, really. I have an old green bag that houses all of the things I've found just for this purpose. Develop an eye for things that your students might find interesting or might have limited background knowledge of. Place the object under a document camera or pass the object around. Start with student observations. Then encourage their questions and inferences. With your unobtrusive, guided facilitation, the conversation will become increasingly complex. When modeling this experience for the first few times, I might ask: What do you notice about this object? What seems to be important here? What do you wonder? Who might use this object? Do you think it is from the past or present? What is your evidence? If you need ideas for the first few times you try this exercise, use a shoehorn, a crumber, or a guitar pick.

Strategic Segues

We want to give as many opportunities as possible for original thinking, and we want to make it easy to do so. One of the most helpful resources for thinkers is a menu of thinking stems. Many of the authors featured in this very book, myself included, include variations of thinking stems in their own work. There's a reason for that. Whether kids are writing, talking, or responding to reading, these stems can ease students into sharing their thinking without having to wonder where to start. A few multipurpose stems are:

- I'm noticing . . .
- I wonder . . .
- Maybe . . .
- Now I'm thinking . . .

With thinking stems available on charts, on bookmarks, in their journals, or wherever, kids who need this kind of support can choose a stem that helps them say what's on their mind. And just like with any support, the need for these stems will diminish over time as students move toward more confidence in thoughtful expression.

So as you transition from one lesson or subject to another, encourage students to refer to the thinking stems before you move on to something new. They can quickly talk about their new thinking with a partner, creating some closure for what was addressed. They will be naturally using the language of the strategies with just a few thinking stems and a quick turn-and-talk.

Closing up Shop: Another Day Is Done

Great is the art of beginning, but greater is the art of ending.

—Robert Heinlein

The last few minutes of the day are some of the most important. Too often, however, they slip away without a real sense of closure. As a teacher, I want my students to leave my classroom each day not with jumbled thinking about the series of seemingly disjointed experiences they've had, but with the pleasure and meaning that thoughtful closure can bring. The end of a day is an ideal place for determining importance and synthesis. Through reflection and conversation, everyone can make the day's experience more meaningful.

Psychology can teach us a lot about the ending of a learning session. In fact, there's a name for this: the closure principle. Closure helps us contextualize experiences we have, and when there is closure in a person's thinking, meaning is created that is longer lasting than if closure is absent. Even a brief period of closure at the end of a school day can help maximize the chances that students will be metacognitive about the day's happenings, and make meaning of new learning.

There are dozens of books about how to best begin the school day. Books about routines and procedures, books about morning meetings, books about classroom management. Not so much support is available to us when it comes to how to best end the school day. Ironic, it seems, if you think about Robert Heinlein's quotation on the previous page. So let's consider a few ways to close out the school day, ways that emphasize reflection and encourage kids to wonder, infer, connect, summarize, and synthesize.

The Six-Word Synthesis

Perhaps you've already latched onto the "six-word" craze in your classroom or in your personal reading and writing. If so, you know how simple and powerful this little thought-provoker can be. If not, you'll surely want to give it a try very soon. Here's what I know.

Legend has it that Ernest Hemingway took a dare from a reader: to write a short story using only six words. Hemingway did not shy away from the challenge, writing the six-word story that prompted thousands of people around the world to write sparingly but think deeply. Hemingway's story prompts us to question and infer: "For sale: baby shoes, never worn." Decades later, books, magazines, radio, and television programs have capitalized on this technique that pushes both the writer and the reader to think.

Using the idea of a six-word story can translate into powerful synthesis in the classroom. At the end of a busy day, ask your students to cluster into small groups and reflect upon the day. Ask kids to think about what mattered most or about something important or interesting they learned during

> Maybe this is trivial, but six-word auto-biographies are a great warm-up activity for teacher workshops. The best one I ever heard: "Bottle blonde. Everyone knew. Never cared."
> —Smokey

the day, but the synthesis must consist of exactly six words. It doesn't have to be a six-word sentence; it can be a six-word phrase or a series of six adjectives or verbs. Believe me, it sounds easier than it is! Students will surely engage in meaningful discussion as they identify and synthesize meaningful information and experiences from throughout the school day. Their six-word syntheses can be shared during the last few minutes of class or can be saved for the next day's opening thoughts, connecting the learning from one day to the next. And it works across the curriculum, as these student examples illustrate:

- You put together when you add. (math, kindergarten)
- Chlorophyll allows plants to get energy. (science, fourth grade)
- Preterite and imperfect are past tenses. (Spanish, tenth grade)
- Why did Martin have to die? (reading, third grade)
- Gregor Mendel discovered how genetics works. (science, sixth grade)
- People in communities help each other. (social studies, second grade)
- For loudness, bow by the bridge. (orchestra, middle school)
- Boo Radley stayed shut up inside. (English, ninth grade)

My friend Elizabeth teaches fifth grade. After finishing a Gary Paulsen read-aloud, Elizabeth asked her students to do a "six-word book report." Written on sentence strips, the syntheses ranged from the literal to the amazingly deep. One student wrote: Boy all alone in the woods. Another wrote: Courage and determination save the day.

Just one warning about these six-word thinking boosters: They are addictive. You and your students will find yourselves thinking and talking in six words, even when you don't intend to! Writing and sharing these syntheses are engaging, but most importantly it gives students time to determine importance with regard to new learning and synthesize it in a creative way.

The Day in Review

It's the universal, robotic interchange between parent and child:

PARENT: So what did you learn at school today?

CHILD: Nothing.

Or sometimes it goes like this:

PARENT: So how was school today?

CHILD: Fine.

At different times in my life I've asked these questions and given these answers. It's a mindless interchange, and frankly it bothers me. I tell kids that if they are lucky enough to have someone in their lives who asks these questions, then they need to be considerate enough to give thoughtful answers. At conferences and parent nights, I encourage caretakers and guardians to be sure to ask these questions daily, because as a class we are going to spend time crafting the answers. Sometimes I even role-play with kids at the end of a school day, asking them, "So what did you learn today?" I ask them to turn-and-talk as I cruise around listening in. Other times, when time is more abundant, I'll project a three-by-three grid onto the board, and fill the nine squares with student responses to the age-old question. It can be cool to share these ideas with kids the following morning, too, to bridge the days together. Or keep these responses over a week's time and review them together on Friday. Teachers and kids alike are amazed when they stop to reflect upon and synthesize new learning. Once again, this idea can support students as they make sense out of the many things they learn across the span of a school day. It is a simple yet powerful way to determine importance and make meaning.

Reflect with a Strategy Menu

Another tool for synthesis at the end of a busy day is simply to ask students to select from a strategy menu. Post options and allow kids to make their thinking visible and/or audible. Kids can jot down thinking on index cards, mini–white boards, sticky notes—or share aloud with a friend. Menu options might include:

- one new word you heard today
- one important fact you learned
- one opinion you have about something you read
- one question that lingers
- one quick sketch that symbolizes new learning

Wrap up the day by asking students to find a classmate to whom they have not spoken today, and exchange thinking before returning to their seats.

Sapere Aude!

So there you have it—a string of ideas for spreading thinking across and into the day, beyond the categories of content, into the cracks and crevices of the typical school schedule. That's really all I can give you: ideas, and perhaps a few questions too. Think about your typical routine. Think about how many opportunities your students have to practice the concept of *sapere aude*, courageous thinking. Provide them every chance you can to talk, question, reflect, connect, infer, visualize, synthesize, and talk some more. Use all of those little places in the day to allow kids every chance to make meaning of their learning lives.

Just one more thought. Consider the words of famous American baritone Thomas Hampson: "Singing is not about timbres or category labels, singing is about fascinating acoustical properties like the colors of the human voice which derive from thought and emotion." I see thinking and comprehending in much the same way. Comprehension is not about subjects or category labels. Comprehension is about fascinating thinking, derived from reading, writing, talking, and (just as any musician will tell you) a whole lot of practice. With opportunities for these lavished across the school day, our students will begin to think deeply and courageously. *Sapere aude!*

Courageous thinking! I'm excited for you to teach me how to pronounce it. I'm hanging this phrase above my writing desk. Courageous thinking! Sapere Aude! Great words make life so much better. Thanks, Tanny.

—Sam

References

BWH Ventures, LLC. n.d. "Home Page." http://www.randomfunfacts.com (accessed October 14, 2010).

Mental_Floss. n.d. "Amazing Fact Generator." http://www.mentalfloss.com/amazingfactgenerator/ (accessed October 14, 2010).

Ritchhart, Ron. 2002. *Intellectual Character: What It Is, Why It Matters, and How to Get It.* Hoboken, NJ: Jossey-Bass.

Snapple Beverage Corp. 2010. "Real Facts." http://www.snapple.com/real-facts/ (accessed October 14, 2010).

Snapple Beverage Corp. 2010. "Retired Facts." http://www.snapple.com/retired-facts/ (accessed October 14, 2010).

Swartz, Robert J. 2008. "Energizing Learning." *Educational Leadership* 65 (5): 26–31.

Tishman, Shari. 2008. "The Object of Their Attention." *Educational Leadership* 65 (5): 44–46.

Visual Thinking Strategies. 2010. "Home Page." http://www.vtshome.org (accessed October 14, 2010).

Young. 2010. "Learn Something Every Day." http://www.learnsomethingeveryday.co.uk (accessed October 14, 2010).

Toward the Next Generation of Comprehension Instruction

A Coda

P. David Pearson

My colleagues—the editors and authors of this diverse array of chapters—have written an important book about reading comprehension instruction, and at just the right time. It is important because it achieves two essential goals on behalf of all those professionals committed to comprehension as the core of reading instruction. First, it reasserts the fundamental, research-based principles that have guided responsible comprehension instruction for nearly three decades. Second, it responds, in both explicit and implicit ways, to the recent criticisms of comprehension instruction, especially instruction that helps students learn how to use comprehension and metacognitive strategies to understand otherwise puzzling text,

As important as these goals are, they are not the real genius of this book. Its real genius is that it is written by teachers, for teachers. All of the authors in this book know what classrooms are like—either because they teach in classrooms every day or because they spend a lot of time working with teachers in classrooms and in professional development settings. This means that authenticity and integrity pervade every chapter in this book. Teachers will immediately sense this authenticity on their way to realizing that this book offers an endless supply of useful suggestions for creating comprehension inside classrooms.

Achieving the Major Goals

Research-Based Principles

In the spirit of honoring the importance of reading to learn, I will frame my synthesis of the research-based principles on which this book is based as an account of what I learned from reading the chapters in this important volume. I have organized them as a set of principles that I, being a focused and highly strategic reader, inferred from reading across all the chapters. I believe, and I hope, they are an appropriate summary (maybe even a synthesis) of the wonderful ideas in this text.

Teaching Comprehension Is a Moral Enterprise

Let's begin with the broadest and, I think, most important principle. Teachers don't enter into the kind of instruction privileged in this volume just so students can and will read better. They do it because they know that comprehension opens a world of opportunity—that the ability to make sense of text, to engage with the big ideas of literature, and to learn about how the world around them works makes it possible for students to live a good life, a life in which reading is a never-ending source of learning, enjoyment, and reflection. We may not think about it every day when we enter the classroom, but it really is true that we teach comprehension to create a competitive workforce for the global economy, to promote a literate citizenry worthy of our democracy, and to guarantee that each student we have the privilege of serving has the tools to live an "examined" life. It is useful sometimes to step back and ask ourselves why we do what we do. The authors of this book invite us to do just that. Actually a few of them—including Zimmermann, Upzack Garcia, and Commins—*insist* we do just that.

Comprehension Instruction Begins and Ends in the Hearts and Minds of Students

We've known about the impact of knowledge on comprehension for several decades; that was the fundamental message we learned from schema theory in the 1970s. And many of the authors of this volume have published eloquent accounts, both in this volume and in previous works, of how we can use knowledge to promote comprehension. What has changed in the last few years is that we are much more aware of the complementary idea that knowledge is as much a consequence as it is a cause of comprehension: Knowledge begets comprehension begets knowledge begets comprehension. . . . This is the kind of virtuous cycle we would like to promote in schools instead of the vicious cycle we are all too well aware of—the one in which reading failure prompts reading avoidance prompts failure, and so on. Put differently, we can and should say that good comprehension instruction puts the interests, needs, and knowledge resources of students at the heart of comprehension instruction. In her chapter, Marjorie Larner truly enacts this principle when she directly asks students themselves how comprehension instruction has affected them as learners.

Reading to Learn Is Always a Part of Learning to Read[1]

They don't always say so out loud (as Gina Cervetti, Anne Goudvis, and Brad Buhrow do), but one of the goals that the authors of this volume share with me is to do everything possible to downplay the commonly expressed distinction between learning to read and reading to learn. I have tired of hearing the phrase that in grades 1–3, kids learn to read, and after that they read to learn (Pearson and Cervetti in press). The authors of this volume reject that idea, either explicitly or implicitly. In its place they champion the idea that learning from reading should be part of the reading equation from the outset of kindergarten and first grade. Kids should always be reading content that is worth knowing. They should encounter ideas that promote the acquisition of knowledge, insight, human understanding, and joy. Even though this book is more about reading than writing, I would add (and I think that all the authors would agree) that students should also be writing about things that matter, about those very understandings, insights, and moments of joy. Then and only then will they learn that reading and writing are tools for learning—a message some of our commercial curricula seem hard-pressed to promote.

If we want to promote this idea that reading to learn is always a part of learning to read, we need to really emphasize the tool metaphor—that reading and writing (and I would add language, especially what we have

---

[1] These ideas first appeared in a revision of my own perspective on the Radical Middle that I wrote for the second edition of Rona Flippo's book *Reading Researchers in Search of Common Ground* (in press). They appear here with the permission of the author and the editor.

TABLE 1: LANGUAGE PROCESSES AS LEARNING TOOLS				
		DISCIPLINES		
		Literature	Science	Social Studies	Mathematics
Learning Tools	Reading	✔	✔	✔	✔
	Writing	✔	✔	✔	✔
	Language	✔	✔	✔	✔

come to call *academic language*) are tools for learning. And they are best put to service in acquiring knowledge and inquiry skills in disciplines like science, social studies, mathematics, and literature. As a vivid example of this principle, in her chapter, Tanny McGregor talks about extending the use of the thinking tools of language throughout the school day. By the way, I think it is better to think of literature (not language arts but literature) as a discipline on a par with the subject areas of schooling.[2] Then the process parts of the language arts (reading, writing, and language) are released from the sole grasp of literature and are available for all the disciplines. Think of it as a matrix with disciplines across the top and tools for learning down the side, as depicted in Table 1.

Were we to take such a matrix seriously, we would have very different basal reading programs than those currently on the market because the distribution of disciplines and genres would be much broader in scope than is currently the case. This broader scope would have the side benefit of broadening the appeal of basal content to a wider range of learners than is possible with the literature-centric basal programs in today's market. But what is really important about this reconceptualization is that it means that the acquisition of knowledge, understanding, insight, and (yes) joy would always provide a context for honing our language-based learning tools. Wouldn't that be a great expectation to hold—that when we learn new ideas, we improve our language skills!

---

[2] I agree with those who argue that the subject matter of literature is the human experience itself—life and death, love and hate, friendship and betrayal, harmonizing with or harnessing the natural environment, and so on.

Comprehension Is as Dependent on Affect as It Is on Cognition

There is no denying the importance of cognitive activity and outcomes in the comprehension process. I just said as much in acknowledging the importance of knowledge. And I have spent most of my career championing cognitive connections between the texts kids read and the background knowledge they bring to the classroom. But we have not (or at least I have not) always paid as much attention to the affective side of understanding as we (I) might, focusing more on the ideas that students gain from reading rather than on feelings or motives.

In nearly every chapter in this volume my fellow authors encourage us to broaden our view of comprehension, to worry as much about the *will* and *thrill* of reading as about the *skill*. This perspective comes packaged in many forms, each with different terms. In the chapters that emphasize literature, including those by Leslie Blauman and Chryse Hutchins, we are reminded that encouraging aesthetic responses to literature is core to the literary experience (my preference has always been to deal with aesthetic response before more everyday comprehension responses so as to encourage personal responses while they are still fresh in students' recollections). We are also reminded that even when students read the informational texts of social studies and science, they can—if teachers ground the experience in "hands-on" science or "minds-on" social studies—promote a high degree of engagement. Reading about how the natural or social world works need not, should not, be *boring* (to borrow from the most popular of adolescent terms to describe school!). Finding ways to connect these texts to students' lives is one way of achieving engagement, as is providing choice. Not everyone has to read the same text about gravity or the War of 1812; it makes for interesting discussions, in fact, when students bring different perspectives and knowledge sources to the table. Students can even choose the ways in which they want to demonstrate their understanding; Susie can answer some constructed response questions, Miguel can write an essay, and Darien can make a PowerPoint presentation about the very same text. And each form of response represents an opportunity to assess student comprehension.

Scaffolding Is the Central Instructional Metaphor in Guiding Students Along the Path of Independence

When Wood, Bruner, and Ross (1976) coined the scaffolding metaphor as a way of describing what expert tutors do to promote problem solving among students, they could not have possibly imagined how popular the term would become as a way for educators to describe the pedagogical journey from teacher-dependent to completely independent learning on the part of students.

The instant I read Wood et al.'s account when it appeared in the mid 1970s, I was smitten. It captured exactly what I was trying, albeit clumsily, to communicate to teachers about the genius of instruction. I soon incorporated the term into my teacher lexicon—along with prior knowledge, comprehension strategy, inference, and metacognition—as terms to describe the basics of comprehension instruction. It was the core concept behind another popular metaphor, *the gradual release of responsibility* (hereafter GRR), that Meg Gallagher and I coined in 1983 to describe the genius of the work that Joe Campione and Ann Brown were doing with learning-disabled students at the Center for the Study of Reading.

What was, and is, so compelling about the scaffolding metaphor is that it captures most of the important insights we have developed about good pedagogy. Here are my top four insights.

1. *We reduce the amount of scaffolding* across *time (and lessons) as students develop greater independent control in applying any strategy, skill, or practice we want them to use with regularity.* This is the most common and obvious of insights about scaffolding, the very core of the GRR framework. But it does *not* mean, as many infer, that we always begin a sequence with modeling, then moving to guided practice, and finally independent practice. We could begin a sequence by asking students to "try it on their own," offering feedback and assistance as students demonstrate the need for it. James Baumann, an instructional researcher who has made significant contributions to comprehension research, once asked me in a conference session on strategy instruction, "David, how much explicit instruction should a teacher provide?" My response: "As little as possible." And I meant it sincerely. There is no inherent virtue in explicit instruction and modeling. We offer if and when students demonstrate less than completely independent control over an activity; and we provide just enough scaffolding so that students can perform the activity successfully. It is a "Goldilocks" phenomenon—not too much, not too little, but *just the right amount.*

2. *We vary the amount of scaffolding offered* within *any given lesson as students demonstrate the capacity to control the strategy, skill, or practice.* It is extremely powerful for a group of students,

within the context of a single lesson, to demonstrate to themselves that they can do more on their own by the end of a lesson than they could at the beginning.

3. *We can and should vary scaffolding between students within a single lesson.* Part of the genius of the gradual release of responsibility framework is that it applies in so many situations. We have already suggested that we can vary the scaffolding provided to students across lessons and across time within a lesson. But we can also differentiate the nature and amount of scaffolding across students within a given lesson. For example, in a discussion about a story or an informational text, one student may benefit from a clue about what page to look at to find information relevant to answering a question, a second may be helped by restating the question in different words, and a third by turning an open-ended (Why did Henry take Jake's backpack?) into a forced choice question (Did Henry take Jake's backpack for revenge or money?).

4. *We are prepared to revert to greater (or lesser) scaffolding as text and task demands create varying scaffolding needs.* This, for me, is the most powerful and important insight about scaffolding. If we accept the general notion that reading comprehension represents an interaction between a reader, a text, and a "task" within a sociocultural context (RAND Reading Study Group 2002), then we must accept the idea that our comprehension "ability" varies with the text and task. And the path to progress is not always a straight line: Show me a reader who is a master comprehender today, and I'll show you one who isn't tomorrow. All I have to do is to up the ante on the complexity of the text, the obscurity of its topic, or the cognitive demand of the comprehension task. As teachers, we must always be prepared to revert to greater scaffolding when one of these elements (text, topic, or task) creates greater demands on readers. Just as surely, we must be prepared to withdraw that scaffolding when these "stars" of comprehension are more positively aligned. It is this insight that I had in mind when I responded to Baumann's query with the "as little as possible" explicit instruction answer. And this is precisely what Debbie Miller has in mind when she admonishes us to release responsibility a little faster than we have in the past.

Responding to the Critics of Strategy Instruction

In some ways, it is clear that an underlying purpose of this book is to respond to the criticisms that have been leveled at comprehension instruction, particularly strategy instruction, over the last several years. Keene, in the opening chapter, lays out a compelling account of all the things we have learned because we have been engaged in strategy instruction as a profession for the past thirty years. And there is an assumption, in most of the chapters, that others in the profession are questioning some of the basic assumptions about strategy instruction. The response is effective, I believe, because the authors of the chapters in this book realize what I also know to be true—that the critiques offered of strategy instruction are often a critique not of thoughtfully designed and executed strategy instruction, but of some hypothetical caricature of strategy instruction. So my fellow authors have redoubled their efforts to lay out first principles to guide our efforts, along with compelling examples of what good strategy instruction should look like. I think they have accomplished that goal. This book is justified on these grounds alone.

In my personal view, the fundamental reason why strategy instruction has been vulnerable to critique is that when it gets implemented in commercial reading programs (which is surely the site of its most widespread implementation), the dynamic, adaptive, and responsive character it has in the hands of the authors of the chapters in this volume is replaced by rigidity and inflexibility. Even worse, if and when it becomes the object of assessment (as is highly likely in our current hyper-accountability context) it is likely to become even more set in stone. Risking the label of a troglodyte, I would remind readers that when I wrote about comprehension strategies with Roehler, Dole, and Duffy (1992), we cautioned teachers that (a) good reading strategies are as adaptable as they are intentional and (b) good strategy instruction is as adaptable as it is intentional. Both reading strategies and the instruction we offer to support them cannot survive in an environment that requires strict adherence to accountability demands.

So I would argue (indeed I have quite recently [Pearson in press]) that strategy instruction, especially in the ways in which it has been put into practice in the modern curriculum (e.g., basals and kits), stands in need of reform. It may not be as effective as conventional discussions that, in one way or another, focus on knowledge acquisition (McKeown, Beck, and Blake 2009; Wilkinson and Son 2011). And it may breed an excessive reliance on abstract, content-free, metacognitive introspection about strategy use (Pearson and Fielding 1991).

When strategy instruction becomes too generic and abstract, too "isolated" from the goal of acquiring knowledge and insight, it is in danger of becoming an end unto itself—what Pearson and Fielding (1991) speculated might become "introspective nightmares." We get these nightmares when the enactment of the strategy becomes more complicated than the ideas that the strategies were supposed to help students acquire. I am not arguing that we should throw out all forms of strategy instruction. To the contrary, I remain committed to high-quality strategy instruction, instruction that demonstrates the purpose and utility (what they buy you in terms of learning goals) of strategies at every step along the way. Put differently, I endorse the dynamic, adaptable, thoughtful model of strategy instruction put forward in the chapters of this book. So I am completely on board with Ellin Keene's conceptualization of the outcomes and dimensions of understanding or Debbie Miller's advice to move more rapidly toward independence, Cris Tovani's notion of a tool kit for getting yourself unstuck, and Samantha Bennett's integration of comprehension instruction with planning and assessment. These fellow authors convey precisely the approach to strategy instruction we must take to compensate for the more "compliant" enactments we find in some of the commercial attempts to promote strategies, especially those that couple it with standards and assessments for strategy use.

To ensure that strategy instruction gets off to a good start, students must acquire "insider" knowledge about why and how we use strategies, as Ellin Keene and Cris Tovani (among others) have always contended. And they benefit greatly from the instant feedback demonstrating to them that strategies are useful—that pulling out just the right tool to help you over a hurdle at just the right moment makes you a smarter, more effective, and more strategic reader.

In a sense, strategies suffer from the same rap as phonics rules. Ideally they are only a means to an end. It's when phonics rules or strategies become their own goals that the system self-destructs. In such circumstances, both teachers and students are more likely to engage in mock compliance. Thus the strategies get put into a special "school talk" box that is hauled out only when the assignment requires it and then put back on a shelf well out of reach for everyday reading. The only way to block mock compliance is to provide guided apprenticeships that help students learn how, when, and why to apply strategies so that they can see their transparent benefit.

A Final Plea

I close this coda with a plea to all readers of this wonderful book on reading comprehension. And the plea is simple: Don't get too enamored with comprehension as the sole solution to all the problems of modern reading instruction. Comprehension instruction can make the critical difference in student engagement and achievement, but only if it gets enacted in an ecologically balanced instructional program, one that ensures that students get a fair shot at a lot of other reading and language skills and understandings. Writing in 2002, Nell Duke and I argued that comprehension instruction, especially ambitious strategy instruction (which we fully embraced and championed), could only be nurtured in a pedagogical surround that paid adequate attention to phonics and word recognition, vocabulary, rich discussions of text, sound writing instruction, opportunities for students to read a wide range of texts and genres independently, high-quality assessment, and motivation and engagement. To that list, writing from today's perspective, I would echo my colleagues Stephanie Harvey, Anne Goudvis, Brad Buhrow, and Gina Cervetti in keeping knowledge acquisition high on one's pedagogical agenda. I know that the authors of this volume share this view of ecological balance. I encourage all those who read this volume to embrace such a view. If and when you do, you'll find that your comprehension curriculum will be more powerful and more fruitful than ever. Happy teaching—and learning.

References

Duke, Nell, and P. David Pearson. 2002. "Effective Practices for Developing Reading Comprehension." In *What Research Has to Say About Reading Instruction*, 3d ed., edited by A. Farstrup and J. Samuels, 205–42. Newark, DE: International Reading Association.

McKeown, Margaret G., Isabel L. Beck, and Ronette G. K. Blake. 2009. "Rethinking Reading Comprehension Instruction: A Comparison of Reading Strategies and Content Approaches." *Reading Research Quarterly* 44 (3): 218–53.

Pearson, P. David. In press. "An Update on Life in the Radical Middle: A Personal Apology for a Balanced View of Reading." In *Reading Researchers in Search of Common Ground*, 2d ed., edited by R. Flippo. Newark, DE: International Reading Association.

Pearson, P. David, and Gina N. Cervetti. In press. "Literacy Education: Should the Focus Be on 'Reading to Learn' or 'Learning to Read'?" In *Curriculum and Instruction: Debating Issues in American Education*, edited by C. J. Russo and A. J. Eackle. New York: Sage.

Pearson P. David, and Linda G. Fielding. 1991. "Comprehension Instruction." In *Handbook of Reading Research*, vol. 2, edited by R. Barr, M. L. Kamil, P. Mosenthal, and P. D. Pearson, 815–60. New York: Longman.

Pearson, P. David, and Margaret C. Gallagher. 1983. "The Instruction of Reading Comprehension." *Contemporary Educational Psychology* 8: 317–44.

Pearson, P. David, Laura Roehler, Janice Dole, and Gerald Duffy. 1992. "Developing Expertise in Reading Comprehension." In *What Research Says to the Teacher*, 2d ed., edited by S. J. Samuels and A. E. Farstrup, 145–99. Newark, DE: International Reading Association.

RAND Reading Study Group. 2002. *Reading for Understanding: Toward an R&D Program in Reading Comprehension*. Santa Monica, CA: RAND.

Wilkinson, Ian A. G., and E. Hye Son. 2011. "A Dialogical Turn in Research on Learning and Teaching to Comprehend." In *Handbook of Reading Research*, vol. 4, edited by M. L. Kamil, P. David Pearson, Elizabeth Moje, and Peter Afflerbach. London: Routledge.

Wood, David, Jerome S. Bruner, and Gail Ross. 1976. "The Role of Tutoring in Problem Solving." *Journal of Psychology and Psychiatry* 17 (2): 89–100.

Books Recommended by Our Contributors

Allen, Jo Beth. 2007. *Creating Welcoming Schools: A Practical Guide to Home-School Partnerships with Diverse Families.* **New York: Teachers College Press**.

Great teachers get to know, appreciate, and build upon what students bring with them from home. This book provides teachers with an abundance of ideas to connect with children and their families from all backgrounds. NC

Allen, Patrick A. 2009. *Conferring: The Keystone of the Reader's Workshop.* **Portland ME: Stenhouse.**

Patrick's book is a huge step forward in thinking about conferring with students. His approach is clearly spelled out on these pages with numerous examples of students' progress in reading. His humorous voice combines with a range of practical tools to make this a must-have for reading teachers. EOK

Allington, Richard. L. 2008. *What Really Matters in Response to Intervention: Research-Based Designs.* **Columbus, OH: Allyn & Bacon.**

An excellent critique of current approaches to RTI. Replace "RTI" with "second language learners" as you read, and nearly all the points and suggestions are applicable. Addressing the needs of diverse learners is an all-day, every-teacher responsibility. NC

Apple, Michael, and James Beane. 2007. *Democratic Schools: Lessons in Powerful Education,* 2d ed. Portsmouth, NH: Heinemann.

This updated version of Apple and Beane's stirring classic adds new stories of schools that take democracy seriously and treat students as citizens, not consumers in training. A must-read for anyone who feels part of the progressive tradition in American education. Elsewhere, Apple continues to document the corporate invasion of our schools, while Beane has given us vital models of curricular integration and inquiry. HSD

Ayers, William, Gloria Ladson-Billings, Gregory Miche, and Pedro Noguero, eds. 2008. *City Kids City Schools: More Reports from the Front Row.* New York: The New Press.

If you were deserted on a desert island with your urban school, and you could only have one book, I would strongly recommend *City Kids City Schools: More Reports from the Front Row.* Filled with practical ideas for the classrooms, research and statistics, essays from related fields of social justice, politics and history, spoken word, poetry, memoir, and fiction, this is a beautifully written relevant thought-provoking collection of varied genres that will stimulate discussion, deepen understanding, and inspire deepening capacity to reach every child in our schools. ML

Beers, Kylene, Robert Probst, and Linda Rief, eds. 2007. *Adolescent Literacy: Turning Promise into Practice.* Portsmouth, NH: Heinemann.

How can you not love a book that includes writing about adolescent learning from some of the most learned and practical people in the field today? I think this book sets a new standard for edited volumes. It covers a very wide range of topics and is so reader friendly and useful. EOK

Bomer, Katherine. 2010. *Hidden Gems: Naming and Teaching from the Brilliance in Every Student's Writing.* Portsmouth, NH: Heinemann.

Katherine's beautiful book about student writing holds many insights for reading teachers as well. She espouses a "cup half full" approach to understanding individual learners and building from their strengths that is very relevant across the content areas. EOK

Bracey, Gerald W. 2009. *Education Hell: Rhetoric vs. Reality, Transforming the Fire Consuming American's Schools.* Alexandria, VA: Educational Research Service.

This collection of Bracey's hard-hitting essays about the state of education during the NCLB years exposes how "accountability masquerading as reform" is destroying our public school system. Bracey begins by detailing the history of American school reform efforts over many years, focusing on the recent "descent into test mania" and ending with a chapter on the essential role public education plays in a democracy. AG

Brookhart, Susan. 2008. *How to Give Effective Feedback to Your Students.* Alexandria, VA: ASCD (Association for Supervision and Curriculum Development).

Working on my latest book, *So What Do They Really Know?*, I searched high and low for people in the field who could help me get smarter about giving students useful feedback. Discovering Susan Brookhart's book, guided me, fed me, and suggested ways to improve the way I give feed-back. If you want to not only grade your students' work but also help them improve their understanding, this is the book for you. CT

Casanova, Ursula. 2010. *Si Se Puede! Learning from a High School That Beat the Odds.* **New York: Teacher's College Press.**

In this time of endless litanies about "failing schools" and plummeting morale, there is good news on the high school front. Cibola High in Arizona has transformed itself into a true community of learners, and a place where cultural and linguistic diversity are a source of strength and excellence and test scores are on the rise. The book includes many practical ideas, shared by the teachers, school leaders, and students, of how this unique school continues to flourish. AG

Conrad, Lori L., Missy Matthews, Cheryl Zimmerman, and Patrick A. Allen. 2008. *Put Thinking to the Test.* **Portland, ME: Stenhouse.**

As students are learning to think strategically in all areas of the curriculum, why not extend comprehension instruction into the test-taking arena? After years of classroom experience developing lessons in strategic thinking, the authors offer groundbreaking ideas on how kids can be taught to think effectively as test takers. Each chapter offers concrete lessons, student samples, and anchor charts, going well beyond the standard test-prep fare. CH

Darling Hammond, Linda. 2008. *Powerful Learning What We Know About Teaching for Understanding.* **San Francisco: Jossey-Bass.**

Linda Darling Hammond and an impressive group of thoughtful scholars offer an extensive exploration of the best K–12 researched-based classroom practices on children's learning and teaching for understanding. SH

Darling-Hammond, Linda. 2010. *The Flat World and Education: How America's Commitment to Equity Will Determine Our Future.* **New York: Teachers College Press**.

This book demonstrates that without significant changes in the ways that teachers are prepared, schools are organized, and knowledge is disseminated, children in the U.S. will not be able to hold their own in the changing global context. NC

Dweck, Carol. 2007. *Mindset: The New Psychology of Success.* **New York: Ballantine.**

When school doesn't go the way I want it to, the thinking in this book fortifies me. Carol Dweck's synthesis of research re-enforces my belief that "Smart is not something you are. It is something you get." CT

Mindset really got me thinking about how children perceive intelligence. Do they see their intelligence as something that is fixed—I'm born with a certain amount and that's it, or, do they see intelligence as something that's more malleable—I have the power to make myself smarter through hard work, effort, and determination? This book and its implications for teaching, learning, and living will change you—I so wish I had had it when my own children were little! DM

Escamilla, Kathy, and Susan Hopewell. 2009. "Transitions to Biliteracy." In *International Perspectives on Bilingual Education: Policy, Practice, and Controversy,* edited by John E. Petrovic, 69–94. Charlotte, NC: Information Age Publishing.

This chapter discuss the need for a paradigm shift in the current thinking about how to teach emerging bilingual students in the United States. The authors address the idea that all languages are resources to help bilingual students in their academic development and that in fact bilingualism is a positive outcome for all students. The article recounts a study in which emerging bilingual students are being taught in settings where they are allowed to be the simultaneous bilingual children they are and instructors are working to develop a positive trajectory toward biliteracy. AUG

Gallagher, Kelly. 2009. *Readicide.* Portland, ME: Stenhouse.

In this eloquent and thoughtful tirade, high school teacher Kelly Gallagher describes exactly what's happening during too many English and reading classes in our middle and high schools (and we would add elementary schools as well). He calls it "readicide"—"the systematic killing of the love of reading often exacerbated by the inane, mind-numbing practices found in schools." Fortunately, the book is full of wonderful teaching ideas for what teachers who keep kids first and foremost in their minds must to do about it. AG

Hyde, Arthur. 2006. *Comprehending Math: Adapting Reading Strategies to Teach Mathematics, K–6.* Portsmouth, NH: Heinemann.

From inferring to visualizing, Hyde shares how comprehension strategies can help kids think deeply about solving story problems as well as open-ended mathematical tasks. This information is a boon for everyone seeking effective ways to "braid" mathematics, language, and thinking into a vibrant learning experience for students in the elementary grades. CH

Jones, Stephanie. 2004. *Girls, Social Class and Literacy: What Teachers Can Do to Make a Difference.* Portsmouth, NH. Heinemann.

Jones takes on the major social issue of poverty in our public schools. She discusses why and how to honor students' connections as well as their disconnections to their reading. By affirming these disconnections, Jones helps us understand how to validate students and their life experiences by allowing them to talk and write about topics that matter to them, even if they are uncomfortable and difficult for the teacher to hear. Jones leaves the reader with ideas of how to take action with their new knowledge of their children. BB

Kempton, Susan L. 2007. *The Literate Kindergarten: Where Wonder and Discovery Thrive.* **Portsmouth, NH: Heinemann.**
Blending academic rigor with movement, art, and play is a challenge. How to model the language of thinking for emerging readers and writers is another concern. Sue effectively answers these questions by sharing writing samples, wall charts, music selections, book titles and precise language, which will help teachers successfully weave thinking and learning into a creative kindergarten classroom. CH

Krashen, Stephen D. 2003. *Explorations in Language Acquisition and Use.* **Portsmouth, NH: Heinemann.**
Krashen discusses the idea of linguistic input and the comprehension hypothesis. His research and ideas around free voluntary reading ring true. We must keep kids engaged, excited, and curious about their world. BB

Meier, Deborah. 1995. *The Power of Their Ideas: Lessons for America from a Small School in Harlem.* **Boston: Beacon Press.**
I still go back again and again to these reflections from a pioneer of the small schools movement. As we read Deborah Meier's reflections on leading Central Park East in Harlem, we glimpse the continual learning and revision of leadership and the crucial role of how we connect to each other in creating a powerful and genuine learning community. ML

Page, Scott E. 2007. *The Difference: How the Power of Diversity Creates Better Groups, Firms, Schools, and Societies.* **Princeton, NJ: Princeton University Press.**
This professor from Yale shows how groups that include diverse perspectives outperform homogeneous groups of like-minded individuals. *The Difference* provides a rationale to fight for inclusive schools and learning communities. ML

Perkins, David. 2010. *Making Learning Whole: How Seven Principles of Teaching Can Transform Education.* **San Francisco: Jossey Bass.**
I'm still savoring this book! It has sticky notes sticking out every which way and it's at the top of my bedside table stack. Right now I'm wondering about it in relationship to lesson design and my work with children and

teachers—how can we avoid teaching isolated elements of a discipline, and instead, create "junior versions" of the whole game? Filled with big ideas, this book keeps me coming back for more. DM

Pink, Daniel. 2009. *Drive: The Surprising Truth About What Motivates Us.* **New York: Riverhead/Penguin.**

Drive is essential reading to help all of us increase our capacity to engage and grow by focusing on structures that allow humans to be their best selves: autonomy, mastery, and purpose. I've found when I help teachers and schools focus on increasing these elements in planning, instruction, assessment, professional development, and collaboration, everyone is more engaged in learning and life. SB

Pink talks about motivation and internal and external rewards—which one do you think drives and motivates us? He believes we're motivated by the power that comes from making our own choices, learning and creating new things, and doing better "for ourselves and the world." The implications for the classroom are enormous. DM

Pollock, Mica. Ed. 2008. *Everyday Anti-Racism: Getting Real About Race and School.* **New York: The New Press.**

If you are looking for authentic perspectives, practical ideas, and real stories from a variety of educators engaged in the real struggle to increase our capacity to serve students from diverse backgrounds, this is a great resource to provoke new thinking and conversation on the way to more effective practice that reaches every student. ML

Pressley, Michael. 2006. *Reading Instruction That Works: The Case for Balanced Teaching,* **3d ed. New York: Guilford.**

I turn to this book over and over for syntheses of the research and insight into Mike Pressley's impressive range of knowledge about reading. He seriously considers approaches to reading that have been widely discussed among practitioners. EOK

Ravitch, Diane. 2010. *The Death and Life of the American School System.* **New York: Basic Books.**

The author, a prime architect of the Bush era education plan, reviews the state of American public education since the passage of NCLB, revises her thinking in light of current evidence, and reverses course in this honest and courageous book. SH

Ravitch analyzes research and draws on interviews with a broad range of stakeholders to question the current direction of reform in public education. She focuses on the impact of school choice on public schools, describes quality teaching, and engages in a data war with advocates for charter and traditional public schools. Ultimately, Ravitch advocates for a greater focus on excellent curriculum and the revival of neighborhood schools. SZ

Ritchhart, Ron. 2002. *Intellectual Character: What It Is, Why It Matters, and How to Get It.* **San Francisco: Jossey-Bass**

Ritchhart's classic text on building intellectual character through classroom environment, routines, and pedagogy far surpasses any writing that had been done at the time with respect to raising expectations for student engagement and intellectual challenge. EOK

Samway, Katharine D., and Denise McKeon. 2007. *Myths and Realities: Best Practices for English Language Learners,* **2d ed. Portsmouth, NH. Heinemann.**

Samway and McKeon provide the reader with easy to understand information to clear up the many misunderstandings around the teaching of English language learners. The book provides information on second language acquisition, assessment, placement, and programming and much more. BB

Singleton, Glenn, and Curtis Linton. 2006. *Courageous Conversations About Race: A Field Guide for Achieving Equity in Schools.* **Newbury Park, CA: Corwin Press.**

This is the book I go to for practical ideas and resources to lay the groundwork for communities to be able to talk honestly about issues of race for ourselves and our colleagues with an outcome of raising our awareness and sensitivity in practice. ML

Steineke, Nancy. 2002. *Reading and Writing Together: Collaborative Literacy in Action.* **Portsmouth, NH: Heinemann.**

Kid-kid collaboration is at the core of our best comprehension lessons. But how do we make sure that every kid in our class can work productively, reliably, and congenially with every other student? In this overlooked book, high school teacher Nancy Steineke explains the steps skillful literacy teachers can take to ensure a collaborative classroom community all year long. HSD

Wink. Joan. 2010. *Critical Pedagogy: Notes from the Real World,* **4th ed. New York: Addison Wesley Longman.**

Joan Wink takes the work of McLaren, Marx, Freire, and others and synthesizes critical theory. Wink invites readers to make connections and create their own definitions of what critical pedagogy is and why it is so important. Critical theory helps us remember that only when we continue to talk and have dialogue with people who have viewpoints different from our own can we have hope for a democracy. BB

Wolf, Daniel. 2009. *How Lincoln Learned to Read: Twelve Great American and the Education That Made Them.* **New York: Bloomsbury USA.**

What, really, is a "good education"? Wolf provides an honest look at how life experience, gender, and social class contributed to as well as limited the education of twelve great Americans. He takes a critical look at our nation's history and examines the untold stories of what it means to be educated in America. BB

Wolf, Maryanne. 2007. *Proust and the Squid: The Story and Science of the Reading Brain.* **New York: Harper Collins.**

A fascinating exploration into how reading changes our brains, not to mention the ways we think, communicate, and learn. Wolf, a cognitive neuroscientist, researches the historical, biological, and linguistic aspects of how we read and write—noting that these skills are relatively new in the evolutionary scheme of things. Her insights into dyslexia and other reading and writing difficulties uncover many surprising complexities in this skill we humans sometimes take for granted. AG

Wood, George. 2002. *Time to Learn. How to Create High Schools That Serve All Students.* **Portsmouth, NH: Heinemann.**

Here are lessons from a small school in Appalachia that is doing so many things right. Now a demonstration site for the Coalition of Essential Schools, Federal Hocking High School's faculty have become pioneers in literacy across the curriculum, and their principal George Wood has cofounded the essential Forum for Democracy and Education, www .forumforeducation.org. HSD

Zhao, Yong. 2009. *Catching Up or Leading the Way.* **Alexandria, VA: ASCD (Association for Supervision and Curriculum Development).**

The Michigan State professor, schooled in China, explores the current state of American education and asks us to seriously consider what we are doing playing catch up with third-world countries. Zhao questions why Americans are determined to become an exam-centered system (like China, Singapore, and others) when the U. S. is known the world over for creativity, innovation, and the ability to think outside the box. SH

Zhao brings a unique perspective to what is right and wrong about education in America. He wrestles with the critical question: Are schools emphasizing the knowledge and skills that students need in a global society, or are they actually undermining their strengths by overemphasizing high-stakes testing and standardization? Zhao stresses the need for our education system to encourage creativity and problem solving in preparing students to be productive global citizens. SZ

Articles Recommended by Our Contributors

American Association for the Advancement of Science. 2010. Special issue, *Science, Language and Literacy* 328 (5977): www.sciencemag.org/special/education2010/.

This themed issue of the AAAS journal advocates that we teach "science inquiry skills and literacy together, through collaborative and critical discourse." The authors—scientists, researchers, literacy specialists, and others—tackle topics as diverse as the challenges of academic language in science reading, reasoning and communicating in science, and what it means to be "scientifically literate" in a changing world. AG

Ash, Doris. 2008. "Thematic Continuities: Talking and Thinking About Adaptation in a Socially Complex Classroom." *Journal of Research in Science Teaching* 45 (1): 1–30.

Ash studied the talk and reasoning of fifth and sixth graders as they engaged in a science unit on endangered species. She shows how deep involvement in content-area themes created "thematic continuities" that scaffolded students' appropriation of science talk and science thinking. She documented how science understanding, everyday discourse, and science discourse interact over time in ways that ultimately moved students toward more scientific ways of communicating and reasoning. GC

Association of Supervision and Curriculum Development. 2008. "Teaching Students to Think." Special issue, *Educational Leadership* 65 (5).

This amazing issue is appropriately titled *Teaching Students to Think,* but every article actually teaches *teachers* to think, as well. Provocative yet practical, this collection of research overflows with ideas to support comprehension instruction. And with the entire issue available online, we can easily take advantage of these rich resources again and again. Visit www.ascd.org to find archived issues of *Educational Leadership.* TM

Compton-Lilly, Catherine. 2009. "Unpacking Artifacts of Instruction." *Literacy Teaching and Learning* **13 (1 and 2): 57–79.**

Compton-Lilly explores how the contents of student book bags or backpacks can inform teachers about students' literate identities—ones that are often not visible in the official school day. BB

Hargreaves, Andy, and Dennis Shirley. 2009. "The Persistence of Presentism." New York: Teachers College Record at Columbia University. Available at: www.tcrecord.org/content.asp?contentid=15438.

This article rocked my world by introducing me to the theory of presentism—the short-term perspective that prevents teachers and schools from becoming the kinds of thinking-based, learning-based, improvement-based organizations that can truly change lives and powerfully educate ALL children. We all need to think hard about ways to combat presentism and help teachers and administrators have the courage and will to do what matters most (see Schmoker, page 264) to give all students the power to interact with, influence and transform their world. SB

Pianta, Robert C., Jay Belsky, Renate Houts, Fred Morrison, and The National Institute of Child Health and Human Development (NICHD) Early Child Care Research Network. 2007. "Teaching: Opportunities to Learn in America's Elementary Classrooms." *Science* **315: 1795–96.**

Take a huge sample population and mix it with extensive observations of student learning experiences, and what do you get? A snapshot of how America's kids spend their days in school. The findings are bleak. Yet they offer up a challenge to teachers and administrators everywhere: We can improve the learning lives of American children with simple, direct attention to the quality of instruction. TM

Purcell-Gates, Victoria, Nell K. Duke, and Joseph A. Martineau. 2007. "Learning to Read and Write Genre-Specific Text: Roles of Authentic Experience and Explicit Teaching." *Reading Research Quarterly* **42 (1): 8–45.**

Purcell-Gates, Duke, and Martineau examined, among other things, the relationship between classroom-based opportunities for authentic reading and writing in science, and second- and third-grade students' reading and writing growth. The researchers defined authentic literacy events as those that served a communicative or real-life purpose beyond school-based practice. In one example of an authentic science writing activity, students in one classroom visited a pond and then prepared a brochure for public distribution about what lives in ponds. The authors found strong relationships between the degree of authenticity of reading and writing activities during science instruction and growth in students' reading and writing of science texts. GC

Schmoker, Mike. 2009. "What Money Can't Buy: Powerful Overlooked Opportunities for Learning." *Phi Delta Kappan* **(March): 524–27.**

Schmoker lays down the gauntlet for all of us in this short article. He says, "Enough!" We don't need any more research, we don't need any more data, and we don't need any more money. What we need is the courage and will to do what matters most—and he gives us five simple practices that would radically change education if we just stay focused and stop chasing the next, new, shiny "fix." Courage—where will we find it? SB

Shanahan, Timothy, and Cynthia Shanahan. 2008. "Teaching Disciplinary Literacy to Adolescents: Rethinking Content-Area Literacy." *Harvard Educational Review* **78 (1): 40–59.**

Shanahan and Shanahan call into question the idea that even excellent early literacy instruction automatically supports students in acquiring the complex literacy skills needed to engage in content-area instruction in middle and secondary classrooms. They report the results of an exploratory study designed to identify the specialized reading skills within different disciplines. They found, for example, that mathematicians focused on precision of meaning and therefore paid careful attention to every word, while historians approached comprehension as the uncovering of a particular author's perspective on historical events. The authors call for advanced literacy instruction that engages students with these practices. GC

Wagner, Tony. 2008. "Rigor Redefined." *Educational Leadership* **66 (2): 20–25.**

"Rigor Redefined" is a call for all schools to listen more carefully to the demands of the world outside of academia. In this provocative article, Tony Wagner interviews business and community leaders to find out what qualities they look for in potential hires. Readers discover that they aren't looking for employees who can rattle off isolated facts and content standards. Read this amazing article to find out how Wagner puts the term *college and work ready* into its proper place. CT

Selected Publications by Our Contributors

Samantha Bennett

Bennett, Samantha. 2007. *That Workshop Book: New Systems and Structures for Classrooms That Read, Write and Think*. Portsmouth, NH: Heinemann.

Bennett, Samantha. 2009. "Time to Think: Using the Workshop Structure So Students Think and Teachers Listen." In *The Right to Literacy in Secondary Schools*. New York: Teachers College Press.

Leslie Blauman

Blauman, Leslie. 2011. *The Inside Guide to the Reading-Writing Classroom, Grades 3–6: Strategies for Extraordinary Teaching*. Portsmouth, NH: Heinemann.

Brad Buhrow

Buhrow, Brad, and Anne Upczak Garci. 2006. *Ladybugs, Tornadoes and Swirling Galaxies: English Language Learners Discover Their World Through Inquiry*. Portland, ME: Stenhouse.

Buhrow, Brad. 2009. In *Comprehension and Collaboration: Inquiry Circles in Action*, Stephanie Harvey and Harvey Daniels. Portsmouth, NH: Heinemann.

Gina Cervetti

Cervetti, Gina N., and Jacqueline Barber. 2008. "Text in Hands-on Science." In *Finding the Right Texts: What Works for Beginning and Struggling Readers*, edited by Elfrieda H. Hiebert and Misty Sailors, 89–108. New York: Guilford.

Cervetti, Gina N., Marco A. Bravo, Elfrieda H. Hiebert, P. David Pearson, and Carolyn A. Jaynes. 2009. "Text Genre and Science Content: Ease of Reading, Comprehension, and Reader Preferences." *Reading Psychology* 30 (6): 1–26.

Cervetti, Gina N., Carolyn A. Jaynes, and Elfrieda H. Hiebert. 2009. "Increasing Opportunities to Acquire Knowledge Through Reading." In *Reading More, Reading Better*, edited by Elfrieda H. Hiebert, 79–100. New York: Guilford.

Cervetti, Gina, P. David Pearson, Marco A. Bravo, and Jacqueline Barber. 2006. "Reading and Writing in the Service of Inquiry-Based Science." In *Linking*

Science and Literacy in the K–8 Classroom, edited by Rowena Douglas, Michael Klentschy, and Karen Worth, 221–44. Arlington, VA: NSTA.

Darling-Hammond, Linda, Brigid Barron, P. David Pearson, Alan H. Schoenfeld, Elizabeth K. Stage, Timothy D. Zimmerman, Gina N. Cervetti, and Jennifer L. Tilson. 2008. *Powerful Learning: What We know About Teaching for Understanding.* San Francisco: Jossey-Bass.

Nancy Commins

Commins, Nancy L., and Ofelia B. Miramontes. 2005. *Linguistic Diversity & Teaching: Reflective Teaching and the Social Conditions of Schooling.* Mahwah, NJ: Lawrence Erlbaum.

Commins, Nancy L. 2006. Contributing expert in *English Language Learners at School: A Guide for Administrators,* edited by Else Hamayan and Rebecca Freeman. Philadelphia: Caslon Press.

Commins, Nancy L., and Ofelia Miramontes. 2006. "Addressing Linguistic Diversity from the Outset." *Journal of Teacher Education* 57 (3): 240–46.

Commins, Nancy L., ed. 2007. *Immigrant Integration: Educator Resource Guide.* Colorado Department of Education English Language Acquisition Unit and the Colorado Trust.

Commins, Nancy L. 2008. "Responding to Linguistic Diversity." *The School Administrator* 65 (10): 10–14.

Miramontes, Ofelia, Adel Nadeau, and Nancy L. Commins. (1997) 2011. *Restructuring Schools for Linguistic Diversity: Linking Decision Making to Effective Programs,* 2d ed. Teachers College Press.

Harvey "Smokey" Daniels

Daniels, Harvey. 2001. *Literature Circles: Voice and Choice in the Student-Centered Classroom,* 2d ed. Portland, ME: Stenhouse Publishers.

Daniels, Harvey, Marilyn Bizar, and Steven Zemelman. 2000. *Rethinking High School: Best Practice in Teaching, Learning and Leadership.* Portsmouth, NH: Heinemann.

Daniels, Harvey, and Nancy Steineke. 2004. *Mini-Lessons for Literature Circles.* Portsmouth, NH; Heinemann.

Daniels, Harvey, and Nancy Steineke. 2011. *Texts and Lessons for Content-Area Reading: With More Than 75 Articles from* The New York Times, Rolling Stone, The Washington Post, Car and Driver, Chicago Tribune, *and Many Others.* Portsmouth, NH: Heinemann.

Daniels, Harvey, Steven Zemelman, and Nancy Steineke. 2007. *Content Area Writing: Every Teacher's Guide.* Portsmouth, NH: Heinemann.

Harvey, Stephanie, and Harvey Daniels. 2009. *Comprehension and Collaboration: Inquiry Circles in Action.* Portsmouth, NH: Heinemann.

Zemelman, Steven, and Harvey Daniels. 2004. *Subjects Matter: Every Teacher's Guide to Content-Area Reading.* Portsmouth, NH; Heinemann.

Zemelman, Steven, Harvey Daniels, and Arthur Hyde. 2005. *Best Practice: Today's Standards for Teaching and Learning in America's Schools,* 3d ed. Portsmouth, NH: Heinemann.

Anne Upczak Garcia

Buhrow, Brad, and Anne Upczak Garci. 2006. *Ladybugs, Tornadoes and Swirling Galaxies: English Language Learners Discover Their World Through Inquiry.* Portland, ME: Stenhouse.

Anne Goudvis

Goudvis, Anne, and Stephanie Harvey. 2005. *Reading the World: Content Comprehension with Linguistically Diverse Learners.* Video. Portland, ME: Stenhouse.

Harvey, Stephanie, and Anne Goudvis. 2005. *The Comprehension Toolkit: Language and Lessons for Active Literacy.* Portsmouth, NH: Heinemann.

Harvey, Stephanie, and Anne Goudvis. 2007. *Strategies That Work: Teaching Comprehension for Understanding and Engagment,* 2d ed. Portland, ME: Stenhouse.

Harvey, Stephanie, and Anne Goudvis. 2008. *The Primary Comprehension Toolkit. Language and Lessons for Active Literacy.* Portsmouth, NH: Heinemann.

Harvey, Stephanie, Anne Goudvis, and Judy Wallis. 2010. *Small Groups Lessons for the Comprehension Toolkit and Primary Comprehension Toolkit.* Portsmouth, NH: Heinemann.

Pearson, P. David, Stephanie Harvey, and Anne Goudvis. 2005. *What Every Teacher Should Know About Reading Comprehension* (video). Portsmouth, NH: Heinemann.

Stephanie Harvey

Harvey, Stephanie, and Anne Goudvis. 2005. *The Comprehension Toolkit: Language and Lessons for Active Literacy.* Portsmouth, NH: Heinemann.

Harvey, Stephanie, and Anne Goudvis. 2006. *Read Write and Talk: A Practice to Enhance Comprehension* DVD. Portland, ME: Stenhouse.

Harvey, Stephanie, and Anne Goudvis. 2007. *Strategies That Work: Teaching Comprehension for Understanding and Engagment*, 2d ed. Portland, ME: Stenhouse.

Harvey, Stephanie, and Anne Goudvis. 2008. *The Primary Comprehension Toolkit. Language and Lessons for Active Literacy.* Portsmouth, NH: Heinemann.

Harvey, Stephanie, Anne Goudvis, and Judy Wallis. 2010. *Small Groups Lessons for the Comprehension Toolkit and Primary Comprehension Toolkit.* Portsmouth, NH: Heinemann.

Harvey, Stephanie, and Harvey Daniels. 2009. *Comprehension and Collaboration: Inquiry Circles in Action.* Portsmouth, NH: Heinemann.

Harvey, Stephanie, and Harvey Daniels. 2009. *Inquiry Circles in Elementary Classrooms.* DVD. Portsmouth, NH: Heinemann.

Harvey, Stephanie and Harvey Daniels. 2009. *Inquiry Circles in Middle and High School.* DVD. Portsmouth, NH: Heinemann.

Chryse Hutchins

Zimmermann, Susan, and Chryse Hutchins. 2003. *7 Keys to Comprehension: How to Help Your Kids Read It and Get It!* New York: Three Rivers.

Ellin Oliver Keene

Keene, Ellin Oliver. 2002. "From Good to Memorable: Characteristics of Highly Effective Comprehension Teaching." In *Improving Comprehension Instruction.* Edited by Cathy Block, Linda Gambrell, and Michael Pressley, 80–105. San Francisco: Jossey-Bass.

Keene, Ellin Oliver. 2006. *Assessing Comprehension Thinking Strategies.* Huntington Beach, CA: Shell Educational Publishing.

Keene, Ellin Oliver. 2007. "The Essence of Understanding." In *Adolescent Literacy: Turning Promise into Practice,* edited by Kylene Beers, Robert Probst, and Linda Rief, 27–38. Portsmouth, NH: Heinemann.

Keene, Ellin Oliver. 2008. *To Understand: New Horizons in Reading Comprehension Instruction.* Portsmouth, NH: Heinemann.

Keene, Ellin Oliver. 2010. "New Horizons in Comprehension." *Educational Leadership* 67 (March): 69–73.

Keene, Ellin Oliver, and Susan Zimmermann. 2007. *Mosaic of Thought: The Power of Comprehension Strategy Instruction,* 2d ed. Portsmouth, NH: Heinemann.

Marjorie Larner

Larner, Marjorie. 2004. *Pathways: Charting a Course for Professional Learning.* Portsmouth, NH: Heinemann.

Larner, Marjorie. 2007. "Leaps." In *Connections,* The Journal of the National School Reform Faculty. Bloomington, IN. Available at: http://www .harmonyschool.org/www/pdf/connections/2007.spring.leaps.pdf. Accessed December, 2010.

Larner, Marjorie. 2007. *Tools for Leaders: Indispensable Graphic Organizers, Protocols, and Planning Guidelines for Working and Learning Together.* New York: Scholastic.

Larner, Marjorie. 2008. "Access to Power: From School to Life." In *The Right to Literacy in Secondary Schools: Creating a Culture of Thinking,* edited by Suzanne Plaut. New York: Teachers College Press.

Larner, Marjorie, Andrea Cipoletti, and Debbie Deem. (ND). *Students at the Center: How to Have a Good Conversation: By Fifth Graders at Aspen Creek K–8.* In *Connections,* The Journal of the National School Reform Faculty. Bloomington, IN.

Larner, Marjorie. (ND). Series featuring student writing in *Headfirst Magazine.*

Tanny McGregor

McGregor, Tanny. 2007. *Comprehension Connections: Bridges to Strategic Reading.* Portsmouth, NH: Heinemann.

Debbie Miller

Miller, Debbie. 2002. *Reading with Meaning: Teaching Comprehension in the Primary Grades.* Portland, ME: Stenhouse.

Miller, Debbie. 2005. *The Joy of Conferring.* DVD. Portland, ME: Stenhouse.

Miller, Debbie. 2006. *Happy Reading!* DVD. Portland, ME: Stenhouse.

Miller, Debbie. 2008. *Teaching with Intention: Defining Beliefs, Aligning Practice, Taking Action.* Portland, ME: Stenhouse.

P. David Pearson

Pearson, P. David. 2009. "The Roots of Reading Comprehension Instruction." In *Handbook of Research on Reading Comprehension,* edited by Susan E. Israel and Gerald G. Duffy, 3–31. London: Routledge.

Pearson, P. David, Gina N. Cervetti, and Jennifer Tilson. 2008. "Reading for

Understanding and Successful Literacy Development." In *Powerful Learning: What We Know About Teaching for Understanding,* edited by Linda Darling-Hammond, Brigid Barron, P. David Pearson, Alan H. Schoenfeld, Elizabeth K. Stage, Timothy D. Zimmerman, Gina N. Cervetti, and Jennifer L. Tilson, 71–112. San Francisco: Jossey-Bass.

Pearson P. David, and Linda G. Fielding. 1991. "Comprehension Instruction." In *Handbook of Reading Research,* vol. 2, edited by R. Barr, M. L. Kamil, P. Mosenthal, and P. D. Pearson, 815–60. New York: Longman.

Pearson, P. David, and Margaret C. Gallagher. 1983. "The Instruction of Reading Comprehension." *Contemporary Educational Psychology* 8: 317–44.

Pearson, P. David, and Dale D. Johnson. 1978. *Teaching Reading Comprehension.* New York: Holt, Rinehart and Winston.

Pearson, P. David, Laura Roehler, Janice Dole, and Gerald Duffy. 1992. "Developing Expertise in Reading Comprehension." In *What Research Says to the Teacher,* 2d ed., edited by S. J. Samuels and A. E. Farstrup, 145–99. Newark, DE: International Reading Association.

Duke, Nell, and P. David Pearson. 2002. "Effective Practices for Developing Reading Comprehension." In *What Research Has to Say About Reading Instruction,* 3d ed., edited by A. Farstrup and J. Samuels, 205–42. Newark, DE: International Reading Association.

Fielding, Linda G., and P. David Pearson. 1994. "Synthesis of Research: Reading Comprehension: What Works." *Educational Leadership* 51(5): 62–67.

Susan Zimmermann

Zimmermann, Susan. 1996. *Grief Dancers: A Journey into the Depths of the Soul.* Golden, CO: Nemo Press.

Zimmermann, Susan. 2002. *Writing to Heal the Soul: Transforming Grief and Loss Through Writing.* New York: Three Rivers.

Zimmermann, Susan. 2004. *Keeping Katherine: A Mother's Journey to Acceptance.* New York: Three Rivers.

Zimmermann, Susan, and Chryse Hutchins. 2003. *7 Keys to Comprehension, How to Help Your Kids Read It and Get It.* New York: Three Rivers.

Keene, Ellin, and Susan Zimmermann. 1997. *Mosaic of Thought: Teaching Comprehension in a Reader's Workshop.* Portsmouth, NH: Heinemann.

Keene, Ellin, and Susan Zimmermann. 2007. *Mosaic of Thought: The Power of Comprehension Strategy Instruction,* 2d ed. Portsmouth, NH: Heinemann.

Extend the conversation on comprehension

with key professional books from these experts

Mosaic of Thought
The Power of Comprehension Strategy Instruction
2ND EDITION

Ellin Oliver Keene and
Susan Zimmermann

978-0-325-01035-9 / 2007 / 312pp / $30.00

Comprehension & Collaboration
Inquiry Circles in Action

Stephanie Harvey and
Harvey "Smokey" Daniels

978-0-325-01230-8 / 2009 / 336pp / $28.50

To Understand
New Horizons in Reading Comprehension

Ellin Oliver Keene

978-0-325-00323-8 / 2008 / 320pp / $27.50

The Inside Guide to the Reading-Writing Classroom, Grades 3–6
Strategies for Extraordinary Teaching

Leslie Blauman

978-0-325-02831-6 / 2011 / 288pp / $25.00

Comprehension Connections
Bridges to Strategic Reading

Tanny McGregor

978-0-325-00887-5 / 2007 / 144pp / $19.00

That Workshop Book
New Systems and Structures for Classrooms That Read, Write, and Think

Samantha Bennett

978-0-325-01192-9 / 2007 / 240pp / $25.00

DEDICATED TO TEACHERS™

CALL **800.225.5800** • FAX **877.231.6980** • **Heinemann.com**